Training for
ULTRA
RUNNING

Training for

ULTRA
RUNNING

ANDY MILROY

DB
PUBLISHING

This edition published in Great Britain in 2013 by DB Publishing, an imprint of JMD Media.

ISBN 9781780913247

Printed and bound by Copytech (UK) Limited, Peterborough.

Contents

Introduction

In 1987 the original edition of 'Training for Ultras' was developed as an attempt to satisfy the oft-expressed request of would-be and novice ultra runners for advice on training. The popularity of that publication indicated that there was a need for another such booklet. The articles in the first booklet came from British runners. For this second booklet I collected material from runners from across the ultra running world, to get a range of training ideas from different running environments.

In 1993 the original booklet 'Training for Ultras' was developed into a more comprehensive and larger publication. This again proved very popular but the basic stapled format had reached its limit. Moving to a larger paperback version has been debated over the last decade, but finally a revised edition incorporating articles from all the booklets has been produced. To the original articles additional material has been added on the training of Yiannis Kouros, Takahiro Sunada, the fastest 100km runner on the road in the world and Giorgio Calcaterra, multiple winner of the World 100km.

The 1970s and 80s were a golden age for Ultrarunning with great runners like Cavin Woodward, Don Ritchie, Tom O'Reilly, Mike Newton, Eleanor Robinson and Hilary Walker from Britain and Bruce Fordyce, Bernd Heinrich, Bryan Smith, Dick Tout and Sandra Barwick setting world and national records at distances from 30 miles to 6 days. We are fortunate that they took the trouble to record their training at the time to preserve it for posterity.

More importantly many of the contributors achieved performances that are still unmatched today. Don Ritchie's 6:10:20 for 100km and 3:48:35 for 40 miles, Sandra Barwick's 6 day and 1000 mile bests, Bruce Fordyce's 50 mile road best are still unsurpassed, and nobody has attempted to break 50 miles and 100km world bests en route to taking the 100 mile record like Cavin Woodward! Cavin's 6:25:28 for 100km is still reckoned as a very good performance today – and that was just his split time.

Perhaps discovering how Don Ritchie trained might inspire another runner to run 11:30 for 100 miles and maybe even 6:10 for 100km. .

The advice offered in the following pages varies enormously. No two runners are alike. Ultra training is dictated by many factors - temperament, ability, build (height/weight), resilience, time available, environment and experience. Obviously it would be counter-productive for someone who has just started running to attempt to emulate the training of an elite 100km performer. Runners should extract from the articles those elements they think they can use, those which suit their own personal requirements.

I would like to thank all the contributors to the booklet for their willingness to share their hard-won experience.

I hope this new book will prove to be as useful as the original edition, to both future and current ultra runners. The advice within is both varied and sometimes contradictory - use what suits you. Every runner is different. Any comments and feedback on the training schedules and strategies would be welcome.

Note: Some of the drinks recommended in the articles may no longer be widely available. There are new drinks which have been developed which some runners use, however I do not have any real information on these, other than the product descriptions. One very experienced present day runner gave the advice that most ultrarunners just dilute existing sports drinks (and Coke) by about 50% and use that. To a degree it is a question of trial and error, what suits you personally, and what your stomach can tolerate under the stress of different events. Developing your drink/feed strategy should be an essential part of your preparation and training.

I would like to thank all the contributors to the booklet for their willingness to share their hard-won experience. I would also like to thank Ian Champion, Chairman of the RRC, for his input and for checking the text.

Thanks also go to Jurgen Schoch for the graphical analysis of the 24 hour splits in the Appendix.

Good Luck,

Andy Milroy July 2013

Getting Started

Moving up to Ultradistance can be intimidating. Here is advice from Stephen Moore who was a former fell runner. He later became one of the most experienced and consistent 100km in the world, setting age group records at 30 miles, 50km and 40 miles in the Barry 40 mile track race.)

As I was standing the start line at a 10 mile road a fellow competitor turned to me and asked, "How on earth do you get started in the ultra scene, it seems like running into the unknown but I quite fancy it." With the starter's gun poised I quickly suggested "You start with a visit to a psychiatrist!" On reflection I was not too helpful and as a number of runners have expressed the same enquiring thought, perhaps this is an opportunity to give a more serious and helpful response. I would like therefore to structure my comments by addressing the psychological issue of making a commitment then developing a long term plan, taking a look at the training necessary, considering the preparation of the race and then on to the race itself. But first let us start that journey . . . .

Into the unknown

Perhaps the hardest part of all is getting to the start line of your first ultra. If you do decide you will 'do it' and commit yourself to it, then I'm convinced that like me, you will be glad you made the effort. Now all this makes it sound as if it is not difficult, but it is. And it will be even more difficult if you decide to commit yourself and the following day stand on the start line of a 100km race! No, it's not a 100 yard dash. It is essential to take the matter seriously on the one hand and yet ensure you enjoy it on the other. This can be achieved by some long term planning and building up over a period, so as not to put the body under too much stress. You need to take one step at a time to avoid injury. Just as you should not run before you can walk, so it's best not to tackle an ultra before you have run a marathon. If you have not run a marathon or even a 10 mile road race then I suggest that you use a marathon as a milestone to achieving your ultimate objective.

I will assume you have progressed from a 10 mile to a marathon race (if you have not there are many programmes in regular running magazines which you could follow) and if you are to get started you need to plan your first ultra. Ideally it would be up to say, 40 miles so that at a later stage you progressed to say a 50 miler or the 100km (62 mile) although some have successfully moved directly from marathon distance to 100km.

Whatever the distance, the plan can be much the same; the first step is to get the race date in your diary, preferably 12 months ahead. The second step is to plan a training programme building up both your long training run and weekly mileage restricting increases to a maximum of 10%. The third step is to insert into the plan a series of races, 10km and 10 mile and 1/2 marathon distance for speed and a few marathons for stamina. If you get this far and complete your long term plan, you are well down the road to your first ultra and ready to start . . . .

Training

The committed ultra runner knows that the most important aspect of training is to train the body into thinking that the most natural thing in the world is to run. It's time out; it's miles in the legs but it's also enjoyment. Just as races may hurt (and if they do the result should be satisfying), so ultra training (leaving speed work aside) should be more relaxed and rewarding. Quiet lanes, towpaths, trails and long days in the hills can be ideal (not so ideal if you are a female on your own) but so often time is at a premium and one has to make do with a short early morning run before catching the train to work, then a run in the rain, when in Winter one has to take advantage of the street lighting.

It certainly helps to be a member of a local club for companionship and competition, yes, even when you are meant to be training! Variety is important and to run with different club runners can provide different routes, speeds and stories.

I have deliberately steered clear of suggesting distances for your longest run or miles per week, for two reasons. First, when I joined Horwich R.M.I. Harriers in 1981 and the secretary asked me what mileage per week I was doing and I said 20, he then proceeded to tell me he did 60 to 70 and I was on the verge of deciding not to join. He later told me that he asked only to see what sort of competition I might provide - 20 miles must have been the correct reply as I was allowed to join! Secondly, distances covered by ultra runners in training vary immensely, longest runs from 20 to 40 miles in one session, weekly mileages from 50 - 150 miles or more; so much depending upon what suits the individual in terms of comfort, quality, commitment and time.

Some use races as long training runs but that does not help if you are getting started. There is another psychological issue here in that the closer you have run in training to your race distance and the more miles you have put in, the more confident you may be. On the other hand, if you purely target miles then your speed could suffer. If you are committed as I assume you are and are putting the miles in training the only word of caution is to listen to your body. If you succumb to an injury, rest, or better still arrange for it to be correctly diagnosed and treated, otherwise you could make it worse and there would be no point in making any . . . .

Preparations for the race

The advantage of developing a long term plan is, that apart from training, you have plenty of time to prepare for the big day. If you are lucky you will have a partner or friend who has provided encouragement and been with you when you have reconnoitred the route so that you, and just as important, your partner or friend ("handler" is the normal ultra definition) will know exactly where to meet you so as to provide you with food/drink/clothes and a change of shoes if necessary, or, if nothing else, threats/abuse to ensure you honour your original commitment!!

As part of your preparation, training is important but it's just as important to rest before the race. You also need to be topped up with energy; depletion and carbohydrate loading is an option often talked about but for your first ultra I would suggest you prepare your food and drink as you did for your marathon. If you want further guidance you could do no better than read Steve Wootton's book 'Nutrition for Sport' published by Simon & Schuster. I would, however, suggest you prepare a list of exactly what you want to eat/drink and at which point it will be needed, to assist your handler - you may be too tired to take decisions at a later stage on the race day. Additionally, prepare a check list of things to take/use on the day of the race. It is, however, beneficial to ensure you put back into your body what you are taking out and top up regularly with liquid and some form of carbohydrate fuel. Do not, whatever happens, experiment in your first ultra, your long training runs or marathons are the times for you to act as your own guinea pig!! Finally, when your training programme comes to an end and preparation is complete, don't forget to rest and have some early nights before the eve of the race, for on your last night it may be difficult to get to sleep. It's all part of the preparation for . . . . . .

The Race

At last the big day has arrived, the nerves play their part but rather like an airline pilot before take off, you progress through the routine of the checklist; drink before the race, once on your way take the first half steadily; run your own race; do not necessarily try to keep up with others; the objective is the finish line not to remain with the leaders until half way! When it is all over, use it as experience. Learn from your mistakes, so that it is only your first race that is into the unknown, then you can do much better the next time.

Hilary Walker gradually established herself as one of the most formidable 24 hour performers in the UK, male or female, and in 1988 set new world bests for 100 miles, 24 and 48 hours. Her career was one of steady development, from a good average performer to the dominant runner. This article reveals how she has developed her present training and racing schedules.

When asked to provide an article on Ultra-training, I thought it would be of more use if I had a slightly different approach from the others who had provided their valuable tips from their established, very successful viewpoint. Instead, I would give an idea of what you can do as a beginner with the minimum of training (like me to start with) and then to compare it with what I do now.

I started running from scratch in 1982 and ran my first real ultra in 1985 having run a number of marathons (about 15) in between. I have never done any speed work - this shows up in my abominable short distance times and unimpressive marathon performances. My usual training pace has been between 7 - 8 minute miling as I still regard myself as a fun runner and train at a pleasurable pace. However, I do take part in races from one mile upwards and these provide me with some semblance of speed work and I am still finding that my pace is increasing as time goes by.

For those new to 'ultra' and haven't got too many miles in the legs, my first note of caution - don't overdo it. It is much better to enter a race undertrained rather than having to scratch through injury. I actually used my first 24 hour race as an indicator of whether I could do 100km in 12 hours which was the cut-off point for the Lincoln 100km, which I intended to run for charity. No problem - and I had only been doing a maximum of 60 - 70 miles a week for the previous six months. The weekly mileage was structured around a 20 mile long run at the weekend with at least a 13 miler sometime in mid-week. I managed to cover 105 miles in that 24 hour race with my longest run prior to that being the South London Harriers 30 miler the previous year. After that first 24 hour race at Feltham, my mileage remained about 50 - 60 miles per week for the rest of the year. I ran a very hot Woodford 40 in 5:40 and did 9:45 for the Lincoln 100km. Then I ran the Chorley 24 hour race on this same mileage but now that I had some ultras 'under my belt' I ran 126 miles easily. It can be seen that although my mileage remained low, my legs 'remembered' the earlier ultras and remained 'OK' throughout the 24 hours. In addition they also recovered more quickly after the event. The first time at a new distance is always the worst for me!

Since my first year of ultra in 1985, I have slowly increased my average weekly mileage so that at the start of the ultra season in 1988 I had had a year of 100 miles per week on average. Usually I will run between 20 and 30 miles one day at the weekend and in the week I will run between 10 to 15 miles in the morning and 5 to 8 in the evening, which includes travelling to and from work (otherwise I would never fit it in with a busy job and leaving myself with my evenings free for some of my other interests!)

These miles have stood me in good stead in a year when I did nine ultras. However, on my present mileage I need to vary the terrain and routes where possible to prevent over-use injuries. My only problems come from going round too many left hand bends (hence my appeal for track races to change direction every few hours) and I know that I am not the only one to benefit from this.

To avoid injuries and to get excellent stamina training I recommend long distance cross-country runs - such as those walks excellently organised by the Long Distance Walkers Association (they are the best value for money that I have ever met). However, I wouldn't want to wish too many runners onto their walks especially if they aren't sympathetic to their aims. For those just starting ultra I would recommend actually walking these 25 - 40 milers as an excellent and enjoyable way to getting used to being on one's feet for hours on end. To those at a higher level of fitness, running them is excellent training. They are tiring as the terrain can be very tough but at the end of the day the legs haven't been battered by miles of unremitting roads and pavement and there shouldn't be any residual stiffness. But a note of caution, you can't let your mind drift while running! The brain and the eyes have to navigate the route using a route description which can often be pretty cryptic so that I have often been known to do a few miles more than what was originally intended.

I use these events primarily in winter months as training whereas in the summer I use the shorter ultra races to keep my legs attuned to the longer distances. My racing schedule for 1988 gives some idea of how I have varied my ultra events:-

March	Barry	40 miles
April	Solihull	100kms
May	Apeldoorn	24 hours
June	Lincoln	100kms
August	Swansea	42 miles
August	Preston	24 hours
October	London to Brighton	53 miles
November	Blackpool	48 hours
December	Rotherham	47 miles

I could be accused of racing too much but notice how I intersperse the longer ultras with the shorter ones which I don't race flat out. 1988 has been my most successful year to date with my best results coming towards the end of the year. These races have been run on a background of about 100 - 110 miles a week with one month (July) of 140 miles a week - but I don't find the time to fit that in except for a short spell in mid-summer when my long suffering friends find me turning up for dinner in my running gear with a rather large appetite!

Mention of appetite brings me onto food - a preoccupation of high mileage runners! Others have given their valuable opinion on what they find the can and cannot eat and it is very much a personal taste. I eat almost everything in large quantities!! I usually listen to the dictates of any craving I may have, because more often than not, there is an underlying physiological need. Potatoes form the basis for my carbohydrate intake and - health freaks throw up your hands in horror - I eat a fair amount of fats. Well, as efficient ultrarunners will be using both fat metabolism as well as their glycogen stores it isn't really surprising. In races I eat the usual bananas and rice pudding while taking a walk but my staple energy source is either one of those complex carbohydrate products like Leppin or dextrosol tablets. The latter I can manage even when my stomach is too upset to cope with normal food.

So what would I recommend to 'ultra-aspirants' from my own experience in a nutshell? Well, you can actually survive and enjoy your first ultra on 50 - 60 miles a week and you will find the subsequent ones easier as your legs remember their previous experiences. My own turning point towards enjoying ultras came when I realised that unlike shorter races, you don't just enter a downward spiral of increasing tiredness. You can often look forward to feeling stronger later on when you are in the middle of having a bad patch. If things get really bad, then you can distract yourself by sharing in the good friendships and camaraderie to be found amongst the others sharing the same experience...... You will never be the same again!

Patti Finke, an exercise physiologist who has held US age group records at 50km and 50 miles. She directed running clinics and seminars on marathon running, together with her husband Warren who twice set US 100km track bests. Her views present a programme for ultrarunning based on scientific knowledge and practical experience.

Occasionally we all need to step back and assess what we are doing. Ultramarathoning probably requires more thought and assessment than other running commitments. Patti's article outlines a programme for ultramarathoning that is based on the application of some of the principles of exercise physiology combined with the practical experience of elite ultramarathoners.

Programme Basics

The first step in any programme is to define your goals. I use goals in the plural sense because a series of goals should be set: long, medium and short range. An example might be a 50 miler in four months, a training run marathon in two months, and working to increase weekly mileage. An important aspect of goal setting is to have the goals be realistic and achievable. Being able to meet goals and go on to set new ones is a rewarding process and helps keep up the motivation for day to day training. A weekly running plan can be built into a long range plan to achieve your long term goal.

Once your goals are set you should think about the basic training principles of overload and specificity. Overload does not mean overtraining; overload means exercising at a level which causes the body to make specific adaptations to function more efficiently. Think of a rubber band - as more load is applied it stretches more and becomes easier to stretch, but too much load can cause it to break. To keep from breaking, i.e. becoming injured or over trained, I add a third principle: rest, or rebuilding. Overload and rest form the basis for the hard/easy programme that uses variations of frequency, intensity and duration to achieve these principles. Frequency is how often you run, and duration is the time spent on an individual run. After a hard workout, rest or an easy workout is important because it gives the muscles a chance to repair themselves and/or adapt. In a programme of increasing mileage or of building basic endurance, hard may be the long slow run or any long run, while easy may be a shorter distance run at the same pace. For the long time runner with an established mileage base, hard may be a shorter workout of increased intensity such as hill work, fartlek, or some kind of interval running.

This brings us to the principle of specificity. Specificity refers to adaptations of both metabolic and physiology systems, depending on the type of overload used. Running is obviously the specific training for running but, by using variations of frequency, duration, intensity and terrain, you can see that there are different kinds of running that may utilise different sources of energy and bring about different kinds of adaptations. This is where goalsetting is so important:

you need a training programme designed for the kind of races you want to run to allow yourself to maximize performance and eliminate wasted effort.

Physiology Basics

An understanding of the physiological principles and adaptations can help you decide how to set up a programme. Energy for work comes from the generation of a substance called ATP (adenosine triphosphate) and the source of this energy is the breakdown of the food we eat. The main energy sources used in running are carbohydrates (glycogen) and fat. As these products are broken down to form ATP, hydrogen is given off, goes through a transport system and requires oxygen to form water which is excreted. Carbohydrate is readily available as a source of energy in the muscle and is utilized mainly for faster running. However, the total glycogen stores can provide only enough energy for one and a half to two hours of running. There are almost unlimited quantities of fat available to use for energy, but as fat metabolism creates more ATP, more oxygen is required to combine with the hydrogen given off, making fat metabolism the energy source of slower running and rest.

There are several adaptations made by training that increase the utilization of oxygen. Some of these changes occur at the level of the local muscle and include better utilization of oxygen through increased size and number of mitochondria (little energy factories within the cells) and an increase in their aerobic enzymes. Then the muscle can more easily use and mobilize fat for energy, which helps to preserve the carbohydrate stores and develops a greater ability to utilize carbohydrate and a greater storage capacity for it. Some muscle fibre that can be used either for aerobic or anaerobic exercise can be adapted to use oxygen better. There is also an increase in the number of capillaries for better nutrient supply and better waste disposal as well as an increase in the amount of muscle tissue.

Adaptations of the cardio-vascular and respiratory systems are also important results of training. The heart muscle increases in volume and weight and the volume of blood increases. Resting and sub-maximal heart rates are decreased; the volume of blood the heart pumps with each beat (called the stroke volume) increases, and this is turn increases the amount of oxygen that can be extracted from the blood through better distribution of blood from the working muscles.

One of the most important changes is an increase in the maximal oxygen intake, called VO2 Max, a quantitative measure of a person's capacity for aerobic energy transfer. Variables that determine VO2 Max are heredity, sex and body composition (the amount of lean body tissue), age and training. Obviously you can do nothing about several of these variables, but improvements of 20-25 percent in maximal oxygen uptake because of training have been observed. Training can also improve your ability to run at a higher percentage of your VO2 Max.

Training Terms explained
To describe a programme we first explain some terms:

Continuous Training - Training, in this case running with continuous activity without rest intervals. This type of training can be high intensity training of moderate duration (continuous fast running) or low intensity of an extended duration (usually known as long slow distance LSD). LSD is the usual form of endurance training. Both types of continuous training will be explained more fully in terms of effort below.

Fartlek - Speed play is a type of continuous training in which the runner speeds up or slows down at will. If fartlek is run on hilly terrain, the pace may remain the same with the running of the hills requiring increased or decreased effort. Fartlek is done to keep training fun and interesting and is usually considered a hard workout.

Race Pace - The goal pace for the race you want to run.

Easy - This is a description of effort and is used to describe the runs where rebuilding occurs. Easy can refer to either pace or distance. Easy is a pace about 75 percent of the pace that the distance would be run in a race or a distance of less than one tenth of the weekly mileage. This concept can be difficult to define when the weekly mileage is high. Later in this article an example of the training week and a table of suggested paces are given. Many runners do not realise the importance of easy runs and do not get adequate rest. The consequence is that they cannot get the benefits of the hard runs because they are too tired.

Hard - This term is also a description of effort and describes training when the principle of overload applies. When the element used in training is speed, the pace should be 85 - 90 percent of race pace. This type of hard run is mainly to improve VO2 Max. Exceeding 90 percent does not give more training effect, but increases the risk of injury or overtraining. When a hard run is defined in terms of distance, it is a run of two hours or more, preferably up to race duration or distance, which is done at an easy pace. This type of run gives improvements in aerobic metabolism with increased aerobic enzymes and better fat utilization and also, perhaps, influences muscle composition. Running these long runs at high speeds is not good training technique because the harder effort tends to favour glycogen metabolism and the combination of long and fast creates a high risk for injury.

The basic training for all distance racing is endurance training. The runner must have the stamina to cover the desired distance. Cardio-vascular endurance must come first. Then the specific muscles become stronger, followed by the connective tissues and tendons or ligaments. Injury often occurs because the runner feels that he has the stamina to run the number of miles, but actually lacks the muscular and connective tissue strength which develops much more slowly. Mileage should be increased about 5 percent per week. Another more workable scheme is to increase 10 percent, then run this number for two weeks, giving one week of stress and one of rest and then increase again by 10 percent. Only when adequate stamina has been obtained should other types of training be used to sharpen. A typical training week includes a long weekend run and one or two hard midweek runs interspersed with four easy or rest days. Two of the rest days usually follow the long run. A notable omission in the explanation of the training terms above is any kind of interval training. I can see no reason why the runner training for an ultra would need or want the stress and injury potential of interval training. A matrix of training is shown below to help pick the type of training desired. Note that the (easy) rest runs should be both short and slow. The options for hard runs are long slow distance and fast shorter runs often called 'tempo runs'. The fourth option 'long fast distance' should not be used.

	SHORT (less than 10 percent of weekly mileage)	LONG (2 hours or more)
SLOW (75 percent effort)	Easy	Hard
FAST (85 percent effort)	Hard	XXXX

With an understanding of the basics we are now ready to put together the physiology and programme principles to design a programme to meet your needs.

Application to Ultramarathoning

One of the first myths of training to dispel is the often heard 'No pain, no gain'. It is possible to train and improve by hard work that does not include pain. It is impossible to reach your goal if you are injured sick or exhausted. A good training programme works to prevent these complications. Dick Brown the coach of Athletics West, feels that his role is to keep his athletes healthy since an injured runner cannot train at all. There is no one right way to train and each runner needs to learn how his or her body reacts to different overloads and what works best. But remember, overtraining does not work for anyone, and a rest day is definitely in order when there is:

1) an increase in resting heart rate of 5 beats per minute;
2) a sudden weight loss of five or more pounds;
3) a feeling of excessive thirst
4) a sluggish or extremely tired feeling; or
5) the beginnings of illness such as sore throat or cough.

Endurance, both cardio-vascular and musculo-skeletal, is the major need for running an ultra. The abilities to utilize oxygen well and burn fat well are also necessary. For a good performance the runner also needs to be able to run at a high percentage of his or her VO2 Max for long periods of time. The programme outlined below utilizes specificity and overload to gain these necessities. Most of them are best gained by long slow distance interspersed with lots of rest and rebuilding.

Race time (min)				
10km	30:00	35:00	40.00	45:00	50:00
15km	46:22	54:06	1:01:50	1:09:33	1:17:17
Marathon	2:20:47	2:44:17	3:07:45	3:31:13	3:54:42
Training pace (min/mi)				
4mi	5:40-6:14	6:37-7:16	7:33-8:19	8:29- 9:21	9:27-10:23
8mi	5:58-6:34	6:57-7:39	7:57-8:45	8:56- 9:50	9:56-10:56
16mi	6:16-6:54	7:19-8:03	8:22-9:12	9:24-10:21	10:28-11:30
32mi	6:37-7:16	7:42-8:29	8:49-9:41	9:54-10:54	11:00-12:07

If you run a race at the times listed in the top half of the table, then you should be training between the paces listed directly below. For instance, if you can race 15km in about 62 minutes you should run a 4 mile easy run between 7:33 and 8:19 pace and a 32 mile run at a pace between 8:49 and 9:41 per mile.

The weekly mileage bases that I recommend are at least 65 miles for a marathon, 80 miles for a 50 miler and 100+ for longer races. These mileage bases need not be run for at least 6 to 8 weeks before the event. Due to the differences in needs between the marathon and ultras, the mileage bases are run in different but specific patterns. This programme is not just to allow completion of the event, but also to allow the competitor to feel good and enjoy the run. Isn't that what running is all about? Doing this weekly mileage necessitates commitment, adequate rest days, adequate sleep, good nutrition, careful monitoring of body feelings, and most of all, an understanding family. It is possible to complete an ultra on less mileage than the recommendations above: however, it may be painful. The specificity part of the plan is extremely important if fewer miles are contemplated.

A programme for the marathon includes one long weekend run and two midweek speed workouts specific to that distance. The ultramarathoner needs to focus on endurance, not speed, meaning that the hard runs will be of long duration at an easy pace rather than being of high intensity. These runs often require 24 hours or longer for recovery. Many elite ultramarathoners do only two and sometimes only one hard session per week. The basic training week that I recommend is divided into two parts as outlined below:

(1) The weekend - typically half the mileage is run in two back-to-back long runs, one considerably longer than the other. I do not recommend runs much longer than 35 miles because they tend to be overtraining and bring about more breakdown than can be regained unless you get lots of rest (i.e. be a professional athlete). The programme of one really long run followed by a fairly long run is a way to overload without overtraining. This plan does not really give your body enough time to recover between the runs, forcing it to adapt without causing injury. It thus simulates very long single runs without the same risk of injury.

(2) The rest of the week - the first two days after the long run are both rest days. The pace for training runs can be obtained directly or by interpolating using the above chart. Another long run is done midweek followed by two more slow-paced rest days. Monitoring recovery heart rate on those days can help you tell if you are running slowly enough and getting enough rest.

This is a good time to keep a running diary with notations of resting heart rate (HR), recovery HR, weight, mileage, and a general comment on how you feel. Learning how your body reacts to overload and when to rest is important in maintaining health. Recovery consists of two phases, short term and long term. During the short term phase the HR drops rapidly from the exercise rate to one about 20 - 30 beats per minute above resting. This usually takes one to five minutes after warm down. The long term phase may last for varying periods depending on the total stress of the run. Monitoring how long it takes for your HR to return to resting is a good way to see when the run has been too hard and a rest day is in order. Usually this long term period should be several hours, but it may last up to 24 hours after a long run, the guidelines for time and numbers are different for each individual and a diary can help you determine your particular body normals.

Examples of typical training weeks are given below:

	80 mile week	100 mile week
Saturday	26 - 30 miles	34 miles
Sunday	10 - 14	16
Monday	4	6 - 8
Tuesday	6	8
Wednesday	15	18 - 20
Thursday	8	8
Friday	7	8

One good way to keep down the possibility of injury is to run as much of the weekly mileage as possible on soft surfaces. The best plan is to do the long runs on trails. This can also add the element of fartlek if the terrain is hilly. Running with even effort over the terrain utilizes the hills to increase VO2 Max. I realise that you are not all as lucky as we are in the availability of nearby trails, but a drive for the long weekend run could certainly be worthwhile. Remember that training time on hilly trails will be a minute per mile or more slower than on roads, and training times from the above table must be adjusted accordingly.

Some of the major questions asked by runners following this type of programme are of the form:

'What happens if
- I missed a day because of illness or injury?
- I need a rest day and my schedule calls for a hard day?
- I missed a whole week of training?
- My .... hurts. Should I run on it?'

The answer is, 'Learn to listen to your body and to respond to its needs.' If something is painful while you're running on it, obviously you shouldn't be. Missing a day or even a week will not cause you to fall into immediate decay. Do not feel guilty, do not be compulsive, and do not add missed workouts to a future day's schedule. If your body tells you it needs a rest, listen. The major goal is to stay healthy and enjoy your running, not to rack up as many miles and consecutive days as you can. If you have missed workouts it may be necessary to drop back to an easier schedule for several days and gradually return to the previous one.

Each workout should consist of at least a five minute warm up (a fast walk or slow jog) before the run and a five minute cool down (again a slow jog or better, a walk). A high mileage programme makes a stretching programme almost a necessity, especially for the muscles of the lower back and the entire backs of the legs. I suggest that this slow stretching programme be done after completion of the workout at least three times a week; more would be better. Other supplemental types of exercise can also be beneficial, if time consuming. Specific stretches and supplemental programmes will not be covered here.

The Race

If you have followed the prescribed training regimen you should be well prepared for the race. I feel that there are two basic strategies in ultra racing.

1) the 'money in the bank theory' - this is to go as fast as you can for as far as you can and finish any way you can; and

2) the 'tortoise approach' - start slowly, keep going at that pace and finish strong.

The first strategy tends to burn much of the available glycogen very soon (in one and a half to two hours) and unless you have great reserves of fat-burning capacity this tends to be painful. This technique can give a large early lead and be psychologically advantageous. Some ultramarathoners of note are very good at this, e.g. Don Ritchie and closer to home, Warren Finke. This can be a very good strategy but requires the runner to be extremely good at monitoring his body and its reserves. It rarely results in superior times, however, and record track performances by both these runners were done at extremely even pace. (Note: Ritchie ran 5:15:58 for the first 50 miles in his 11:30:51 100 miles world best performance - Ed.)

The second strategy is the best approach for the less experienced and long-time fat burners. (I classify myself as a basic turtle and have been known to have the fastest mile splits in the last five miles of a 50.) When using this approach it is best to determine your overall realistic goal for a race and figure the average pace per mile. I start at this pace or 10 - 15 seconds per mile slower and speed up after I've warmed up. the entire race can then be run at a comfortable pace (often a familiar long run training pace.)

Alternating walking and running has been a previously suggested strategy. This idea has several drawbacks. First, you will never win or even run a particularly good time. Second, it alternates usage of different sets of muscles and can be an extremely painful experience. The walking muscles may not be as well trained and can become sore from overuse. It also encourages poorly trained runners to attempt an event beyond their capacity. While walking, the running muscles seem to become stiff and tight from not being kept warm nor getting an adequate blood supply with essential nutrients nor, in my opinion, getting rid of any accumulating lactic acid. I have not seen any physiological studies that cover this and describe what is happening, but experience (my own and numerous others), does not seem to recommend this strategy.

An exception to this is in trail racing, especially for those of us without a high VO2 Max. If you cannot back off to an aerobic pace uphill, walking may be more efficient and less taxing physically. If you need or plan to walk in a race, incorporate periods of walking into your training. I almost always walk the steep patches in my weekly long runs both to save energy and to keep my uphill walking muscles in shape.

No matter what strategy you pick, a pre-race plan should be written down and an attempt made to follow it. The paces picked should be realistic and achievable, not wishful thinking. Remember that the race's important part is not the first 20 miles but actually the last 5 or 10. That's where adequate training and preparation are most important.

The purpose of this programme has been to outline a safe and successful training programme for the ultramarathoner. An explanation of the principles behind the programme has been provided so that the runner can understand why various suggestions have been made. The programme is applicable to most kinds of ultras with modifications of mileage base or specifics (i.e. more trail running for trail racing). If you understand the basic principles as out-lined above you should be able to design a training schedule for any race you want to run. I hope that by following the programme you can be satisfied with your performance and also enjoy the event you've attempted. But you must always remember that one of the major reasons for running is enjoyment and any programme must incorporate fun and variety to keep it enjoyable.

Bruce Fordyce established himself as the foremost 50 mile runner in the world. To date he has won the tough Comrades Marathon (90kms) eight times in a row, and for three successive years won the London to Brighton as well. He currently holds the fastest time for 50 miles on the road for both point to point and loop courses. In 1989 on his 100km debut he set the fastest time yet on a course measured by calibrated bicycle - 6:25:07. His sheer consistency indi-cates that Bruce has a very good idea of what it takes to be successful in the shorter ultras.)

"If at first you can't succeed, you can always become an ultramarathoner." To me there is no doubt that until fairly recently this statement was an accurate assessment of most ultramarathoners and ultramarathons. Many runners of average to mediocre talent were attracted to ultramarathoning because it offered a refuge from the intense competition and extremely high standard found in the 'normal distance races'. The longer and more bizarre the race, the weaker the competition was likely to be - and so it was possible to be a big fish in a relatively small pool of ultramarathoning.

This is changing now. There is more media attention focused on the 'ultras', and a better quality runner is being attracted to the sport. This is particularly the case at the shorter end of the ultra scale, at the 50 - 100 kilometre range. Increasingly, races at these distances are becoming precisely that - races, rather than extended survival trips. South African road running (at all distances) is dominated by one race, the 90 kilometre Comrades Marathon. In May, when the Comrades is run, there is national interest in the race, and unusually, by world standards, an ultramarathon is one of the nation's biggest sporting events. As a result, the Comrades has produced a large number of runners who have specialised in racing 50 to 100 kilometres, and who have become rather good at it. Beyond that distance there is very little interest. My article will be specifically on preparation for the Comrades range of distances, because as a totally inexperienced 'megamarathoner' I am not qualified to speak for the longer distances.

Preparation for races at these distances must be aimed at producing racers rather than 'survivors'. The Comrades, the World 100 kilometre championships, the 56 kilometre Two Oceans, the London to Brighton, to name a few, are races where a runner has to be prepared for several hours of hard cut-and-thrust tactical racing. My training is designed to cope with surges, tempo changes, 3 minute kilometres and steep hills. For those who wish to read no further let me say that with the exception of one or two longer training sessions it is not very different from the training required for the standard 42 kilometre marathoning. After all, the top men 100 kilometre specialists have to be capable of running marathons in the 2:20 to 2:10 range, I prefer also to deal with training principles rather than specific distances, since individuals vary in their ability to cope with different training loads.

1. To race effectively at these distances it is essential to race selectively and sparingly. Just as the World's top marathoners race perhaps two or three marathons in a year, so should the World's top ultramarathoners. I have never been impressed with quantity. Any of the top 100 kilometre runners who are prepared to bore themselves - and the running community in general, can churn out a series of 7 hour races. I would prefer to run perhaps two 6 1/2 hours in a year. I am impressed by quality. Top ultramarathoners are exhausted when they hit the finish line. They cannot contemplate racing again 'next weekend'. They have given their all in one supreme effort. Thompson Magawana nearly collapsed when he finished the 56 kilometre Two Oceans in 3:05. It was months before he effectively raced again - but he had peaked for this one big effort, passing through 42 very hilly kilometres in 2:15 and 50 kilometres in a World record 2:43. World class ultramarathoners peak for one or two special performances in a year.

2. It is now an accepted fact that it is impossible to maintain peak training, and benefit from this training, for more than 8 - 10 weeks (Noakes 1985). This

means that any increase in training for a specific race must begin only in that time period and not before.

3. Again chose quality rather than quantity when training. Train for speed not distance. Speed is the killer. It is infectious. It has spread. To win mile races you have to be fast. To win marathons you have to be fast. The top ultramara-thoners now are showing that to win ultras you have to be fast as well. When Ian Thompson won the 1980 London to Brighton in record time he came to the race as an Olympic marathoner. He was prepared and trained to tackle the standard marathon. He was devastating at 53 miles. For those who enjoy rac-ing, it is possible to kill two birds with one stone by racing at short distances. One can enjoy racing whilst working on speed at the same time. I have had a lot of fun racing at all distances on the track and road while preparing for ultramarathons. The idea is not to be able to sprint fast, after all most ultramar-athons are decided long before the final metres are run, but to be able to raise cruising speed I know that if I can race 10 kilometres in under 30 minutes, I am going to find 32 1/2 minute kilometres fairly easy.

4. As part of this quality training, do some hill work, even if the coming race is on a flat course. Leg strength is vital for ultramarathoning and one of the best ways to get that strength is to run up plenty of hills. Once a week I like to include a specific hill session, striding several repetitions up a steep 400 metre hill.

5. Don't do too many long runs (over 30 kilometres), and when you do, keep them at a slow pace. I find that the long runs simply tire a runner too much and cut adversely into the whole week's training. Thompson, Halberstadt, Maga-wana and others have shown that the long runs aren't that important. It is not the distance covered that matters, but the time on the legs.

6. Be sure to include plenty of rest. Whenever I am unduly tired in training I take a day's rest. In the days immediately before a major race I ensure that I taper my training sufficiently so that by race day I know that I am well rested. I have a feeling that the longer the race the longer the taper needs to be.

7. Read as much as you can about our sport. Motivated people know their subjects. Top ultramarathoners need to know theirs. Read Tim Noakes. Professor Noakes's book ***Lore of Running*** is the closest we will come to having a bible for our sport. It is essential reading, and it covers everything and more about ultramarathoning.

Strategies

Planning how to structure one's training to optimise the time available is not easy. The there are numerous strategies suggested below:

Bernd Heinrich has a formidable record over ultra distances in the United States. In his first ultra he set a new 100km best, and has subsequently annexed all the US track records from 100km up to 24 hours. He has done this within a very limited ultra racing programme by preparing and peaking for specific events. His obvious ability, sub 2 minutes for 800 metres and 2:22 for the marathon has, of course, been a major factor in his success, but his training methods have enabled him to produce excellent performances over a wide range of events.

I have been running since I was a small boy, because it has always been fun. When I was in high school I was into physical development and running was my route of choice. It became an obsession, although it had little to do with competition.

I started running 'seriously', for competitive goals, only 31 years ago, when I was a junior in high school trying out for our cross-country team. I made the team and earned a varsity letter. The next year I won ten straight meets in a row, setting numerous course records.

In college (University of Maine) I ran for three years, earning three varsity letters a year on many championship teams. We ran cross-country in the fall, indoor track in the winter and outdoor track in the spring. In track I ran the two mile. I was not an outstanding two miler. Usually I ran between 9:45 and 10:00. My best was 9:24. At that time, the early 60's, we rarely, if ever, went over 5 miles in a work-out even for cross country and we seldom topped 30 miles per week. Unlike my team mates I ran all summer as well as during all other vacations.

After college I continued to run, after taking a year off. The heavy burden of constant competition in college left me psychologically drained. I ran regularly for about ten years, but I never once competed. I had no desire ever to compete again. I just liked to run. Eventually I joined an informal running 'club', which met on the Berkeley track (in California) every afternoon. We did mostly speedwork, repeat 220's, 440's, half miles, that sort of thing. I became intrigued by speed-running, because I had never done it before. A dream developed to break 2:00 for the half mile. And one day I did it in a solo run, with a friend holding the stop watch. I was 35 years old. This is still one of my most memorable runs, because throughout college I 'knew' I could never go better than 2:05, although I once did two 4:30 miles back-to-back in a work-out.

Having worked speed-running through my system, I got another dream, to run the Boston Marathon. To qualify I ran in a small unknown race, tying for first place with a friend, in 2:33 for my first try at the distance. I felt very strong at the end. This surprised me greatly, because until then the distance seemed untouchable to a mortal like me. The confidence I gained (after running 2:24 at Boston) was sufficient to give me a final, far-out ultimate dream, to go for the US Olympic marathon trials (in the US, the Olympic representatives are chosen in one designated race the Olympic trials) as I turned 40. I now topped 100 miles per week in training for the first time in my life. I figured on doing an all-out run, to do my very best, and then never run competitively again. Well my time was 2:22:36, and from the effort I put I was confident that I did the best I could do at that distance. I felt content not to run it again. However, I had again done most of my passing at the end of the race. That was a clue that perhaps I should try a longer distance.

Perhaps I had failed as a middle-distance runner, but now already having run daily for almost 33 years, I felt I ought to at least give an ultramarathon a try. This was just to ease my conscience.

I picked my race carefully. It would have to be a flat course, at a cool time of the year, preferably at the end of the summer, when I could fit in heavy training. It was the Chicago AMJA 50 mile, 100km in October 1981. The day I started training for this race was a momentous event for me. (The starting gun was almost anticlimactic.) This, I promised myself, would be the only ultrarun I would do in my life. My commitment and effort could not have been less had I planned to assault Mt. Everest. However, shortly after beginning my training I tore a knee cartilage (my left one was already gone). This only increased my sense of urgency - that and age. It gave me a do-or-die attitude. Well, as I said, the race itself was anticlimactic. I was in the best shape of my life when I stepped up to the starting line, and I finished the 100km in 6:38:20. I had planned on being at least 15 minutes faster. But as it turned out I set several records anyway. My first serious ultramarathon was possibly my best. For this race I had necessarily started training with low mileage (because of the knee operation). Week after week through the summer I ran, holding myself back for fear of injury, but gradually working up to 100 - 120 miles per week. The last month was the hardest. I did a 20 mile loop every day, now pushing myself for time. My best training run for the 20 mile training loop was 1:52, but I ran the distance in 2:00 flat routinely. Four days before the race I depleted by running 40 miles. It was also the day after my fastest run, after a week of carbo-depletion, and on an empty stomach with no food along the way. Needless to say, I was far weaker at the end than I was at the end of any race. But three days of carbo-loading did wonders.

I did eventually break the promise I had made to myself (and to my wife) not to run others. I realised that if I bothered to get in shape again I could easily pick up other ultra records. How

would I feel just 2 - 3 years hence, when I would be 45 years old, and the decades thereafter, if I did not get them while I had the chance? I could not come up with a good excuse. Laziness was not something I wanted to live with for the rest of my life.

I would continue to run all my life, but to prepare for and to race for a record was leagues above "normal" running, just as preparing to climb Mt. Everest is different to preparing to take a hike in the Sierras. The one you can only do once, and it is no 10km or marathon that you can keep banging away at.

Training to achieve the very best that you are capable of requires knowing precisely what the limiting factors are to the performance. You also need to know accurately your strengths and weaknesses at any one time, and whether what you are doing at any one time is helping or hindering your progress.

We know a great deal about the factors limiting performance in the sprints (100m - 1000m) and middle distance (10km - marathon). But ultra-marathoners are a different sort of animal, and I honestly still do not know the optimum training regime. The more I read the more confused I get. All that I can say here is that I have guessed, gambled and acted vigorously on my own hunches.

In general, starting out fit and healthy, I train for less time than I did for the AMJA ultra. Three months is about my limit. I seldom run more than once a day, preferring long slow runs to repetitive fast ones. In general I eat before I run, and go at about race pace or faster. Since I peak in my mileage relatively early in my training regimen, I get added stress on the same mileage by mixing in a few longer runs, and/or by running faster. I never stretch, do weights, or do anything else besides straight running. I figure if I do enough mileage then the training will find, and stress, the weakest link to good performance. There is no sense strengthening X when Y will actually be the limiting factor. I figure the only way to uncover Y is to simulate the type of race as closely as possible. In order to find out if I was overstressing myself on 140 miles per week, I once did 200 miles per week for two weeks. I felt just fine. This was a tremendous psychological boost for me, because I had been very much afraid of overtraining.

Over a 32 year running "career" (purely amateur) I am sure I have had sufficient time to achieve my limits. I have experimented with all sorts of regimes, and I have trained specifically for sprints, middle-distances and ultramarathons, all at different times. I do not think any of the three mix. Of course, a good runner can do all three. But not to the extent that he/she tries to mix them, then they will sacrifice in terms of ultimate performance in any one. When I ran my 1:59 half mile I was totally incapable of running a marathon (in under 2:45 I would guess), and when I ran my 2:22 marathon I was incapable of doing a 2:00 half mile. Similarly, when I ran my 6:38 100km, I could not have done a 2:25 marathon. The point is, I have never been a "2:22 marathoner running an ultramarathon". When I could run a 2:22 marathon I was handicapped, I was too specialised for speed at that distance and before I could run my best ultramarathon it was necessary to do considerable painful retooling.

As I said, I have no scientific proof that what I was doing to retool was right, but I needed to believe it was the right thing in order to carry through with it. What follows, then, is my training regimen and its rationale. In retrospect I am not convinced now that it was the best, but at that time I had to be convinced, so I cannot offer alternatives.

Although I routinely carry a background conditioning of 20 - 30 miles per week I have seldom trained for more than three months at a time. I only train with one specific race in mind. The race can only be 2 - 3 months into the future, because otherwise it is difficult for me to concentrate on it every day. This contrasts with other, non-ultra races, of which I have done even twice per day. And of course I regularly run marathons daily, as a form of training, sometimes going all-out.

The day after having cast the die to commit myself to a specific ultra race, I'll go out and typically run a 20 miler. It is always a big hurdle. The last five miles can be sheer agony. But I finish and congratulate myself on making the distance on 'no' training. This little victory right at the start tells me : "Go for it - you can do it".

From then on I do no more speed work. I'm confident of my speed. It is endurance that I need. My theory is that a chain is only as strong as its weakest link. In the second or third week I'm already close to the mileage I'll do for the rest of the training period. My attention is on putting in mileage. I always start my runs slow. If I'm not feeling well, I keep getting slower. If I feel O.K. I might speed up considerably, because I am always in a hurry to get done with the chore. My weakness on the initial training runs is often followed by extreme hunger (I've been so famished that I've stopped at a farmhouse on a lone country road to beg for a crust of bread!). I know what the problem is. The low speed and weakness are due to glycogen depletion, and the hunger sensations come when even the blood glucose finally dips low. Rest and food will reverse the symptoms immediately.

At this point conventional wisdom holds that you slack off, rest a day or two, until you carbo-load again so that you can run relaxed and fast. At this point I differentiate between marathon and ultramarathon training. If training for the former, and maybe even for a 50 miler, I would do precisely as that wisdom dictates because I would want to train my carbo-loading and carbo- burning capacities. An ultramarathon is a different ballpark. There is no way you can store enough carbo for an ultramarathon. In an ultra the weakest link is lipid utilization, and you don't maximally utilize lipids by training for speed (i.e. carbo-metabolism). So I avoid speed like the plague, except at the finish of a long run, if I have any left.

The exhaustion point where I would stop if I were training for a marathon is precisely the point where I begin to start training for the ultra. The mileage until the exhaustion point is useless filler, unless I keep running. I try to put in as much mileage as possible while in the super-exhausted state.

My logic is that an ultra does not even begin until at least 50 miles. The limiting factor is not how much carbo you have on board, (it is a vital link, but not the limiting one, normally), but how well you can dip into your fat stores and eat and digest on the run. So if I'm training for a marathon I run before lunch. If I'm training for an ultra I run after lunch. A speed-runner, in order to achieve speed, should shut off his blood supply to the gut. An ultra runner cannot. So I eat also on the run to train my gut. Also, when I'm carbo-depleted I know that now I'm beginning to dip into the fats. This is the whole aim, although I compromise by training the stomach, too. As to the kind of "fuel" that I use the answer is anything and everything. I let my body tell me what it wants. I figure it knows better than my brain, which is easily biased by the latest fad and fashion.

I should point out that it works both ways. I've learned that the stomach also tries to train me. I ran my 100 mile American record strictly on Exceed, a complex carbohydrate polymer. I thought I had found the magic elixir. Well, the next time I tried it I got violently ill, the mere smell of the stuff made me gag. I had to drop out of the race. I think the reason was that my body remembered the intense pain of my record-setting run and associated it with the drink I used. It said "I refuse to take any more". And it didn't. By the way, I ran my Chicago AMJA 100km record on cranberry juice with the same result. I can't use cranberry juice again, either. I then also thought that I had found the magic elixir, to be quickly brought up short at 30 miles in the next race I tried it. So you see now why it was that I had to drop out of two races! After that I brought all kinds of strange foods, hoping one would not be "recognised" by my body. In my 24 hour run I ate/drank anything I could get my hands on and I developed a super craving for fresh grapes in the last hour. Although I tried both the cranberry juice and Exceed in training, and loved both, I had generally drunk the stuff at the end, as a "reward" for finishing, so it was associated with feelings of pleasure. In the race I tricked my body but it only let me do it once per given food.

My training logs often show slower and slower running times from one day to the next. But you can't expect a car to run when it is out of fuel, so I'm not concerned. I never get muscle soreness when I'm forced to be slow because I'm running on empty. Muscle soreness occurs sometimes on days when I'm carbo-loaded and feel fast and strong, when I push it to the finish. I always cut back from muscle soreness but never from fatigue. Pain = injury. Fatigue = low fuel. I realise that by this regimen my marathon speed will be getting slower and slower, because the fast marathoner still has to rely largely on carbo-metabolism, which I'm trying to avoid. I'm thinking about surviving the second and third, 50 mile instalment of the race. The first 50 miles are not the limiting factor. I've used the same training regimen regardless of the distance of the race. I don't think there is any difference between a 100 mile and a 24 hour race. In fact, when I ran my 156 3/4 miles for the American record at 24 hours, I had planned all along to go for the 100 mile record in that race. I only changed my mind, to stay the entire 24 hours, half an hour before the start of the event, when I knew from the weather reports and temperatures that day would be in the 80's. That made "speed-running" for 100 miles out of the question. But I figured on making up at night, when it would be cooler.

I suspect the ideal would be to train by regularly running ultra races (provided that they are not more than two weeks apart so that you don't lose what you gain before building on it). However, I do not like to leave my work (equals fun) of teaching, research and writing. Each run would take a couple of days out of my schedule. By running day after day in a carbo-depleted state, I am physiologically chronically up at that point for the race where endurance is critical. It is not a fun type of training.

To summarize, in effect I try to get the ultra-experience by running each day before fully recovering from the previous day. I use the previous 20 - 30 mile run to bring me "instantly" to the critical phase of training (for lipid utilization) on the next day, without actually running that 20 - 30 again that day before I feel pain. If I ran only when refreshed and fast every day, then I would be training for races like the marathon, or some other distance irrelevant to my goal.

Tony Jones coached Carolyn Hunter-Rowe (holder of the world track bests at 30 miles, 50 km and 40 miles and the U.K. 100km road best and winner of the 1993 and 1998 IAU 100km World Challenge), and Hilary Johnson (holder of several world ultra age group records.

The character of an ultra runner used to be that of an ageing middle-distance runner. As the athlete gets older and slower so the distance for competition becomes greater in the belief that longer, slower training is kinder to the body. The joints, bones and sinews complain and the ability to hurt during training may be less strong. So the young speedster, champing at the bit, gently mellows, spending extra hours in like minded company putting in the miles. The 1500m time becomes less relevant than the 10k time and this is an indication of possible marathon times.

These views I have accepted as the norm. It has taken me some time and altered conviction to question them.

I have been involved with coaching some of these more mature athletes for the last 10 years. I admit to having had an entrenched pig-headed, old dyed-in-the-wool athlete's attitude as to what older athletes could do and what age bestowed on an athlete.

I have been reluctant to believe the results of my experiments with speed-work for mature, non swift athletes. So what have I tried and what have I discovered?

I started with mainly female athletes who needed retraining after raising their families and trying to cope with all the extra responsibilities and body weight this brings, not to mention restriction of time. The athletes I chose to coach did possess a drive and internal energy, plus an inbuilt need to push themselves to higher levels of achievement. They needed a rapid response programme so they did not become disillusioned but showed marked and immediate improvement.

Two problems were paramount; too little time, too much weight. To alleviate the no time problem the programme had to be rapid i.e. in short sessions and effective. To alleviate the overweight problem, the programme had to burn fat as regularly as possible. I had to look carefully at exercise physiology in order to attain my twin aims. I found that to burn fat, speedwork triggers enzymes in the body which encourage growth in the white, fast-twitch fibres. these are the fibres primarily concerned with the breakdown of fatty acids circulating in the body, to release energy for use by the muscles.

The prevalent "long slow running" theory would give these athletes nothing. To gain improvement the sessions had to be short and sharp. This would build a strong and capable cardio-vascular system and lay firm foundations for further improvement.

The need for a strong heart, able to pump an adequate amount of oxygen-carrying blood around the body in unblocked capillaries, is paramount in any hopeful athlete. Any weakness in this area must be treated seriously and medical advice taken.

Schedules;

All speedwork should be balanced out with other training regimes in operation concurrently.

eg; i) long steady runs   17 miles plus
     ii) sustained runs   8-12 miles
     iii) hill work
     iv) sub-distance races, pre-race build-up
     v) speed sessions

I will concentrate on the latter. They can be broken down further;
A. speed/speed...........ie intervals
B. speed/endurance
C. fartlek........... speedplay

Firstly A.

This is a shorter distance workout, usually not more than 2 mins with an equal recovery time or distance e.g. 8 x 300m with 300 jog interval or 200m walk continuous. This type of training best facilitates the enzyme production to encourage growth in the fast-twitch fibres. This greater preponderance of white fibres than previously will mean a greater ability to run faster more easily, will enable leg cadence to be increased and will guarantee better finishing speed to end a race. Other examples are 18 x 200 in 3 sets of 6 with a 200m jog interval plus a full lap walk between each set. All these intervals should be done on a track or measured course. When this is not available, a lamp-post to lamp-post course is just as good. Take a 2 mile warm-up, then do a 20 lamp-post session, sprint-jog times 3.

Secondly B.

Speed-endurance. There are 2 levels here.

The reps get longer and the recovery time shorter.

The reps get shorter but the sets increase.

Shorter recovery time improves lactic acid tolerance.

Increased reps improves strength also.

Ideas for the former include 12 x 400 with 200 jog interval.

8 x 800 with 400 jog int. These should be run at the athletes 10k road time.

Examples of the latter include 5 x 4 x 200m fast or 4 x 4 x300m fast.

Also under this heading is included pyramid running.

These sessions can be constructed within any constraints prevailing at the time. They begin with a short distance, followed by a longer distance started after a set interval. A longer distance follows, usually after the same interval, then a max distance. After this the distances are repeated in reverse order. These can be run in town or country and will benefit any athlete. For an ultra runner a pyramid of 200, 400, 600, 800, 1000, 800, 600, 400, 200 x 2 or 3 would be considered the norm.

Thirdly C.

Fartlek. Speed-play. These are still speed sessions but are relaxed and should be done at random but with bursts of 3 to 5 mins fast. Fartlek is undertaken on any type of terrain, road, country, woods, dunes, fells etc. This is a good transitional session between intervals and distance training because the pace is the athlete's own dependent upon terrain. These sessions increase the VO2 max and train the body to cope with varying levels of lactic acid, increasing the race pace tolerance level of the body to lactic acid. The 3 - 5 min bursts should be at 10k race pace and the number done should increase rather than the distance between each one

To summarise;

The athletes who undertook the speedwork sessions improved rapidly on VO2 levels and on their ability to cope with higher grade training sessions. Their ability to race, rather than run races, became readily apparent.

It is important to realise that the overall distance run is not always of overall importance. To improve cardio-vascular performance takes several routes. Running 8 x 200 is not the same as 4 x 400. Heart beats per min. are important here, so to ensure an adequate blood supply at the end of an ultra an athlete needs to ensure the heart has been trained to supply a tired body's needs. The athlete can only do this by making sure that the training was specific enough to raise the heart and lung level to crisis proportions. The only way to do this is with speed training.

Ultra running signifies an inability to do over distance training. Ultra runners know that each race is a gamble, a challenge. They realise that this race is a much a mental challenge as a physical one. It is important to them to know that their training is correct. At the end of an ultra race all athletes hurt. It is those who know that their training is good who will prevail.

Don Turner in the 60s and early 70s was highly regarded as an ultra runner. He started running ultras at an early age, second in the 1959 Brighton and third in 1961. He travelled to South Africa as part of an RRC team to tackle the Comrades and finished third. His experience comes from a time when British ultra runners were dominant. Perhaps it is time to re-consider high mileage training for ultras.

My advice is normally that there is little advice that one can give - it is something you have to work out for yourself, everyone is different with different circumstances - and I personally couldn't see how anyone could attempt the Brighton, say , without clocking 100 miles a week. Reading some of the other contributions here it is apparent that very fine performances can be achieved by some runners on considerably less than that mileage - much depends on quality of training.

I followed Arthur Newton's principles in training and went to his house to meet him in Ruislip. We all trained in Dunlop "Red Flash" plimsolls which had a certain amount of cushioning but they did have the merit that they were all the same and were always readily available when you wore a pair out. I am convinced that many of today's foot troubles are caused by too much support so that your action is changed and by the inability to keep buying the same type of shoe.

My aim soon after starting running was to run a marathon and to this end I built up mileage slowly and steadily working mainly in partnership with John Smith of my club. I don't think either of us would have coped with the chore of training without the other's encouragement. The only way I knew to improve - and I was only a plodder - was to cover more and more mileage at a slow pace 'a la Newton' to become stronger and able to bear a much faster pace in a race. I eventually got through my first Brighton and then got the peculiar notion in my head that I wanted to run the RRC 100 miles - I don't think I had any idea of covering it in any particular time, I just wanted to do the distance and I thought that I had to get the training up as much as possible to be fit enough to cover that distance.

That Summer John Smith and I were running about 150 miles a week comprised of 30 miles Sunday, 26 miles Monday evening, 26 miles Tuesday evening, 15 miles Wednesday evening, 26 miles Thursday evening, 15 miles Friday evening and a race on Saturday. I began to realise that this could not only be the way to get fit but to really start recording decent times when I ran 2-44 for the Peterborough Marathon and then slotted in my normal 26 miles training the next day. I also found that we got so fit that we loved the hot weather - the AAA Marathon at Watford was won by Chris Fleming-Smith in 2-36 and I beat people that day who were real stars to me, and this spurred me on to 180 miles a week training reaching a peak of 200 in late August.

The South London 30 was also run in a heat wave that year and 3-16 was very satisfying to me, but still I never dreamed that I could reach top class. But I was so confident for the Brighton, some 4 weeks before the 100 miles that I decided to 'give it a go' and if I blew up then I would steady up and still be confident of finishing. At 30 miles I was 12th, and then I felt so good and so full of running that I charged through the field from 30 miles to 50 miles such that at times I was almost sprinting and telling myself to save a bit. I all but caught the winner in Brighton but it was not to be. The time was 5-46 and

I had proved that long slow training can bring class performances. Although superficially I recovered quickly, the race was still in my legs four weeks later but I never had any trouble in finishing the 100 in 13-43. Incidentally, I got up about two hours before the start of that 100 mile race and ate a large plateful of shepherds pie and baked beans, with rice to follow - carbohydrate loading!

Over the next five or six years I trained up to 150 miles a week at peak periods but never to the extent of that first year. You learn a bit about yourself all the time and the confidence you gain probably makes you put that much more into your training so that the quality is slightly raised. But most of my running was done at 8 miles per hour and I ran 1-21 for 15 miles, 2-30 for a marathon and 5-37 for the Brighton on that.

I don't think many athletes really like training without the lure of races ahead. You can only train to suit yourself and in the environment and conditions in which you find yourself. I used to train only once a day in the evenings, except Saturdays and Sundays. When I went to Scotland I kept to a similar routine running 12 miles after work each day, then 25 miles Saturday and 30 miles Sundays - they were lonely runs! Then when I worked at Guildford 20 miles from home, I used to drive to work Monday, leave the car at work, run home, and run in the next morning, then drive home - the same on Wednesday and Thursday - 80 miles in the week + weekend training - not bad. This was interesting training too, because you were getting in 2 x 20s evening and next morning, then a relatively long rest to the next evening. In latter years I have found running home from work the easiest way to get a run in without taking too much time and there is always an incentive in running home - one way - and a satisfaction nowadays in proving you can get home on your own two feet without waiting for public transport.

We used to get up to all sorts of gimmicks too to make training more interesting. We have run to Worthing (50 miles) and then run in a relay there, we have run to venues for track matches when there is a team coach going, or run-home from such venues, we have been picked up by coaches on the more distant trips but it can get a bit hairy when you are running along waiting for the coach to pick you up 40 miles from home when you're bursting to go behind a tree and daren't leave the road! Then we have run a series of races on successive weekends - a marathon, a 20, a 48.5 miles and a 30 mile on successive weekends more as an exercise in itself to learn more about the effect on you than to think you can do well in them all.

As one gains more experience and knows oneself better I think you can cut down the mileage and up the quality - I think this involves more risk of injury. I don't think I would ever have achieved the performances I did without the high mileage I put in. But it's not for everyone - I recognise that. What I do know too is that long distance runners, and ultra-ones even more so, make the best bunch of friends you can ever have, who stay with you for a lifetime.

Although 1975 was perhaps Cavin's greatest year, nine years later he was still able to defeat a very high class European field in a track 100km. Cavin was a very individualistic runner, both in the way he always set out lead from the gun, and in his training. An account of the latter appears below.

I have been running now for twenty-three23 years, and probably reached my peak in the mid-70s, but my approach to training has always been the same throughout my running career.

I have always disliked training and it is only the thought of the race at the weekend which forces me to maintain my daily routine (for that is what training has become).

There is no way that I could train for weeks at a time in an effort to produce one good performance at the end; and I believe that runners who do that can find that, as well as missing out on many enjoyable races during the build-up period, there is always the chance that something can go wrong on the "big day" and all your sacrifices will have been in vain. Let's face it, anything can happen - you may catch a cold on the day of the race, the conditions could turn out to be treacherous, or you could misjudge the race and blow up altogether and have to pull out and start all over again.

My philosophy has always been "to be race fit, you have to race" and that is why, throughout my athletic career I have always tried to participate in at least one race a week, providing I am not injured. That is not to say that I have to be 100% fit. I have run many, many races with the idea of treating it as a training run or as a "bleed out" for a marathon or ultra race the following weekend, and therefore I do not put pressure on myself to do well every time I go out to race. This means that if I have a 'below par' run one weekend, I do not get too despondent, but can then look forward to improving in the following race, knowing that I only have seven days to pull myself back together again.

I have never run further than 20 miles in training, and the most training I have ever covered in one week is 75 miles plus a race at the weekend.

My schedule for the week prior to my world best for 30 miles in 1975 was as follows:-

Sunday				20 miles
Monday	a.m.	3 miles;	p.m.	10 miles
Tuesday	a.m.	3 miles;	p.m.	10 miles
Wednesday	a.m.	3 miles;	p.m.	10 miles
Thursday	a.m.	3 miles;	p.m.	4 miles
Friday	Rest			
Saturday	World Best Performance 2-43-52 for 30 miles			

Prior to my Brighton win later that year I incorporated an intensive racing programme into my preparation. my racing schedule for the five week-ends up to and including the Brighton was as follows:-

Week End	1.12 miles	- 1-03-22
	2 SLH 30	- 2-55-20 (2nd)
	3 Highgate Marathon	- 2-28-47
	4 Nuneaton 10	- 52-54 followed by the
	Rotherham Marathon	- 2-34-35 the next day
	5 London to Brighton	- 5-12-07 (1st)

I prepared three schedules for the Accolade 100 mile track race in 1975 - one to break Derek Kay's 11.56.56 by 20 minutes, one to break it by 5 minutes and one to break John Tarrant's UK record of 12.30. On the fastest schedule I aimed to reach 50 miles in 5.05 but if I was going well I would aim to break the 50 mile best of 5.01.01. My one big problem with this race was I did not know if I could cover the distance. The longest race I had run had been the Brighton, so I knew I could run 50 miles, so I decided to go for as fast a time as possible for 50 miles and then 'hang on' as long as I could to see if I could cover the 100 mile course.

By 40 miles I was 3 minutes 42 seconds ahead of plan so I pushed on to run 4.58.53 for 50. I was nine minutes ahead of schedule at 60 miles and set a world 100km best of 6.25.28. In fact I did not realise I had broken this record until I had gone through the 100km point, as I relaxed somewhat after breaking the 50 mile record. I had not intended to break the 100km world best and on reflection wonder if I could have improved on this time had I set my mind on attempting it. However, by 70 miles I had slipped back to only six minutes inside my schedule and by 78 miles I only had a 2 minute cushion. Dr John Brotherhood had checked my urine and said I was suffering from fatigue and moreover my temperature was dropping too quickly. He advised me to put on some extra clothing, which I did. I warmed up and from the 150km point I picked up the pace and in fact finished 18 minutes 02 seconds inside Derek Kay's record.

I know that in the early stages of the race the critics were saying that I was going too fast to be able to crack the 100 miles and that my tactics of "running as fast as I could for as long as I could" would not pay dividends. But I hope I proved that running even-paced is not the only way of winning races and breaking records. I would like to think that if a runner wants to try to run ultras fast from the start against the wishes of his coach/trainer he could convincingly argue that that was the way Cavin Woodward did it.

My build up to the 100 miles, four weeks after my win in the Brighton was as follows:-

Week   1 - 22 miles
                 2 - 71 miles
                 3 - 48 miles (including a 10 mile race)
                 4 - 41 miles and three training free days prior to the race.

The week before the race I used the carbohydrate loading diet.

My normal week of training nowadays comprises a 10 mile run in the evenings, Monday to Wednesdays, 12 miles (pm) on Thursday, 3 miles Friday (pm) and I usually keep Saturdays training-free if I am racing on a Sunday.

If I am racing on a Saturday I do not run on Friday evening but will train on Sunday morning for about 12-15 miles at the most.

During the summer months, when the road season is at its height, I occasionally manage a 3 mile training run in the mornings as well.

My distaste for training is aggravated when I find I have to train by myself and I am sure I am not alone in my opinion that it is far easier to train with somebody and this is the advice I would offer anyone who, like me, finds training a drag. I do not train fast, probably at about 6.30 to 7 minute mile pace and I try to avoid "racing" training runs with fellow athletes. Often I feel that runners put too much effort into their training and then cannot fulfil their own expectations when it comes to racing. I firmly believe that the best results are obtained, not by the amount of mileage or speed of training sessions but by training consistently and racing frequently. I think you are more motivated to train if you know the next race is only a few days away.

I have completed 200 marathons and ultras and as you can see these have been achieved with very modest training. I have never had a coach or trainer, just the support of my wife and family. No one can teach you how to train or race; it is an individual thing which has to be drawn from your own personal experiences and capabilities. I believe I have achieved my ambitions and goals as a result of the abundance of races I have taken part in, balanced with my moderate, unpressured training schedules. Although at times I find it difficult to motivate myself to train, this is far outweighed by the enjoyment I get from racing, especially the comradeship in the ultra circuit - I really do run for fun and when I stop enjoying athletics I will know it's time to stop. I was fortunate to still be featuring "in the frame" of ultra races ten years past my peak. Whatever happens, I will never change my approach to training or my thirst for racing - for me, at any rate, it has worked!

Tom O'Reilly was unfortunate in that his peak as an ultrarunner over the shorter distances coincided with that of one of the all-time greats, Cavin Woodward. Despite that he still won the 1976 Brighton. Injury robbed him of a good 24 Hours performance (he was 5th on the world 100 mile track list with 12 hours 02 minutes), yet in 1982 he ran one of the most controlled 6 days to date to set a new world best. Since then injury and other commitments have restricted his ultra racing.)

I would recommend that an average marathon runner thinking of moving up to the ultras takes the transition slowly and only races when they feel ready. They should get used to running slowly, but not for very long distances, carrying on with fast running in short races. The odd training run at around 50 mile racing pace, about once a week running as you feel, not to an inflexible schedule. It is important to get runs up to 3 hours as often as possible - Saturday and Sunday, plus one or two runs during the week of 12 to 15 miles. Be sensible in your choice of your first ultra races - try the shorter events like the SLH 30, the Two Bridges 36 miles, the Woodford 40 or the Isle of Man 40. [All sadly no longer held but 50km races and the Barry 40 still exist – Ed.]

The majority of my training runs are at 6:30 to 7:30 pace, depending how I feel, how fit I am and the weather. Sometimes I have run 10 - 12 miles at a better average pace than 3 - 6 miles.

My preparation for the 1976 London to Brighton and the subsequent 100km track race involved a 9 week build up to peak mileage, then three weeks easing off to the Brighton. I then built up for a further 4 weeks before easing off 2 weeks to the 100km.

The weekly mileages were:-

w/e 10/7 - 79.4 miles		w/e 11/9 - 120.6 miles	
w/e 17/7 - 102.7		w/e 18/9 - 106	
w/e 24/7 - 89.4		w/e 25/9 - 65.3	
w/e 31/7 - 133.8		w/e2/10 - 88.8	
	(including the Brighton)		
w/e7/8 - 133.8		w/e9/10 - 66.5	
w/e 14/8 - 109.9		w/e 16/10 - 93.8	
w/e 21/8 - 171.7	(record week)	w/e 23/10 - 121.2	
w/e 28/8 - 146.6		w/e 30/10 - 106	
w/e4/9 - 174.6	(record week)	w/e5/11 - 109.8	
	(including 100km track race)		

My record week (w/e 4/9 - 174.6 miles) breaks down as follows:-
Sunday   (am) 50.8 miles (6:04:40)
Monday   (am) 16.8 miles (pm) 6.3 miles
Tuesday   (am) 17.4 miles (pm) 4.2 miles
Wednesday   (am) 10.1 miles (pm) 10.1 miles
Thursday   (am) 9.8 miles   (pm) 10.4 miles
Friday   (am) 16.3 miles (pm) 10.7 miles
Saturday   (am) 11.7 miles
Sunday   (am) 52.9 miles (The Brighton)
                5 hrs 23 mins 32 secs (1st).

The week following the Brighton was:-
Monday   (am) 1.6 miles
Tuesday   (am) 6.3 miles
Wednesday   (am) 6.1 miles
Thursday   (am) 7.3 miles
Friday   (am) 4.3 miles
Saturday   (am) 4.5 miles   (pm) 3.7 miles

The week immediately prior to the 100km race went as follows:-
Sunday   (am) 14.4 miles
Monday   (am) 6.0 miles(pm) 6.6 miles
Tuesday   (am) 6.8 miles
Wednesday   (am) 7.2 miles
Thursday   (am) 4.2 miles
Friday   (am) 2.1 miles
Saturday   (am) 100km track race,
                6 hrs 43 mins 59 secs (1st).

The number of quality long distance races a runner can compete in during the year depends very much on the individual. For myself perhaps 3 to 4 marathons/long distance events. This would be in a 6 month period from May to October; in the full 12 months probably 6 or 7 races but then the additional events would be several months away from the ultras.

It takes me at least a month, probably more to recover from a 30 mile plus race. The six weeks between my Brighton and track 100km I consider a minimum racing gap for me.

I cope mentally with the long training runs by carrying a stereo cassette recorder so I can listen to music, talks etc; talking to training partners is another way to make the miles pass quicker. In the race I try to keep alert to the race - how fast I am running; when will I next get a sponge/drink. Also I have time to think, plan and dream of past events.

For an ultra like the Brighton I try to stock up with carbohydrates in the last 2-3 days. I don't attempt a depletion stage - I tried it and it didn't work for me. I have found the loading should be done at regular intervals, rather than trying to pile it all into one meal.

100km Training

The 100km is the Universal Ultra, held around the world and is recognised for both championships and records by the IAAF. It can also be a high pressure event at the highest levels.

Andy Milroy is a British ultra running historian, founding member of the International Association of Ultrarunners (IAU) and the Association of Road Racing Statisticians (ARRS), and a ultra statistician and writer.

In October 1975 Cavin Woodward, running in a track 100 miles, set a new world best for 50 miles of 4.54.53. Losing concentration he eased off a little but still went through the 100km point in 6.25.28. (He was to carry on to set a new world 100 mile best of 11.38.54). Three years later Don Ritchie reduced the 100km track best to 6.10.20.

In the thirty five plus years since Cavin set his 6.25, the world ultra scene has been transformed out of all recognition. There is now an annual World 100km championships and national 100km championships exist in many countries. The 100km has become the universal ultra, promoted and practised on every inhabited continent. Despite the huge expansion in the number of races, of runners tackling the event, and the great rise in its status, few men have surpassed Cavin's 100km split time. Don Ritchie's 6.10 remains well clear of all opposition. Why should this be? Were Cavin Woodward and Don Ritchie such special athletes?

The answer as to why they produced such good times perhaps lies in their racing programs. In 1975 in the preparation for this 100 mile, Cavin ran eight marathons at sub maximal pace, using them as training runs for ultras (the times ranged from 2.22 to 2.37). He also ran five ultras - two 30 milers, a 36 miler, a 40 miler and the London to Brighton. In between these he ran a mixture of shorter races ranging from a track 5km to 10 miles on the road. Thus the bulk of Cavin's racing was close to or shorter than the marathon. Apart from the 40 miler, he ran only two long ultras that year.

Don Ritchie was perhaps at his peak as an l00km runner between 1977 and 1982. Looking at his racing program for 1977, it was based even more firmly on short races than Cavin's was. Apart from two 50km track races and the 36 mile Two Bridges, the bulk of his races were over 10 to 12 miles, with a couple of 3 and 5km track races thrown in for good measure. He ran just two long ultras – the Brighton and the 24 Hours at Crystal Palace. In the latter event he stopped at 100 1/2 mile having set a new world 100 mile best of 11.30.51.

The following year a prolonged knee injury severely limited Don's racing until June when he ran 6.18.00 for the Hartola 100km. Don has said that he felt superb that day. Between Hartola and the Brighton, Don ran a 13 miler, a marathon, a 40 miler, a 10 miler and the 36 mile Two Bridges. In early October he won the Brighton in a course record, and a month later set a new world l00km track best of 6.10.20.

In 1979, following a 50km, a 40 miler and a marathon Don won the Del Passatore 101km, and three weeks later set a new world 100 mile road best at Flushing Meadow, New York. Recovery from the 100 mile took some time. Injuries then curtailed his training and caused him to retire in both the Brighton and the Crystal Palace 24 hours. 1980 followed a similar pattern - good wins at the Turin - St Vincent 100km and the Del Passatore were followed by injuries which cut short his ultra racing schedule for the year. The battle against injury continued into 1982. At last, late in 1982 Don began to recover, achieving 2.24 for the Aberdeen marathon in September. A week later he ran 6.28.11 to win the tough Santander 100km, the fastest time to that date on a certified course. Three weeks later he entered the RRC 100km track race. In very tough windy conditions he set a new world best for 40 miles before retiring from the battle.

From the above it can be seen that both runners raced only twice or three tines a year at 50 miles and beyond, either through intent or circumstances, building up to such events by using short sub marathon, marathon and short ultra events.

What of the runners who have surpassed Cavin's 6.25.28 on a certified course - what was their racing schedules like? One was the Belgian, Jean-Paul Praet. His coach, Patrick Descheppe, wrote that Jean-Paul's yearly program contained two 100km races, one in June and the other in the autumn. Before the first 100km event he would run one or two half marathons, a marathon, a 50km race followed perhaps by another marathon. This is from March until the first two weeks of May. Following the 100km came three weeks rest with some light training before the build up to the next 100km in the autumn.

Another runner was Bruce Fordyce. In "International Ultra Training" Bruce wrote "Just as the World's top marathoners race perhaps two or three marathons in a year, so should the World's top ultramarathoners.... Any of the top 100km runners can churn out a series of 7 hour races. I would prefer to run perhaps two sub 6 1/2 hours in a year." In 1983 he ran the 56km Two Ocean race as a training run (3.14) in preparation for the Comrades. After setting up a record in that race he took four to six weeks to recover fully before preparing for the Brighton. In the Brighton that year (his third successive win in the event) he set a new world 50 mile road best of 4.50.21. His advice on marathons was to use them as training runs. He would probably only race hard once (over the full marathon distance) in the five months before the Comrades.

In the early 1990s the fastest marathon runner to successfully make the transition to the ultras was Konstantin Santalov, a 2.14 performer. Minutes faster over the marathon than Fordyce, Ritchie, Woodward or Praet, he had the potential to threaten even Ritchie's 6.10. He ran under 6:30 eleven times, four times in 1992, but aside from a sub 6:20 mark set on a course not measured by calibrated bicycle, he never approached Ritchie's 6:10. Arguably he never achieved his true potential at the 100km, due to his extravagant racing policy

It was left to an even faster marathon runner to challenge Ritchie's 100km time. Takahiro Sunada in 1995 competed for Japan in the IAAF World Marathon Cup over the classic Athens marathon course, finishing second behind the former World marathon champion Douglas Wakiihuri, in a personal best of 2:13:16 to Wakiihuri's 2:12:01.

In December at the famous Fukuoka marathon, he finished 10th in another personal best of 2:12:01. He was still only 22 years old. He was still improving at the shorter distances running 13:43:39 in 1996 for 5000 metres.

Most of 1997 was lost through injury when he was forced to have surgery to the plantar muscle. In 1998 he decided to move up to the 100km. This is unusual for an elite marathon runner in Japan where such runners are employed as members of company teams who tend to decide the races these runners compete in.

Sunada recorded the fastest road time on record on a course measured by calibrated bicycle - 6:13:33. Interestingly racing the 100km did not affect Sunada's basic speed he was still able to run sub-14:30 minute for 5000 metres.

1999 did not start well for Sunada. He did not finish the Beppu-Oita Marathon in February, and ran only 2:22:44 in the Nagano marathon in April. Despite this he entered as an individual in the World 100km Challenge in Chavagnes in France. There he set out to run away from the rest of the field, clocking a phenomenal 2:54 for the first 50km. He went through the 60km in about 3:28 but trouble hit at 63km. He finished with a final time of 6:26:06.

Later in the year he returned to the Fukuoka Marathon and again set a personal best of 2:11:03, finishing 8th. Not only did his basic marathon speed seem unaffected by his ultra experiments, indeed it seemed enhanced.

However his Fukuoka performance was then followed by a more mediocre time (2:20:00) at the Tokyo Marathon in February 2000. Unable to compete in the World 100km Challenge that year he entered the European 100km Championships as a guest in Belves in France. He won the open race easily in 6:17:17.

Once again the 100km event did not seem to make an impact on his basic speed. In May he was able to run 14:18:05 for 5000 metres on the track, and in July he finished 8th in the Sapporo half marathon in 1:03:39. In September in the Berlin marathon he finished fourth in a new personal best in 2:10:08.

Sunada's racing strategy has been covered in some depth because he shows that running 100km races can improve marathon performance and that a restricted racing program at the 100km can be effective in terms of running very fast times. Unfortunately his experiments with the 100km ended in 2000.

Perhaps the most dominant male 100km runner to emerge in recent times is Giorgio Calcaterra of Italy. Calcaterra, like Cavin Woodward, likes to race frequently, he competes almost every weekend, and has run more than 1,000 races in his career. Over his career he has averaged 16 marathons a year, with a peak of 31 in 2004. In 2000 he was credited with running 16 marathons under 2:20; his personal best is 2:13:15 in 2000. At shorter distances his personal bests are 14:39 for 5000 metres and 30:00 for 10,000 metres with 1:05:00 for the Half Marathon.

In 2003, Calcaterra took part in the difficult Pistoia Abetone, a 53 km uphill race, winning in 3.41.01, (Mario Fattore, world 100km champion in 2002 and 2003, was second in the same time) In 2004 Calcaterra again won the Pistoia Abetone, this time in 3.30.20. In 2006 he moved up to the 100km.

That year he ran three 100km races plus a 50 mile race and the 78km Swiss Alpine Marathon.He took the national title at Faenza in 6:45:24 but finished away from a podium finish in 11th place (7:04:01) at the World 100km in Korea.

The following year he undertook two 100km races plus the Swiss Alpine Marathon (78km), but it was 2008 that saw him reduce his ultra racing schedule still further. He won the Passatore at Faenza in May and then won the World 100km in 6:37:41 in November.

The following year he contested three 100km races, finishing second in the European 100km at Torhout, despite persistent stomach problems. For six to eight months during the second half of 2009 and the first months of 2010 his training was interrupted by continual back problems during his work as a taxi driver. 2010 again saw two 100km races plus the Swiss Alpine Marathon, but because of the back problem in neither 2009 nor 2010 was he a contender in the World 100km.

In 2011 he was able to revert to the successful pattern of 2008, running only the Passatore before again winning the World 100km in 6:27:32.

Calcaterra has been successful at the highest level when he restricted the number of 100km run in a year.

Does this success with a restricted racing program at 100km apply just to male runners? If we look at the elite female runners who have produced 100km performances of around 7.30 and faster there are three individuals - Chantal Langlace, Ann Trason and Brigit Lennartz. Chantal Langlace was basically a marathon runner who moved up to the ultras a couple of times very successfully. (Her 7.27.22 was on a course that was around 550 metres short so equates to around 7.32 on a full 100km course). I suspect Chantal ran a mixture of shorter races, 10kms, 1/2 marathons and marathons as preparation for the 100km since that would be her standard running fare.

I don't have details of Ann Trason's racing program for 1988 (The year she set a world road best of 7.30). However I have made a careful study of Ultra-running Magazine for that year. She appears to only have completed one ultra prior to Santander, the 100 mile trail race at Leadville where she set a course record of 21.40. That was in late August. Previously she had retired from the Western States 100 miles at 73 miles in late June. Her run in early October at Santander was on a tough hilly course which makes her 7.30.49 even more remarkable.

It is interesting that the following year in ideal conditions on a much faster course she ran 7.33.12, despite the motivation of having lost her world 100km best that year. That year, 1989, she had run a 100 mile track world best in March, a course record in the Western States trail 100 miles in June and in September had run sub 8 hours for 100km en route to a new world road 100 miles best of 13.55.02 and 143 miles 152 yards in 24 hours. So by late October she had a lot more competitive long ultra miles in her legs than she had had a year before.

The woman who took the world 100km road best from Trason was Brigit Lennartz. Dr Karl Lennartz, her father and coach, has written a detailed account of Brigit's racing schedule for 1990, the year when she improved on her own world 100km best. In January she ran a half marathon followed by three 10km races; in March a half marathon followed by a 10km and a marathon in 2.38.15. Over the next month she ran a 15km, a 1/2 marathon, a 10km, a 25km and two more 10kms, leading up to her 7.18.57 100km best in April. A similar racing schedule prepared her for another 100km in June (7.51.50), and then in late July she won the Swiss Alpine marathon (67km). In terms of times Brigit's 7.18 and 7.26.52 place her well clear of the opposition. It is interesting to note that her racing schedule is very similar to that of Ritchie, Praet and Fordyce.

Trason regained the world best with 7:09:44 in 1993. That 100km looks to have been her only road ultra that year. She had won a 50km on the trails, then the American River 50 miler on the trails, and another 50 miler before winning the Western States 100 miler in June. She ran another 50km on the trails before the Amiens 100km.

When Trason broke this record at Winschoten in 1995 with 7:00:48, she had followed a similar pattern of races to 1993. She ran a 50km on the trails then a week later regained her 50km track world best when she ran 3:20:24 at Santa

Rosa. In April she ran the American River 50 miler, again on trails. In June she won the Western States 100 miles on the trails running 18:40:01. On the information currently available, the 100km at Winschoten looks to be her only ultra at the 100km or longer on the roads that year.

The fastest 100km yet on the roads by a woman was set by the Japanese runner Tomoe Abe in the Lake Saroma race in Hokkaido, Japan in 2000. Her 6:33:11 100km was rooted in a strong base as a fast runner at shorter distances - 3000 metres in 9:22:15 in 1989, 5000 metres in 15:53:46 in 1993 and 10,000 metres in 32:55.78. In 1993 she also ran 67:39 for 20km on the road.

She made her marathon debut in 1993 when she ran 2:26:27 and was then third that year in the World Championships marathon at Stuttgart in 2:31:01. The following year she won the Japanese Marathon championships in 2:26:09 which was also a new Japanese marathon record.

She ran no marathons in 1995 but was third in the Japanese marathon championships in 1995In 1997 she was selected to run in the World Marathon Championships but struggling to finish in 29th place, in 2:45:19. .

1998 again saw a relative decline in her performances as the standards in the women's event in Japan rose. Coached byTakeshi and Shigeru Soh, twin brothers who were notable marathon runners in the late seventies and early eighties, they suggested that she attempt a 100km run to convince her that she had extraordinary endurance capabilities.

The example of Takahiro Sunada may also have been influential in persuading the Soh brothers that such a run would be beneficial to Abe's marathon career. Sunada had shown that running such distances as the 100km could have a positive effect on the performance of an elite marathon runner. The 100km race was undertaken as part of Abe's marathon training.

This was the only 100km that Abe was to run in her career. Regrettably it did not lead to a renaissance in her marathon career.

So the evidence from women seems to support the view that restricting the number of 100km run in a year will improve the performance in those run.

An unexpected insight to appear from an examination of Don Ritchie's racing schedule is the effect of enforced rest through injury. In 1978 a prolonged knee injury forced Don to postpone the start of his racing season until the 27th of May. A month later he ran the Hartola 100km in 6.18.00, stating afterwards that he felt superb.

In 1982 injury again restricted his racing mileage, not as severely as in 1979, but enough that he only managed four races of the marathon distance and more, the longest being 53km. From this he emerged to run 6.26 at Santander. (Valmir Nunes, current world Cup Champion, and Konstantin Santalov ran 6.36 and 6.37 on that course this year in a very competitive race). Erik Seedhouse had two enforced periods of rest of that year from his usual hectic racing schedule. Following the first he set a 100km pb of 6.37, following the second he ran the World Cup. A back problem forced him to retire from that race but a week later he set the second fastest time of his career (6.42). Subsequently his times have declined.

The effects of enforced rest have also been observed in elite marathon runners. Prior to the 1984 Olympics Carlos Lopes was hit by a car ten days before the race and was unable to train again before the race. Similarly Joan Benoit's knee surgery forced her to rest at a crucial period in her buildup for Los Angeles. Both runners emerged triumphant.

Thus it would seem that a well planned racing program incorporating no more than two or three 100km a year and adequate rest would pay dividends to any elite 100km runner. This view is also held by Professor Tim Noakes who has carried out extensive studies of South African ultra runners. (The Comrades Marathon in South Africa is the largest ultra in the world, currently attracting around 13,000 runners, and consistently attracting the top distance runners in that country).

Why should this be so? Marathons and Ultra marathons do take time to recover from, particularly if raced flat out. Praet takes three weeks easy running after the June 100km, Fordyce four to six: Tim Noakes reckons it may take months to fully recover from such a race. Racing another 100km before fully recovered from the previous one will eventually lead to runners becoming 'punch drunk'. Drawing from the experience of top marathon runners, the number of top class performances a runner has within him is limited. Life at the top in marathon running tends to be short. Ron Hill remarked that Abebe Bikila lasted so long at the top because he raced so infrequently. The same applies to Ultrarunning. Don Ritchie was remarkable in the sheer longevity of his ultra running career as an elite performer. None of the runners who contested the '77 and '78 Brightons behind him were still forces to be reckoned with when he was still competing internationally in the early 1990s. Most had disappeared from the scene.

Another factor effecting 100km performance is leg speed. Elite 10km runners run 5km and 3km for speedwork, 5km runners 1500 metre events, 1500 metre runners 800 metres and so on. The same applies to the 100km. If a runner runs a whole series of 100km events his body will get used to running at ultra pace, his cruising speed will drop. It is perhaps worth looking at the London to Brighton in this context. In the '70s it was normal for the first 10 miles of the Brighton to be run in under the hour, and often 30 miles was reached in close to three hours. In those days there were a mere handful of ultras for British runners - the Woodford 40 for example. The runners who contested these events were basically marathon runners who ran the occasional ultra.

In later years the pace of the Brighton slowed. I suspect the reason is that there were then around fifty ultras in the UK for runners to choose from. It was runners used to running at ultra speed who latterly ran the Brighton not those used to the faster tempo of the marathon. The message is an elite l00km runner needs to run marathons, half marathons, and 10kms to maintain and develop his leg speed. Run too many 100kms and that speed will be lost.

In recent years the elite runners have increasingly focussed on the World 100km to the exclusion of other major ultras - which has severely limited their racing opportunities. Partly this is due to the demands from federations that runners selected to compete for their country are very controlled in their racing at 100km and further. When these elite runners arrive at the World 100km, the event being very competitive, no one is prepared to take risks. Consequently the necessary fast pace over the first 50km in order to get on terms with Ritchie's 6:10 does not happen. (In that race in 1978, three men went through the first 50km in under three hours.)

So we now have elite runners restricting their racing at 100km, but due to competitive pressure unable and unwilling to run the first half of the race fast enough to give them a chance to finish close to 6:10. However when the World 100km is held early in the year, as happened in 2012, the opportunity exists for elite runners to go for such a time, perhaps in a less pressured event with possibly significant financial inducements to set a new world 100km best.

After running a l00km in 6.25.28, Cavin Woodward ran a further 38 miles to break the 100 mile record on the cinder Tipton track. If the present generation of elite l00km runners want to surpass Cavin's mark and get on terms with Don's 6.10, they have to plan their racing schedule with great care. Unless they do Don's mark could last as an absolute world 100km best well beyond 35 years, well into the 21st century.

At World 100km in Chavagnes in France in 1999 Takahiro Sunada gave an interview with the media on his training. The previous year he had run 6:13:33 for 100km on the Lake Saroma course in Hokkaido Japan.

Takahiro Sunada's training

Q: Have you run in Europe before?

A: Yes, I ran a 5,000-metre track race in Portugal.

Q: Why did you not run the 1998 World Challenge at Shimanto in Japan?

A: It was in October -- right in the middle of the Japanese marathon season. I had too many other running commitments.

Q: How do you plan to run at Chavagnes?

A: I plan to run a tactical race. (Sunada is a 2:12 marathon runner.).

Q: How did you prepare for the 1999 World Challenge?

A: I ran a five-hour training run. Last month, I ran a 2:22 marathon. This time was affected by a strong wind.

Q: Who do you see as your biggest threat?

A: The Russians!

Q: Has running an ultra had any effect on your speed?

A: No, my 100-kilometre pace is my normal training pace. There has been no change in my speed.

Q: How do you feel going into the race?
A: Cold! It is much warmer in Honshu in Japan where I live.

Q: How do you train?
A: My manager plans my schedule. I run 19 kilometres each morning before breakfast at 4 minutes per kilometre. I do interval training on the track twice a week. Also twice a week I does a pace run -- a run of 30 kilometres at the same pace. I train in total 1,000 kilometres per month. I have one day off a week with no running, on Sunday. I work for the Sekisui Chemical Company. They allow me time off to run.

Don Ritchie is regarded by many as one of the greatest ultra runners of modern times. With track World Best Performances at 50km (twice), 40 miles, 50 miles (twice), 100km (6:10:20), 150km, 100 miles and 200km, plus world road bests at 100km and 100 miles he had an unparalleled record in the sub 24 hour events. Added to this is his excellent competitive record both at home and abroad. He had numerous Continental 100kms wins to his credit, (including setting a world road best), and a 100 mile road best in the USA

When I was asked to write down some of my thoughts on training I was a bit apprehensive. Sometimes when things are going badly, and I am not running well, I think then that I know nothing about proper training methods. At times like that an advisor may be useful, to talk things over, as he may see the reasons for your difficulties quite clearly, while you yourself are baffled. There are other periods when running is going well and you think you know exactly what training is good for you.

I have never had a coach, and my training developed by empirical methods to what seems to suit me. There is no one "Right" way to train, and success has been achieved by many different combinations of methods.

The important thing is to believe in the training you are doing, so that your confidence and expectations of success improve along with your physical condition.

As I see it the object of training is to submit your body to stressful situations similar to those likely to be encountered in a race, so that it can adapt to handle the race situation better. It is important to apply the stress in small doses with adequate recovery between applications, so that adaptation can take place.

Too much stress, training too hard, or inadequate rest, will cause deterioration of condition. Also increasing the stress too quickly can lead to problems. When building up to a high mileage you should listen to the feedback from your body, and run accordingly. You get plenty of warning signals from your muscles, as you approach the "Overdose" condition.

It is then time to back off somewhat, remember you are training, not straining. The idea then is to keep the stress level high enough to promote adaptation, but not high enough for breakdown.

It is also important to have consistency in training, and a fairly regular lifestyle. For example it is better to run 10 miles every day, than two tens every second day. Consistency also, in my experience, tends to prevent injuries, and I find the "safest" period is when I have established a steady mileage of 110 miles a week.

Most of my injuries have occurred when there is some dramatic change in training, e.g. starting effort sessions or hill runs, or when building up to a plateau again followed a rest of more than four or five days. I also consider roads the safest training surface.

I have found that I respond best to a fairly high mileage, and average around 100 miles per week. My weekly mileage may be between 20 and 160, depending on the circumstances. I also benefit from Fartlek, on grass and forest roads, and from efforts of one minute to five minutes duration on the road. If you are a person who does not put on weight easily, (I do), then I think it is unnecessary to train so heavily.

To run an ultra marathon you need a good training background, and a suitable mental attitude, i.e. you must be a little crazy.

I like a ten week build-up to an important race, increasing my mileage from 100 to perhaps 160 miles per week. Hopefully this will ensure you can tolerate the discomfort a 100km race will inflict on you.

A certain type of mentality seems to be advantageous. I think you require to be a calm, determined, patient person with a high tolerance for prolonged discomfort, and with a high capacity for delayed gratification.

It is important to stress the value of the weekly long training run. In my opinion this is a key session and should be of at least two hours duration but not too long otherwise enjoyment is lost and it becomes a drudge. I find my 31 mile course on the road and Forestry tracks suits me and I try and do this twice or three times a month. Longer training runs are too time consuming and I do not think they contribute any more to improving one's condition.

I have been running since 1962 with only injury induced rests so I must enjoy it. I think it is very important to make the training varied and enjoyable. We are fortunate in the area where I live that we have undulating forestry roads, beach, golf courses, disused railway lines and quiet roads. Consequently longer runs of 20 to 30 miles can be very pleasurable. I change my training throughout the year, changing the emphasis on the type and intensity to prevent boredom. Up to mid May I normally work towards a marathon then vary training to aim at a 100km before easing back in the summer holidays when I race every week at 10 miles or half marathon. In August I start working towards a 100km again. This variety keeps my enjoyment going.

My normal training programme would involve running twice a day, Monday to Friday, with single runs on Saturday and Sunday. Usually the pace is 10 miles per hour, or quicker, and nearly all is done alone.

If I am trying to improve my pace, I will include three "effort" sessions per week. I would do a 10 mile run, broken up by one and two minute hard runs alternating with equal intervals; a 15 mile run, doing 1-2-3-4-5-4-3-2-1 minutes hard, with equal recoveries, then repeating; a further session on hills would be a third effort session.

The following extract from my training record for September and October 1978, will indicate my schedule:-

18TH SEPTEMBER, 1978

Monday	a.m.	8 miles.
Tuesday	p.m.	8.5m back from school.
Wednesday	a.m.	14m to school.
	p.m.	14m back from school
Thursday	a.m.	14m to school
	p.m.	8.5m back, then 8.5m hard in evening with club.

Friday	a.m.	14m to school.
	p.m.	12m back.
Saturday	No run, felt tired.	
Sunday	31 miles in 3-0-48.	
	132.5 miles	

25TH SEPTEMBER

Monday	a.m.	
	p.m.	17.5 miles.
Tuesday	a.m.	14m to school.
	p.m.	8.5m back.
Wednesday	a.m.	14m to school.
	p.m.	14m back.
Thursday	a.m.	14m to school.
	p.m.	8.5m back + 3.5m hard at club.
Friday	No run.	
Saturday	No run.	
Sunday	53.5 miles London to Brighton,	
	1st in 5-13-2 [the fastest average speed for this event]	
	147.5 miles	

2ND OCTOBER

Monday	No run.	
Tuesday	No run.	
Wednesday	a.m.	8.5m to school.
	p.m.	14m back.
Thursday	a.m.	7m to school.
	p.m.	8.5m back + 7.5m with club.
Friday	a.m.	14m to school.
	p.m.	12m back.
Saturday	p.m.	5.75 mile Alves-Forres race 29 mins 1 sec.
Sunday	a.m.	26 miles.
	103.25 miles	

9TH OCTOBER

Monday		18.5m. Mid-term holiday.
Tuesday		10.5m.
Wednesday		31m.
Thursday		24m.
Friday		23m.
Saturday	a.m.	8m.
	p.m.	5.25m cross country race.
Sunday	26.5m.	
	146.75 miles	

16TH OCTOBER

Monday		23.5m.
Tuesday	a.m.	14m to school.
	p.m.	8.5m back + 5.5m hard with club.
Wednesday	a.m.	14m to school.
	p.m.	20m back.
Thursday	a.m.	14m to school.
	p.m.	8.5m back + 7.5m hard with club.
Friday	a.m.	14m to school.
Saturday	a.m.	7m.
	p.m.	2.5m cross country relay leg.
Sunday	a.m.	26m.
	165.0 miles	

23RD OCTOBER

Monday	p.m.	20.5m.
Tuesday	a.m.	14m to school.
	p.m.	14m back.
Wednesday	a.m.	14m to school.
	p.m.	14m back.
Thursday	a.m.	14 m to school.
Friday	No run.	
Saturday	RRC 100km (62.5m) track race at Crystal Palace	

6-10-20, world best performance.

Sunday   No run.

153.0 miles

My training in recent years has been on similar lines but a lower total mileage as I do not run so far to and from work or train with the club twice a week. During this period however I managed to get under 2-20 for the marathon twice, 2-19-34 and 2-19-58 through cutting back on my mileage and trying to run my effort sessions faster. I also race in shorter races in my area, treating them as speed endurance training.

Sometimes I use the carbohydrate loading diet, but I am not convinced of its effectiveness. Done strictly it can cause extreme weakness, and lower resistance to infections, when on the low carbohydrate stage. I have had some bad experiences in the early days, on the strict diet. Now I just eat more vegetables cutting out bread and jam for the initial three days, then I eat a lot of carbohydrate rich foods during the 48 hours preceding the race.

Usually I have two days off prior to the race, but sometimes taper off to say five miles the day before the race. During the race I drink E.R.G. and a long chain polymer glucose drink which I concoct myself, and I may have some of this every 5km or 20 minutes intervals.

I regard stretching as extremely important in reducing the risk of muscle injury. Before training I do not stretch, but begin at a slow pace and gradually pick it up. Following a run I spend about five minutes stretching my calves, quadriceps and hamstrings. I do this sequence before a race also.

I think one's general diet has an influence on performance. Mine is high in carbohydrates and fibre with little meat and quite a lot of fish. This is what I 'feel' like eating and it suits me

Erik Seedhouse credits his current training programme (once-a-day runs, regular long sessions and cross-training) for his series of fast 100Ks. He later finished third in the World Ultra Triathlon Championships!

Having started running at the age of 16, I ran my first marathon at 17. As this proved fairly successful (2.39) I decided to concentrate on the distance and soon found myself averaging in excess of 160km/week at the age of 18! I ran a 2.35 marathon followed two weeks later by a 2.30 Following this race and listening to none of the advice/warnings, I announced to anyone who was interested that I would run 2.25 in the next London Marathon, then six months away.

Six months later, having lived the lifestyle that would have tested the resolve of a hermit and having averaged over 160km/week, I ran 2.25.48 for a U.K. Age -18 Marathon Best; for good measure, I followed this performance with a U.K. Age -18 Half Marathon Best of 1.11.37 the following week.

Just over two years later, I was a burnt-out shell of an athlete; I collapsed following training runs; a 3 km jog would send my pulse racing to 200 beats per minute and walking up a flight of stairs too quickly would leave me breathless: my running had become an addiction, then an obsession before finally developing into the perversion that had practically destroyed me! The heart specialist who examined me after I started experiencing stabbing pains in my chest diagnosed a heart murmur brought about by running too much, too young, too fast (all my training averaged out at well under 3.45 min/km) It was to be nearly 3 years before I raced again.

Today, with a cumulative total of 9 years running experience, a B.A. degree in Sport Studies and a M.Med.Sc. in Sport & Exercise Science I like to think I have a better understanding of training principles than I did then. Having said that, my approach to my first ultra was hardly ideal. Once I had heard about the first 100km Championships in early 1989 I decided that this just might be the distance for me. Rather than give the distance the respect it deserved, however, I ran the London Marathon 2 weeks prior to the event (a p.b. of 2.24.06) followed by a half marathon a week later. These races and the fact that at the time I was training with the 2 Para Combat TV team resulted in a fairly mediocre debut of 7.00.30 but was sufficient to place third and convince me that the event was worth taking seriously.

Since then, after having completed 14 100km races (9 in under 7 hours), a combination of over-racing and illness has resulted in me having completed only one build-up to a specific 100km, the 1992 World Cup 100km in Palamos (6.33.03). I credit this performance to the training programme that has evolved over the years and also the holistic approach that I take to running, the diet, stretching programme, etc.

My usual training time is at around 7.00 am to 7.15 am. This means that my body has gone at least 10 hours without food and as a result it only takes 20km or so to exhaust the glycogen stores in the liver. As one can appreciate, if you are running a 50km training run, then the body has 30km left without any glycogen. This is the key to running 100km races successfully, the training of the body to use alternative fuel sources. By exhausting the glycogen supply, the body is forced to adapt and rely on another form of fuel - fatty acids.

The requirement in ultra running is to be able to use fat fuel as efficiently as possible and by running long distances early in the morning that is what you are doing. As far as speed is concerned, long 'fast' runs are the most effective training because the metabolism of muscle fuel is crucial to optimum performance, as the balance of fuel enzymes (these catalyze chemical reactions within the cells) which break down either glycogen or fatty acids, must be attuned to the race situation. Set against this is the fact that volume is more draining than speed and the trick is to get the best balance. Quality stresses the muscle and the body adapts better. Taking this point into consideration, all my training is performed at/or close to race pace. At the moment 200km/week is about the limit but this will increase up to 250km/week shortly. One aspect of my training that I feel merits particular mention is the fact that none of my training even approaches what could be considered maximum effort; to do so would only invite injury due to the already heavy workload. In my swimming programme, however, I regularly swim at maximum effort, usually for distances of between 2 and 3km, but also anything up to 5km and beyond.

The theory behind the swimming training (or cross training as most people prefer to call it in this instance) is fairly simple and is worth taking into consideration when planning a training schedule (especially one that is high-volume). Swimming engages practically all the muscle groups which can never be a bad thing if you happen to be a runner! Because of this, it significantly improves the blood circulation and the mechanical efficiency of the heart (again, not a bad thing if you are looking to improve your running performance), as a result of more muscle groups being involved. Interesting studies have been performed on twins, one a runner the other both a runner and a swimmer. Needless to say the runner-swimmer had a VO2 max much higher than the runner (30% higher in fact). Everybody has a certain aerobic potential and it is up to the individual to optimise this potential. Swimming is probably one of the best ways for runners to maximize their aerobic potential.

Of course this approach to training flies in the face of the accepted dogma that all training should be totally specific. Unfortunately, those athletes that stick with this approach will never fulfil their maximum potential aerobically. Several studies, among them a study by Loftin et al., 1988 highlight significant evidence that suggests that arm training in addition to normal leg training enhances performance during leg exercise more than leg training alone. Why this should be so is not entirely clear as yet, but the hypothesis centres around the possibility that trained arm muscle may be better able to remove lactate during high-intensity exercise and also be able to store glycogen before an ultra (or other endurance race).

Anybody who follows triathlon will no doubt be aware of the training schedules of the top competitors. Very few of these will train more than 120km/week running as they feel that cycling assists and goes some way to improve their running. Speaking from personal experience as a triathlete I can vouch for that as I have participated in several triathlons without any specific bike training, yet have consistently been in the top 25% bike splits. In Nice for example (4km swim, 120km bike, 32km run) I actually managed to finish in the top 25% of both swim and bike splits and place 2nd U.K. competitor overall - after having passed 87 people on the run! despite having done no bike training whatsoever.

Additional Information:
Diet:

Breakfast	: Muesli, Pure orange juice, milk and tea.
Lunch	: Granary bread with honey, milk, apple and muesli bar.
Dinner	: Pasta, vegetables and fish.
Snacks	: muesli bars, biscuits, fruit, Lucozade, Leppin, scones, crisps. (0vo-lacto vegetarian, but eat fish)

Supplements:
100mg Vitamin C (time release),
Multi-vitamin & Iron,
Cod Liver Oil 276 mg,
Octacosanol - 5000 mg,

Guarana prior to race.

Pre-race : 2 x Ultrafuel (Twinlab) + 2 x muesli bars + tea.

TRAINING
Build-up Training to Palamos:
(peak week: 202km,   lowest week: 164km)

Sun ; 36km	Mon ; 10km
Tue ; 20km	Wed ; 32km
Swim: 3km (sub 50min)	Swim: 1.5km (sub 25min)
	10km
Thu ; 32km	Fri ; 16km
Swim: 3km (sub 50min)	
Sat ; 36km	
Total ; 192km	

(8 week build-up = 1475 to 1500km)

Taper: Week 9 : 128km, Week 10 : 100km, Week 11 : 36km

Average training pace: Sub 4.00 min/km : Range : 3.45 - 4.15 min/km

Build-up Training to Cape Town:
(peak week: 240km,   lowest week: 170km)

Sun ; 50km	Mon ; 10km
10km	10km
Tue ; 20km	Wed ; 36km
Swim: 2.5km (sub 40min)	Swim: 1.5km
10km	
Thu ; 32km	Fri ; 10km
Swim: 2.5km (sub 40min)	
10km	
Sat ; 16km	
Total ; 214km	

(8 week build-up = 1575 to 1600km)

Taper and average pace as above

All swim training freestyle and at 80% + effort (heart rate : 150 +)

In future, I will plan to push training volume up to a ceiling of perhaps 300km but only for a short period of the total training phase. Having spoken to athletes such as Konstantin Santalov, Aleksander Masagarin and Valmir Nunes, it seems that all of them include a few high mileage weeks (in some cases, very high, Valmir trains up to 400km/week in his peak week). This is perhaps one of the reasons I was passed at 77km whilst in the lead in Palamos - the fact that I did not have sufficient volume work, despite having averaged over 170km/ week for over 8 weeks.

Here are some details of how other elite 100km runners (sub 7 hours) have trained in a typical week. Although in isolation this does not show their build-up to that particular point, it does give some insight into the components that go into making up their weekly mileage.

Roland Winkler of Germany maintained that the well trained marathon runner can do well in ultra events if he or she can make the required mental adjustments. He saw little difference in his training for the marathon or for the 100km. The furthest he ran in training was 37 miles/60kms. Prior to an ultra race he would rest more, up to three days, but would take almost as long a rest for a marathon. He regarded it as important to race shorter events at a faster pace from time to time. Another German takes a similar view, but recommended a slower training pace than for the marathon with twice weekly runs of 25 - 31 miles.

A leading Finnish runner went for high mileage. Prior to his peak performance, he averaged 160 - 175 miles a week for almost three months. Two weeks before the key event he ran a flat-out marathon (4th in the national championships) then mostly easy runs, the longest 15 miles.

Many West European ultrarunners were influenced by the Waldniel method of the German coach ***Ernst Van Aaken*** He recommended 2000 and 3000m tempo runs at 1 1/2 to 2 minutes slower than one's best time, repeated 5 - 10 times, followed by a few sprints of 60 to 80 metres at the finish of a session.

He also suggested a gradual build-up in the long run over 3 to 5 years to 30, 35, even 50 miles. However Monika Kono, one of the most consistent German ultrarunners preferred to run marathons rather than use fast training for ultra distance.

Here is another typical week from a French runner this time.

Monday	morning - 10 miles steady.
	afternoon - intervals - 6 x 1km in 3:00 - 3:05.
	400m jogging between intervals
Tuesday	1 1/2 hours run in undulating area, about 9 miles.
Wednesday	morning - 10 miles steady.
	afternoon - either hard fartlek or hard hilly runs
	or 5 to 6 x 1200m speed runs in very hilly area
	(anaerobic training) - 1000m jogging between
	intervals.
Thursday	as Tuesday.
Friday	as Monday and Wednesday morning.
	afternoon - either short intervals, 12 x 200m
	very quick or 5 x 2000m in 6:20 - 6:30 with 600m
	relaxed running recovery.
Saturday/Sunday	either race or run for 3 hours (31 - 37 miles)
	in different areas
Weekly Mileage:	112 - 137 miles.

In the week before 100km race

Monday	25km road in 1:33.
Tuesday	2 x 10km (one fast one slow).
Wednesday	13km (5 x 400m fast).
Thursday	50 minutes steady.
Friday	as Thursday.
Saturday	6:27:08 Vogelgrun.
Sunday	6km/ 4 miles jogging - later 40 - 50 minutes steady.
Total	118 miles.

Another from an American

Typical week building up to a major event.

Monday	13 miles easy; Nautilus - weight training.
Tuesday	morning: 15 miles (5:40 - 6:00 minute mile pace).
	afternoon: 7 miles (5:30 - 5:50 minute mile pace).
Wednesday	as Monday
Thursday	morning: 5 x 1 mile (4:50 - 4:55)
	with 400m jog between.
	afternoon: 7 miles (6:00 minute mile pace).
Friday	as Monday
Saturday	Race - 10km to 20 miles, or 13 miles easy.
Sunday	20 -25 miles (6:00 minute mile pace).
Weekly Mileage:	105 - 120 miles.

Another recommends a 15 week build up to a 100km. This would peak in the 12th and 13th week as follows:-

Monday	1 hour run.
Tuesday	30 minutes warm-up followed by 20 x 400m (80 sec) with 2 minute recovery, finishing with 10 minutes hard.
Wednesday	1 1/2 hour run - 20km.
Thursday	30 minutes warm-up followed by 6 x 2000m (7:00 minutes each).
Friday	1 hour 15 minutes run.
Saturday	1 hour run.
Sunday	Long run - 3:30 - 4 hours or 35 - 40km race
Weekly Mileage:	80 - 85 miles.

And among the women:

The South African Frith Van Der Merwe in preparation for the89km Comrades .

Would aim to undertake this kind of weekly regime.

Monday	morning: 6 - 9 miles easy.
	afternoon 6 - 9 miles fartlek.

Tuesday	morning as Monday.
	afternoon 5 miles time trial (sub 30 minutes).
Wednesday	10 - 12 mile club run.
Thursday	8 uphill sprints, 2 1/2 mile jog.
Friday	rest day.
Saturday	18 mile hill running.
Sunday	9 - 12 miles easy.
Weekly Mileage:	80 - 95 miles.

Now for something completely different. Rumours were rife in the late 70's and early 80's of the phenomenal distances Mike Newton covered in training. At last we have a chance to discover the training for his many forays over 100km in Europe.)

I was on my final long run and after going through East Grinstead I got lost. The sixty mile jaunt ended up in a seventy mile nightmare. Over-distance with a vengeance.

A week later in Holland at the '78 Winschoten 100km race, which I won with 6h 43m 16s, an eager young Dutch runner asked me how he could improve his training. I replied, not meaning to be unfriendly, "Get lost." He took it the wrong way and missed my advice.

Life is full of contradictions and mine is no different. In the late '60's, over thirty and overweight, I had become a victim of modern day living. I no longer played tennis and the urge for cricket had died in the wet summer of '69.

My best suit didn't fit anymore, so it was time to stand back and make a cool assessment of the situation. There and then I made a vow to get fit again. Easier said than done!

So it began. Twice a week from Tooting Bec track in rubber soled cricket boots, grey slacks and sweater I would puff my way round the common. I suppose the local athletic community looked on me as a harmless eccentric. However, after a few months I gained their respect when I was able to run with established club runners without any apparent discomfort.

I now became passionately interested in running and so that I could do more even changed my work. I became a part time security guard patrolling a factory in Merton. Any spare time I had I searched the public library for anything on athletics. This thirst for knowledge became compulsive but the only thread I found in all that literature is that you have to work very hard and you must believe in yourself. As I became fitter I lost weight, around a stone and a half and with it a sort of rejuvenation gave me the impetus to look for new challenges. I joined the South London Harriers club and was introduced to the late Tom Richards, silver medallist in the 1948 London Olympic Marathon. He would chat about the 'Brighton' and 'The Isle of Man 40'. He won both these races in the fifties. "Pace kills", he would say in his South Wales accent. "Those who start too fast don't last." This was one of his favourite axioms.

When I joined S.L.H. in 1973 appropriately enough the S.L.H. 30 mile road race was scheduled for the next month. This was to be my first experience of competitive running and foolishly I forgot Tom Richard's sound advice as I kept up with the leaders, Don Faircloth and Cavin Woodward. I stayed with them for about six miles, then I hit the wall. It was absolute hell hanging on for the next 24 miles. Somehow I got through it and finished in 3h 29m the first S.L.H. club member home.

Even in those days I knew that stamina was my strong suit. Over several years this prophetic assessment came to fruition, especially in the 100km races. I always felt that this was a distance I could relate to and it turned out to be so, as in the eighteen 100km races I entered I won nine and was 2nd and 3rd in the rest. In order to achieve this sort of consistency I regularly logged up to 140 miles in a week. I was now a dedicated quantity man.

I suppose my secret for success was to work harder than anyone else, and to run longer than anyone else. Psychologically I expressed it to myself, "It's my training against their training". Certainly I was getting into my stride as by the end of 1974 my rating on the ultra world's list was on the way up.

My particular approach to training is a combination of strength, speed and endurance. A very potent mixture. After trial and error I devised an ambitious programme. Hill work for strength, long slow runs for endurance, track intervals for speed, timed distance trials for endurance and speed and hard core soccer pitch diagonals for speed and endurance. This five pronged attack on the ultras made me into one of the top distance men of the '70s' and '80s'.

Gradually it dawned on me that the more even paced I ran these protracted events the better my overall performance would be. For example the '76 Crystal Palace 100km track race, in which I just lost to Tom O'Reilly in a very close finish. My time was 6h 44m 42s.

A typical track training session looks like this: - 25 x 600 metres in 1m 45s per 600 metres. Then I would ease down for half a lap to around 50 secs. Once I had reeled of those 25 intervals I would go straight on to continuous lap running for an hour, fast straights and allowing a breather on the bends all done at about 80 seconds a lap. I would then repeat the whole thing. The complete training session would last approximately four hours.

In order to handicap myself I would wear a track suit and heavy trainers. Talking about handicapping - I even made myself a weighted jacket to use for training in preparation for the 1977 SLH 30.

For training I would run to Old Coulsdon, do a lap of the course and then return to the Tooting Bec track. The total distance, 30 miles in about 3h 16m. My main concern was my pace or lack of it. Could I develop the necessary leg speed and maintain it? I wanted better than 10mph for the four 7 mile laps. I realised I wanted a combination of speed and endurance so I used asphalt soccer pitch diagonals corner to corner. I would run as many in an hour as possible setting a personal best, then try and beat it. Eventually I reached the lofty heights of 182 diagonals in 2 hours. I measured my pace on the 50 metre diagonals at better than 11 miles per hour, so at last my legs and lungs were getting used to working at a higher capacity.

However I was still not sure of success and felt it was now time to use the weighted jacket I had made. Certainly it was a cumbersome looking object. In its manufacture I had used ten lb. bags of barley seed bought from a local grocer and sewn them into the lining of the jacket. To avoid chafing I stuck on sponge rubber pieces at the most vulnerable places where rubbing would occur. Finally I removed the sleeves to allow freer arm movement. To cover the unsightly bulk of the weighted jacket I wore a large track suit top. When I looked into a mirror I wasn't quite prepared for the shock, as I appeared to have miraculously acquired the portly dimensions of a Billy Bunter. Nevertheless after getting used to the initial awkwardness of the jacket I found it wasn't too much of a problem. With it on I estimated I had to work about 10% harder an hour than normal.

As extra preparation to the SLH 30 I decided to go up to Scotland for the Two Bridges 36 mile road race. The course incorporates the crossing of the Forth Bridge which is quite a stimulating experience. I finished easing down, in 3h. 40m. 14s. This was the confidence boost I needed as a week later at the SLH 30 I ran a strategically even paced race finishing in 2h. 58m. 48s.

In the mid seventies I ran 5h. 37m., 5h. 32m. and 5h. 31m. in successive years for the London to Brighton I couldn't finish better than 4th place. This clearly illustrates the high class of the runners who opposed me.

I never allowed these disappointments in the Brighton to get me down for long, and soon banished any negative thoughts from my mind as I once again took to the open road. To escape the London traffic I would start at 5am from my Streatham home. Long slow distance would be the order of the day at around 7 to 8 mph. I made my way in dawn's early light to the South Circular, then on to the Thames tow paths or the Grand Union Canal, into the Home Counties, Surrey, Kent and Sussex.

My one guiding principle was to log up as many miles as possible. 'Money in the bank' as they say. As I grew stronger a sort of assertion of power took me on to the summits of Box Hill and Leith Hill, the Weald of Kent, across and back over the Downs. I studied the Ordinance Survey maps, avidly memorising a whole range of B roads and country lanes until I was able to traverse the countryside like a modern day Pheidippides.

I would design the run, anything from 40 to 75 miles, undulating or flat, as a kind of topographical parallel to the course to be run. Accordingly, the steep gradients you sometimes encounter during a race will always wear down the unprepared athlete first. In an effort to avoid this possibility I always found hill work a marvellous way to build up leg strength. For instance, a week before the Ewhurst 100 mile road race in 1980 I ran 200 hills using seven different gradients in and around the Norwood area in 4 hours. This was good preparation for the Ewhurst ten lap Challenge which is certainly one of the most undulating courses in Europe.

Once the race started I didn't alter my pace very much from lap to lap. Martin Daykin, at the height of his form, set a cracking pace for 70 miles but fatigue and the hills caught up with him in the end. This enabled me to come through and win in 12h. 55m. 12s, a course record.

To prepare myself for the I.O.M. race in 1978 I ran to Box Hill and then ran to the top and back four times before returning home, 42 miles in five hours.

France, for me, was a happy hunting ground where I won six races. In 1977, my debut sortie was in the Migennes 100km, which I won in 7h.15s. Those Continental races have the quality of a festival about them. The whole atmosphere with the band playing and the banners flying are entirely opposite to the stereotype organisations one gets in the UK. There seems to be less pressure but paradoxically I was always afraid of falling by the wayside. To overcome this possibility I gave myself a thorough preparation.

Six days before the '79 Condom 100km in the South of France I trained as follows:-

Day 1	Timed trial, windy conditions, 51 miles in 5 hours.
Day 2	30 hills, 200 yards each, 1 in 10 gradients, overall duration 2hrs.
Day 3	track work, 60 x 400 metres, in 75 seconds for each 400 metres with a lap jog of 95 seconds, duration 2(r) hours.
Day 4	Depletion run, 12 miles in 1hr. 10 min., on 'Diet' no carbohydrates.
Day 5	8 mile jog in 1 hour.
Day 6	No run, off 'Diet', travel to race.
Day 7	Race.

The Condom 100km course was exceedingly hilly. After taking care of the top German runner Helmut Urbach, I then overtook the Australian Martin Thompson around the 50km mark. I went on to win with comparative ease with 7h. 4m. 34s. this stood as a course record for 10 years. Once again space precludes me from digging below the top layer for an in depth survey of my European exploits.

24 Hour Training

The 24 Hours is arguably the toughest of all ultras. It is an event that is notoriously difficult to get right consistently.

Current British 24 Hour international Robbie Britton:
"I never look at the whole 24 hours or 100 miles [161km], or I'd break down and cry. Mentally I just break it down into any sort of manageable chunk that I can, whether that be an hour or a kilometre. Once I've got through that, I can just focus on the next one."

Dave Cooper on the necessary background for a 24 hours. Dave was one of the most consistent 24 hour runners, seemingly able to churn out quality performances one after another.

Obviously before tackling a 24 hour race an athlete would wish to have many years of training and racing behind him over the shorter distances. Most marathon runners start out as club athletes running in track races in the summer and cross country in the winter with road races and road relays throughout the year. After three or four years they probably try the marathon and if successful will then run three or four of these races each year for several years before extending the distance further. Then via 30 milers and 40 milers they may well move up to the 'Brighton' and the 100km. It is from this point after eight to ten years that they begin to wonder about how they would fare in a 24 hour race. It would seem logical for such an athlete to extend the mileage gradually between each move up in racing distance, say 30 - 40 miles per week during the cross country/track racing phase, 50 - 70 for the marathon, 70 - 100 for the ultramarathon (that is 30 milers up to 100 kilometres) and 100 miles plus per week for the megamarathons, 24 hours, 48 hours, Six Day Race, etc. I include 100 milers in the megas with the 24 hour races for in most of the latter race results you will find approximately half the field actually making the 'ton'.

Training for the 24 hour race

I do not feel that I am in a position to pontificate to other runners with regard to how to train for a 24 hour race. The runner must decide on the training that suits him (or her). I am very aware of the fact that a runner's training is a highly personal thing. We all do the training we enjoy, which gives us the best results for the effort we put into it, that fits into our lifestyle and takes advantage of the area in which we live. What I can do, however, is detail my own training methods and some of the rationale behind them, so that the novice may be in a better position to work out a successful programme of his own.

In general terms it would be wise to run further in training than for the shorter distances. As outlined above if 50 - 70 miles per week is sufficient training for a successful marathon and 70 - 90 for the 'Brighton' or 100km then 100 per week would be the minimum advisable for the 24 hours. With regard to the recommended mileages stated above these would not necessarily take place all the year round, there may well be months with no races in view when my mileage would average 20 - 30 miles per week, even less if injured or unwell or if some personal circumstance should temporarily curtail training.

I would advise building up to a plateau of mileage over a three month period from 40 - 60 miles per month as follows; one week of 50 - 70 miles, one week of 60 - 80, two weeks 70 - 90, two weeks 80 - 100, then hold 100 miles per week for four weeks. Two weeks before the race, 60 - 80, and 40 - 60, respectively depending on how you feel. It depends on the individual how much to taper off before a race of this magnitude but an experienced distance runner should know this. It is always better to taper off your training too much, and be slightly undertrained than go into the race drained of energy due to over training. This is especially true of the first race, later with several races under your belt you can afford to experiment.

The above notes on training can be taken as a rough theoretical guide: now follows a detailed account of my own training. This has tended to change slightly from year to year. I no longer race in the winter, I gave up cross country sixteen years ago. I tend to do less mileage in the winter for in this country very few 24 hour races take place in these months. This, in my opinion, is a pity for longer distances are covered in races organised in cold conditions than in the kind of hot humid conditions we often experience in the summer months.

In cold weather athletes can put on additional clothing and still run fast but when it is hot the weather conditions usually result in reduced mileage for the entire field.

Taking 1985 as a sample year (this is very tempting as my best ever races took place then).

My monthly mileages were:-

Jan 206,

Feb 58 (Yes only 58!),

March 199,

April 478,

May 438 (140),

June 442 (153),

July 367 (145),

Aug 661 (436),

Sept 262,

Oct 205,

Nov333,

Dec 210.

Total mileage: 3859

The numbers in brackets in May, June and July refer to 24 hour races, and that for August a Six Day Race. These distort the mileages for the months in which they appear. In January to March and October to December I would be training four to six days per week but in the other months I would be training every day and only rest due to colds, injuries or for two or three days recovery after a megamarathon.

A typical week in Winter might be:-

Sunday long run - 20 miles,

Monday- 4 miles,

Tuesday - 4 miles,

Wednesday rest,

Thursday - 4 miles,

Friday - 4 miles,

Saturday - rest

Total mileage: 36 miles

A typical week in Summer:-
Sunday long run 6 hills - 20 miles, (for details see below)
Monday repetition running (for details see below)
12 x 400m untimed on road with 1 min jog + 4miles = 8 miles,
Tuesday - 4 miles,
Wednesday - 4 miles,
Thursday am - 20 miles to work; pm - 20 miles home   = 40 miles,
Friday - 4 miles, Saturday - 20 miles.
Total mileage: 100 miles

or
Sunday hill run 6 hills - 20 miles,
Monday - 8 miles,
Tuesday am - 20 miles to work, pm - 20 miles Home   = 40 miles
Wednesday 8 miles,
Thursday am - 20 miles to work, pm - 20 miles Home   = 40 miles
Friday - 8 miles,   Saturday - 20 miles
Total mileage: 144 miles

The long runs of 20 miles run at weekends are over hilly terrain in the Brentwood area of the Essex countryside; this choice is to make the work hard and the scenery aesthetically inspiring! The runs to work are on the flat, through the urban areas of Eastern and Central London from Hornchurch Essex, to South Kensington in the West End. The 4 and 8 mile runs in the week are in the early morning in Hyde Park and take place before work; almost all the running is done on the road. The intensity of the running varies with my objective in so far as racing is concerned. I tend to run hard on the Sunday session 20 milers, either the long run in the winter or the hill run in the summer, the interval running and the runs to work. The runs home from work, the short runs on weekdays and the Saturday morning 20 milers may often be run easily for recovery purposes. My annual mileages during the last seven years have been:-

1981 - 3149,   1982 - 3469,   1983 - 4617,   1984 - 5401,

1985 - 3883,   1986 - 3276,   1987 - 2655.

As an example of a four month build up to a specific 24 hour race I have chosen the period preceding the Chevilly Larue track race near Paris in early June 1985.

As you see below, I have three grades of effort for my training runs, **easy** (for recovery purposes or, when tapering before a race), **fast** (at racing speed) and **hard** (flat out; running as hard as possible. Sometimes I have to slow down or even walk in one of these sessions).

At the end of January running on frozen snow I severely strained my left hamstring muscle. Easy jogging each day after a week's rest to allow the injury to heal, followed this mishap.

Thereafter my training was as follows:-

Sat	23	*FEBRUARY*	6 miles	easy
Sun	24		10	hard
Mon	25		4	fast
Tues	26		4	"
Wed	27		4	hard
Thurs	28		rest	- bad
Fri	1	*MARCH*	"	sore
Sat	2		"	throat
Total mileage 22 miles				
Sun	3		10	easy
Mon	4		4	fast
Tues	5		4	"
Wed	6		4	"
Thurs	7		4	"
Fri	8		4	"
Sat	9		3	easy
Total mileage 33 miles				
Sun	10		20	hard
Mon	11		4	easy

Tues	12		4	"
Wed	13		4	fast
Thurs	14		4	"
Fri	15		4	"
Sat	16		3	"

Total mileage 43 miles

Sun	17		20	hard
Mon	18		4	"
Tues	19		4	"
Wed	20	am	8	fast
		pm	3	"
Thurs	21		8	"
Fri	22		8	"
Sat	23		13	Race

Total mileage 68 miles

Romford Half Marathon (1.35.23)

Sun	24		20	easy
Mon	25		4	fast
Tues	26		8	"
Wed	27		8	"
Thurs	28		8	"
Fri	29		4	"
Sat	30		3	"

Total mileage 55 miles

Sun	31			rest - holiday in Guernsey (flight out).
Mon	1	*APRIL*	3	hard
Tues	2		10	"
Wed	3		8	"
Thurs	4		12	"
Fri	5		12	"
Sat	6		13	"

Total mileage 58 miles

Sun	7		8	" - holiday ends
Mon	8		10	easy

Tues	9		4	fast
Wed	10		4	"
Thurs	11	am	20	miles to work
		pm	20	miles home
Fri	12		4	easy
Sat	13		20	fast
Total mileage 90 miles				
Sun	14		20	hill run (6 x hill)
Mon	15		8	fast
Tues	16	am	20 miles to work	
		pm	20 miles home	
Wed	17		8	easy 112
Thurs	18	12x440+4	8	
Fri	19		8	fast
Sat	20		20	easy
Total mileage 112 miles				
Sun	21		26	Race
London Marathon (3.07.58)				
Mon	22		8	fast
Tues	23	am	20 miles to work	
		pm	20 miles home	
Wed	24		8	easy
Thurs	25	am	20 miles to work	
		pm	20 miles home	
Fri	26		8	easy
Sat	27		20	hard
Total mileage 150 miles				
Sun	28		20	hill run (6 x hill)
Mon	29	12x440+4	8	
Tues	30	am	20 miles to work	
		pm	20 miles home	
Wed	1	*MAY*		
		12x440+4	8	hard
Thurs	2		8	fast

Fri	3	20	easy
Sat	4	70	Race

Total mileage 174 miles*

Preston 24 hour Road Race (3rd 140 miles 1655 yards)

Sun	5	70	
Mon	6		rest
Tues	7	4	easy
Wed	8	4	"
Thurs	9	4	fast
Fri	10	rest	- slight
Sat	11	"	chill

Total mileage 82 miles *

Note: * indicate weeks including 24 hour races; these distort the training mileage for the week with a 24 race starting on the Saturday, the miles for that week are abnormally increased. During the weeks following the race, the mileages decrease, so that a certain amount of equalling out occurs.

The training for the Paris and Solihull (Birmingham) races, a detailed account of which follows this text, proceeded according to plan and the results came well up to expectation. Also the rate of recovery after the Paris race was extremely rapid. Looking back to the first race of the series, the Preston 24 hour road race, here my training also was extremely satisfactory, however, the full value of the training was to some extent thrown away. The resulting 140 miles was achieved, I feel, in spite of rather than because of the very hard training on the last few days before the 24 hour run. My main memory of this race was that I was running feeling tired from the start, I felt drained of energy as if I was running on a very hot, humid day. Actually the conditions were very good. Terry Edmondson ran a personal best of 156 miles, also Mike Newton ran 150 miles which was close to his road p.b.

With hindsight, what I should have done was to have run 8 miles easy on the Monday, 20 miles easy to work on the Tuesday, 8 miles easy on the Wednesday, and 4 miles easy on each of the last two days. The twenty mile run on Friday the 3rd of May was a bad mistake. It must be stated in my defence, however, that I profited handsomely from this error in my next two races. It will be obvious to the discerning reader that I keep a fairly detailed diary of my running activities and use this as a constant source of reference in the planning of my training for future races. I write down details of any failures in the margin notes for I feel we learn more from our mistakes than from our successes.

Sun	12 MAY	5	easy
Mon	13		rest
Tues	14	4	fast
Wed	15	4	"
Thurs	16	4	"
Fri	17	4	"
Sat	18	10	"

Total mileage 31 miles

Sun	19	20	hard
Mon	20	3	easy
Tues	21 am	20	miles to work
	pm	20	miles home
Wed	22	4	easy

Total mileage 115

Thurs	23	8	fast
Fri	24	20	easy
Sat	25	20	hard

Total mileage 115 miles

Sun	26	20	hill run (6 x hill)
Mon	27	20	fast
Tues	28 12x440+4	8	hard
Wed	29	8	fast
Thurs	30 am	20 miles to work	
	pm	20 miles home	
Fri	31	8	easy
Sat	1 JUNE	20	easy

Total mileage 124 miles

Sun	2	20	hill run (6 x hill)

Mon	3	am	20 miles to work	
		pm	20 miles home	
Tues	4		8	easy
Wed	5		8	fast
Thurs	6	12x440+4	8	hard
Fr	7		8	easy
Sat	8		20	fast

Total mileage 112 miles

Sun	9		20	hill run (6 x hill)
Mon	10	12x440+4	8	hard
Tues	11		8	fast
Wed	12		8	fast
Thurs	13		8	fast
Fri	14		3	easy
Sat	15		42	Race

Total mileage 97 miles*

Chevilly Larue Paris 24 hour track race (1st 153 miles 1072 yards)

Sun	16		111	
Mon	17			rest
Tues	18			"
Wed	19			"
Thurs	20		4	easy
Fri	21			rest
Sat	22		5	easy

Total mileage 120 miles *

Sun	23		15	easy
Mon	24		4	fast
Tues	25		4	"
Wed	26		8	"
Thurs	27	12x440+4	8	hard
Fri	28		4	fast
Sat	29		20	"

Total mileage 63 miles

| Sun | 30 | | 20 | hill run (6 x hill) |

Mon	1	JULY		
		12x440+4	8	hard
Tues	2		5	fast
Wed	3	12x440+4	8	hard
Thurs	4		4	fast
Fri	5		8	"
Sat	6		20	"

Total mmileage 73 miles

Sun	7		20	hill run (6 x hill)
Mon	8		10	fast
Tues	9	12x440+4	8	hard
Wed	10		8	fast
Thurs	11		8	easy
Fri	12		4	easy
Sat	13		87	Race

Total mileage 58 miles *

Solihull 24 hour track race (2nd145 miles 72 yards)

Sun	14		58	
Mon	15			rest
Tues	16			rest
Wed	17			rest
Thurs	18		4	easy
Fri	19		4	fast
Sat	20		5	easy

Totalmileage 71 miles*

The last three hours at Solihull were slow compared with the three that preceded them. With six hours to go I made a big attempt to catch Martin Daykin who was five miles ahead. For three hours I did all I could to catch him but was unsuccessful and eased off in the final hours and finished in very good condition. Though I did not win, I had the satisfaction of knowing I had probably pushed Martin to a personal best run of 152 miles, which is a course record for Solihull track.

Hill Running

This is a form of resistance running in which the objective is to strengthen the leg muscles using a steep gradient. The runner does not attempt to run up the hill as fast as possible. He runs the hill with his arms down at his sides and concentrates on his leg action. The stride length should be fairly short, the knee lift exaggerated, and the feet hit the ground with a ball of the foot landing. The runner concentrates on the action of the quadriceps (the large muscles on the front of the thighs) and also the calf muscles.

At the top of the hill a short period, a minute or so of easy jogging to recover, is followed by a hard run down the hill. Here the arm action should be exaggerated, the run fast and hard and no attempt made to modify the action of the landing of the feet. Easy jogging for a minute or so at the bottom of the hill will prepare the runner for another hard run up the hill.

A runner who runs such a hill session up a half mile long hill with a steep gradient 6 to 10 times will have had a very good workout. Such a session should take place once a week in the context of very heavy training and I feel is of more benefit than much longer distance runs at a slow pace. I run 4 ½ miles to the foot of a hill I use in Brentwood Essex, which is half a mile long. I run up and down this six times as described above. Between each run up and down I jog at the top and bottom for a minute to recover. The entire session covers 20 miles and takes 2 ½ hours approximately.

Repetition Running

This is a useful complementary session to the 20 mile Hill Running, it is short but very tough. I like to run it the day after the Hill Running session. Here the objective is to run very fast over a set distance, 220 to 440 yards, the distance does not have to be exact, can be paced out in fact. Each fast run is followed by a minute's jogging before the next sprint. I run 12 fast 440's with 1 minute of jogging between each and follow this with a 4 mile run to total 8 miles.

The benefit of these alternatives to long slow distance runs and the faster runs over the shorter distances (even paced running) is that they strengthen and exercise the leg muscles in a different way and are also of great benefit psychologically. You may have noticed that in both Hill and Repetition Running it is necessary to concentrate to derive the maximum benefit from the exercise. We long distance runners tend to go out for our runs as a kind of duty and if not careful may well develop into plodders running along slowly with our minds elsewhere. Obviously on a long run this is perfectly reasonable. To occasionally set out to run really fast in a session or two per week tends to offset this. Also, surprising as it may seem, to raise the tempo in the later stages of a 24 hour race, if you feel strong enough at the time, can have a very invigorating effect on a runner (and a demoralizing effect on the opposition). It is as if the muscle fibres which are called into play during fast running have been lying dormant and are comparatively fresh. Obviously fast running should be indulged in during such a race for a very limited amount of time and one should desist immediately one feels tired. A runner can of course practice inserting fast hard running in a session of slower running (fartlek) during any training run.

The point is emphasized here, however, to illustrate the fact that even in megamarathons speedwork and fast running have their places, if used in the right context.

The mental side of race preparation (also preconceived ideas)

The reason that many quite ordinary runners, in so far as marathons and ultramarathons are concerned, can achieve astonishing successes in the megamarathons is due to a large extent to their mental attitude. This is especially so in the case of the lady runners. Many of the top quality ultra runners tend to defeat themselves in the first 8 hours or so of a 24 hour race. This is because they are fast and strong enough to run extremely hard in ultra races and achieve fast times well up the field. They approach the ultra as a long marathon and are successful, so they approach the megamarathon with the same attitude. After all this tactic works in the shorter races, why not in the longer ones?

The slower ultra runner has a different approach. Because he is not so fast, he tends to think more in terms of survival than winning the race. He takes a lot longer to finish an ultramarathon over a set distance and has to suffer more because of this, (but of course, due to the fact that the standard megamarathons are durations rather than set distances, all the runners and walkers who stay on the course for the whole period are naturally going to be on their feet for exactly the same amount of time). Those who run hard and fast will suffer more and if the gamble comes off will cover the greatest distances. Those who adopt the more casual (less intense) approach may not cover such big distances but will tend to finish in much better physical condition.

In recent years several extremely talented ultra runners have enjoyed a spectacular debut in the 24 hour race but subsequently have failed to duplicate the performance in later attempts.

As a general rule, however, many of the top ultra specialists fail to do themselves justice in megamarathons. The reason for this, I believe, is that in any congregation of runners, due to their past performances being recognised and ranked, the quality runners go into their first 24 hour race with something to prove, their reputations on the line. This nearly always manifests itself in very fast running. I privately think of this as "the scalded cat" or "headless chicken syndrome". Obviously such runners are very nervous, the adrenalin is pumping, they are in the lead, and each lap gained means more distance between them and the chasing runners. Being aware of a pack running behind them can engender a feeling closely akin to panic. In this state of mind the feeling that one should stop for food or drink may well be ignored, or at least postponed. In many cases, climatic conditions which frequently change, especially at nightfall, are simply not heeded. This type of runner is very often a spent force sometimes after as little as 4 or 5 hours.

Another type of runner who would appear to have much less chance of success is the mountain walker or fun runner, who may have run several marathons and graduated from these into ultra races, but whose attitude is far more casual than the first type. I am not saying that this type of runner does not treat the race with respect or make his preparations carefully; he treats the race as he would a day long trip, his approach is much lower key. Such runners are likely to be still moving well, walking or running, in the second half of the race and have a much better chance of finishing well up the field with a good mileage.

It is generally considered that the 24 hour race is very punishing to the body and this is of course true; but especially so for the strong ultra runner who runs the race in his first attempt with the same intensity that he approaches an ultra race, e.g. the London to Brighton. The 24 hour race if run hard and successfully, that is to say with the minimum of rest breaks and continual running, is probably the hardest race a runner can undertake. The effect on the body can still be felt months later. It is in many ways more severe than either the 48 Hour or the Six day race, for in these races, regular rest periods including actual sleep must be taken.

You can not, in my opinion, train sensibly for megamarathons by running even a portion of the distance. Training runs of 30 miles or more, I sincerely believe, are counter productive. The only way to accustom yourself to these durations is by running several per year along with other ultra races and thereby allowing the body to adapt itself to the stress. Only a small but significant few of the total number of ultra runners seem to be able to do this successfully.

Runners who aspire to these races are very fortunate at the present time for there are now four or five of these races per year in this country, the same number as there were marathons in the early 1960's. This is in marked contrast to the state of affairs ten or more years ago when these races were staged every two or three years and the would-be megamarathon runner would prepare himself for a "do or die" effort, for the opportunity might not come his way again. It may also be called to mind that, unfortunately, none of these races were open to lady runners. We have a lot to be thankful for in the "Enlightened Eighties"! Nowadays we can plan running several races per year and experiment with different tactics for each one, in the hope of finding the perfect race plan.

Above all else in the first race you must try not to be too nervous, to run easily early on at a comfortable pace and save your nervous energy for the final hours of the race. You must have faith in the ability of your body to still be strong in the later stages. There is a great deal of fear in a 24 hour race as night falls and the novice runner begins to realise just what he has let himself in for. The runner with a cool head can sit in the back of the field biding his time, secure in the knowledge that the race itself will take care of all but the strongest of his rivals. Do not try to run the other runners into the ground, let them do the job for you themselves! These tactics are not guaranteed to win the race but will enable you to cover your best distance. Always aim to cover the biggest distance possible on the day and ignore completely what the opposition is doing in the early stages. The time to become competitive is in the last eight hours, if you are still strong.

There are several pre-conceived ideas nearly all runners have before they run their first 24 hour race. Most runners feel that a much larger volume of training will be needed than for an ultra. This I have proved to my own satisfaction, is just not so. The runner who can comfortably finish a 100km with no more than the usual fatigue may well run a good first 24 hour race If indeed he fails, it will probably be for other reasons than insufficient training. Many runners who make the attempt will find themselves unsuited to the duration, either mentally, physically or both. However, you will never find out whether you can measure up to the challenge of the megamarathon if you do not try it; the only way to succeed is to dare to risk failure.

The universal misconception about the 24 hour race is that it will be incredibly boring. This was what prevented me from trying the race years before I did. I was interested in the race, read avidly all the accounts about such races in the Road Runners Club Newsletter but could not conceive myself running in a race that was obviously so tough and so boring. In actual fact it is just as well that I did not race a 24 hour race ten years ago, for irrespective of what my performance might then have been, these races were so infrequently staged that I would have gone round the bend waiting for the next race to appear on the calendar! In actual fact these races are extremely enjoyable and though, of course very tough, are no more boring than any other ultra.

24 hour races are either run on the 400 metre track or on small loops on the road. In this situation the runner, whatever his ability, has complete contact with all the other runners in the race. If you are a back marker in the race, this may be somewhat tedious as the leader comes charging past several times per hour! If you are a decent soul you may feel obliged to move out to let him through on the inside, after all he looks so good he might break the world record. Later on when he drops out you may well regret all the distance you lost by running wide for him! Apart from the contact with all the other runners whatever their ability, the officials, spectators and your handlers are always close at hand. The camaraderie with everybody connected with the race is far greater than in the shorter races. You have plenty of time to learn the other runner's history if you are running with him (or her) for several hours. In the megas there is a sprinkling of comedians so there are plenty of laughs too.

This is not to say that these races are not tough and painful; they most certainly are! You ache, the bones in your feet, your ankles, knees, leg muscles, hips, all over in fact. You become so tired for so long you become sick and tired of feeling tired! But then if these races were easy, being the sort of person you are, you would give them up in favour of something more demanding.

Many runners do in fact make these races easier by their more casual attitude. The hard man approach where the runner runs the race continually with minimal stops and attempts to cover the maximum distance of which he is capable, is not the only method employed. Some runners run for a few hours at a comfortable pace, then walk for a while, then mix walking with running for a few hours, then come off the track for a meal, come back on the track to run and walk for several hours, then come off for another meal and a sleep, and carry on like this in good spirits to the end of the race.

Often two or three runners adopt this low key approach together. They walk, run and leave the track at the same time. One well known duo were been known to leave 24 hour races to visit local restaurants! They, of course, seldom cover big distances but frequently are well over 100 miles and their interest is mainly centred on six day races. They appear in every race available, sometimes racing on successive weekends, a schedule which would hospitalize a runner with a more serious approach. Another point to bear in mind is that this type of runner, though his personal bests may not appear impressive, has been on the scene for a great deal longer than many a top class runner. He also appears to enjoy his running and is cheerful at all times. Food for thought for us all!

Strategy; Walking; Feeding; The role of the handler.
It is a good idea to enter your first race with a good deal of planning done beforehand. Many runners decide not to walk but to run continuously for as long as they can. Others plan to mix walking with running. If you decide on the latter course, do so in a planned way. This is the system that I use, a formula which works well for me. The novice may copy it as it stands or modify it to suit his, or her, own requirements.

Assume for the sake of argument that the race is being run on a standard 400 metre track, break up the race into thirds; three eight hour periods. During each hour of the first eight hours, take planned walking breaks and using the hour as a unit, break this up into 20 minute segments. So at 20 minutes, 40 minutes and on the hour take a walking break, it can be a timed period say 30 seconds to 5 minutes, or a distance; paced out or 100 metres to an entire 400 metre lap. The important thing is that the break is taken regularly and is initiated right from the start of the race, for it is essential to accustom the body to the routine from the outset. At first when you feel fresh and are running well you will not want to stop and walk but after a while you will settle down and will even begin to look forward to the walking breaks.

It is very convenient to have food and drink handed to you whilst you are walking. Also if you take a drink at the start of every 20 minute walking break you will have no fear of becoming dehydrated. When two hours have elapsed it would be as well to take a small item of solid food. This routine established from the outset, should, if things go well be continued throughout the race. The basic idea is to establish a routine to satisfy the needs of mind and body alike so a state of equilibrium is reached where the runner can continue to move over the ground covering distance for an indefinite period of time, running, walking, taking food and drink and only leaving the track for toilet stops, to change clothing and attend to blisters, chafing etc. If at the end of 8 hours the runner begins to feel tired the walking break can be extended to say half a lap and after 16 hours, if need be to a full lap of walking.

Of course the runner who decides to do no walking can still utilise the plan by either stopping for or being handed food and drink at regular intervals. Some runners like to stop for short rests. I feel that it is better to do this at the end of regular periods of time rather than after having covered a certain distance, say 10 miles. For if you adopt the latter course as time goes by and you become more and more tired it will take longer and longer to cover the set distance. Human nature being what it is you will want to take a longer and longer rest. Remember, rest for 2 minutes and a lap is lost, 10 minutes and a precious mile has gone. If you walk you will gain a respite from running, but will still be gaining miles, also your legs will not be stiffening up as they would be after even a short sit down.

In order to run these races successfully a runner needs to have the ability to run easily over long distances, the temperament to cope with the ordeal and lastly, if things go wrong, the strength of mind to set his sights downwards and accept a result that is less than he had hoped for. I have this ability (especially the latter) and on several occasions have won races because of this. Probably one of my abilities so far as the 24 hour race is concerned is the fact that I can not run fast; which of course is really a lack of ability.

The strongest runner can benefit from some walking even if this is just the few yards needed to take food or drink. Walking rests the body but at the same time distance is still being covered. The amount of time lost during a series of short walking breaks is negligible and the benefit gained can be great.

Feeding - This heading includes drinking; in fact I feel that the majority of nourishment taken in a 24 hour race will be in liquid form. At every megamarathon the organisers provide a drinks table and many provide food in addition. The drinks consist of water, dilute orange and lemon squash and often also an electrolyte drink of some kind; sometimes a selection of several. Runners at the same time are encouraged to bring their own drinks. I invariably bring to these races a double litre of lemonade and coke (fizzy drinks) and also a special drink of lemon squash diluted to taste with extra sugar and salt added. The food I take consists of mini Mars bars, fig roll biscuits, small sausage rolls, individual type pork pies, Kendal Mint Cake, shortbread finger biscuits and bananas. During the race I stop every 20 minutes of every hour, at 20 minutes past, 20 minutes to and on the hour and continue to do this more or less for the entire 24 hours.

I take a drink either from the drinks table or my own table then walk 20 paces and then resume running until the 20 minute segment is up. At each stop I take one plastic cupful and in the case of my own drinks this is in rotation, lemonade, coke and my special drink. Every two hours or so I will eat a small snack and I will continue my walking break till the snack is completely swallowed. This routine I have found, will enable me to finish a race as well fed as I was at the start, for the feeding is sufficient and continuous. If the weather is very cold and wet I will try to get hot drinks, tea or coffee made very sweet and also hot soup. If the weather is very hot I will drink larger amounts of the cold drinks available but will not stop more often. I tend to keep myself cool with the sponges invariably provided. It is vitally important to keep one's food and water resources topped up at all times. One must not wait till hunger prompts one to eat, for eating then will be too late. There is a time lag between the ingestion of food and the supply of energy to the muscles. One must stay alert mentally throughout the race especially in the later stages when one becomes very tired in order to anticipate the body's needs.

Dehydration is a two-fold calamity for not only are the muscles depleted of energy because of the lack of glycogen but the liquid loss from the body prevents efficient transport of food and oxygen to the muscles. There is another harmful effect of dehydration which should be avoided at all costs. This is the strain it puts on the kidneys. The first year I ran in the Preston 24 hour Road Race in May 1983 I failed to drink sufficiently and at around sixteen hours when in the lead found that I needed to stop and urinate far more than usual and began passing blood; an extremely painful and alarming experience! I know enough about the workings of the body to realise the seriousness of the situation and began drinking more and walking (it was more painful to run than to walk in this state). Luckily I had a good lead at this stage and was able to do a fair amount of walking till my strength returned.

The kidneys are small delicate organs which filter the blood of waste products. During strenuous exercise these toxic wastes build up in the blood and the kidneys are required to work very hard to remove these toxins before they reach a harmful level. To do this when the total blood volume is lowered due to dehydration will put a fearful strain on these organs and permanent damage can be the result in the long term. So it is always better to drink more than is necessary rather than less. This will mean that you will probably need to urinate more than usual, and will be losing time having to stop. However, this disadvantage will be negligible and more than offset by your knowledge of the body's increased efficiency. Time lost at the beginning of the race will be made up for in the later stages when you will be able to maintain your output in miles per hour, whilst the other runners are quite probably beginning to flag, enabling you to move up through the field.

Attention to feeding can make all the difference between success and failure. Certainly it was one of the reasons for me failing to run during the last two hours in the 24 hour race at Copthall Stadium in October 1981. I had to learn the facts about proper feeding in these races the hard way. Of course, it seems so obvious now, now that the lesson has been well rubbed in, but I feel that many fine runners put off feeding in these races far too long, so that after four or five hours they experience an energy gap. Eating or drinking then, once exhausted, when it is too late, often causes vomiting. The reason for this is quite obvious if you stop to think about it. To digest a meal, even quite a small one, requires a certain amount of energy. If you are exhausted you can not digest even a small amount of food or drink and run at the same time. Take your food early, frequently, in small amounts before you are aware of hunger and you will remain strong throughout the race. This is especially true in cold weather, when the body during fast running loses energy in the form of heat.

Many of the hardier ultra runners tend to run lightly clad in cold conditions, for they revel in hard running, and prefer to run at a slightly faster pace to keep warm. This plan often works well in marathons and ultra races but can let them down badly in the 24 hour run, especially if their feeding is insufficient. Trouble is apt to strike suddenly, their running slows, they begin to feel cold, put on more clothes, feel very hungry, decide to stop and eat.

They find it very hard to resume their former pace; they force themselves by sheer will power to run hard and are forced to leave the track to vomit. This state of affairs can only be remedied by a rest of at least an hour. When they return to the track they are unable to resume running because their legs have stiffened up. I would be willing to bet that I have seen this particular scenario occur a good fifteen times in my twenty three megamarathon races!

It only happened to me once, though I have often come to grief in these races for other reasons. Frequently during megamarathons the weather changes dramatically, it becomes colder, the wind gets up, it begins to rain, often a combination of all three. Many runners refuse to stop and don protective clothing with the results that hypothermia forces them off the track as described above. Another thing that amazes me is that frequently a runner will leave the track after the weather has become cold and wet and will return dressed in a rainproof top and resumes running round the track with the hood up but still with nothing more than his shorts to protect his legs from the rain.

I have become aware that the legs are far less sensitive to cold than the upper body. Cold usually manifesting itself round the chest arms and neck, so it is natural to leave the leggings off till last. It is also true that runners who leave their legs bare frequently complain of stiffening leg muscles when forced off the track. As obviously the most vital part of the body to a runner, is the legs, I now always, when I begin to feel chilly, put on a pair of light weight track bottoms, after which I seldom feel cold; upper body included. Many runners do not like to wear full leg covering, for they feel it inhibits to a great extent the freedom of their running action. I feel this way myself but I usually give in to the dictates of the climatic conditions having experienced the folly of ignoring them.

In all megamarathons whether on the track or road, each lap of the course has to be both recorded and timed. This is the job of the lap recorder. It is necessary to time each lap and subtract the time of the previous lap from it, and this onerous task must be complied with for each runner and for the entire race. It is in the runner's interest to make sure he is seen by his lap recorder on each circuit of the course. I always shout my number to my recorder and get him to shout it back. If he just shouts "O.K!" or "Got You!" he may be logging another runner passing the recorder's table at the same time as I. If he has missed me I will be one lap short at the end of the race. If in doubt, I trot back and check that he got me. Often lap recorders handle two or more runners if they are experienced; or if there are not enough to go around. One must try to remember that in its own way lap recording is just as hard as running a megamarathon and often these dedicated folk have been up all night too! Try not to become too angry if your lap recorder makes a mistake, for without him there would be no race.

The role of the handler

It is a good idea for the handler to try to stay alert at all times for in this type of race as the hours go by a runner can become almost hypnotised by continually running round the track and thereby forget to feed and fail to take notice of changing weather conditions until it is too late. This may well happen to a runner who is supremely fit and well able to run for 24 hours but who becomes mentally drained due to lack of sleep.

It is here that a good handler is worth his weight in gold, can run with his man, talk him through a bad patch, snap him out of a slight daze and make him take care of his body's needs. An attentive handler can save his charge a lot of distance during a race by having ready the right food or drink and can, if need be, walk beside his charge whilst administering it. He can have changes of clothing ready when needed, and give the runner any information he may require about how the race is progressing. A good handler may often anticipate his charge's needs before he himself is aware of them. Many runners and their handlers set up tents beside the track on the grass infield. The advantages of this are too obvious to require much elaboration especially if the weather is bad. Two runners and their handlers may set up their tents alongside each other and during the night one handler may look after both runners, whilst the other is sleeping.

In fact if the weather becomes bad, I mean really bad, either with cold wind and rain or very hot humid conditions, I usually feel good about this for I know that it will affect most of the other runners more than it will me, not because I am any less vulnerable to the conditions than the others but because I always modify my race plan to suit the adverse conditions.

For example, let us imagine that I am running in a 24 hour race on a very hot day in Mid-Summer and the race starts at noon. When fit I usually run at 7 miles an hour in good conditions but running in the heat demands more energy so I find myself running a mile an hour slower than this right from the start, and in addition I feel very tired and uncomfortable. Now my better distances have all been over 140 miles or more, but I know from experience that I will lucky to be much over 130 miles. The other runners all seem to be running as fast as they would if the conditions were cool, which can be very depressing in the early stages of the race. What is wrong with me? Am I the only runner affected by the heat? Perhaps it really is not so very hot after all and I am just having a bad run. The early hours, whilst I am being outdistanced by the rest of the field can be extremely unpleasant. At this time I feel like, either speeding up against my better judgement or packing the whole thing in!

As the hours go by, however, all but a very few of the runners are flagging badly and as night falls I find that without making any effort to increase my pace I am lapping most of the other runners and have moved well up the field. Many of the runners who were running hard when the race started are now walking and several have dropped out of the race. Even on the hottest day the nights are considerably cooler and I always enjoy running at night whatever the weather and at this time I usually find that I can run more strongly, having conserved my energy during the heat of the day. Night time is the friendliest time in these races and I can really get to know the other runners as I circle the track in their company. At long last dawn breaks and I realise that I still have eight hours of running ahead. At this time of the year by eight o'clock the sun is quite hot, but I find that though I have slowed down to five miles per hour, I can still match the pace of anyone on the track and can alleviate my condition with liberal use of the sponges provided. At long last the race is over and though my distance is well down on what I had expected if the weather conditions had been good 120 - 130 miles instead of the hoped for 150, I managed to finish in front of several runners who I would not be anywhere near had the conditions been good. This I feel is what 24 hour running is all about.

With regard to pacing a 24 hour run some fine exponents of these durations run very hard early on and do extremely fast 100 mile times, 13 hours or even faster, this is eight miles per hour pace, but by 16 hours they have slowed dramatically and finish the race at five miles per hour. Other runners start slower, at seven miles per hour and arrive at 100 miles in 14 hours, but continue to run at six miles per hour till the end of the race. Wally Hayward and Ron Bentley both used the fast initial pace to achieve 159 and 161 miles respectively and Jean-Gilles Boussiquet and Dave Dowdle the steady start to achieve 169 and 170 miles.

I do not, of course, have the natural ability of any of these great athletes but my style of racing is the slow steady approach. Terry Edmondson frequently arrived at 100 miles in 14 hours or even faster and has a best of 156 miles. He can run at eight miles per hour comfortably, a mile an hour faster than I can, he tends to 'hang on' in the later stages. In ideal conditions I can run 55 miles in the first 8 hours, 50 in the second and 48 in the third..

The ideal way to run a 24 hour race so far as I am concerned is to make each hour as productive as possible. Obviously you can not expect to run as fast in the last few hours as you did at the start of the race when you were completely fresh, but if you start running at eight miles an hour and feel comfortable running at that pace, there is no reason why you should not be moving quite strongly at six to seven miles per hour at the finish.

Post Race Recovery; How many races can a person run each year?
Back in the 1970s the majority of athletic authorities felt that the 100 miler and the 24 hour run could only be indulged in once or twice at the end of a runner's

athletic career, for the effect of such races would be so severe that permanent damage to the body could well be the result. In those days 48 hour and Six Day Races were unheard of. It was thought that a runner might well ruin his future athletic potential if he ran in a 24 hour race. Since then, especially in the last decade, megamarathons have become commonplace and this has resulted in a more rational attitude. The fact remains, however, that these races deserve to be treated with a great deal of respect.

As has been stated earlier, there are many different ways of approaching a 24 hour race and the man who runs hard in his first race and keeps running for the entire duration is going to suffer a lot more post race discomfort than the man, with a more casual attitude, who has done a good deal of walking and taken several rests. After my first race in which I had run continuously for 22 hours, I suffered dreadfully in the days after the race, my feet were very sore and swollen, I had several blisters, I ached deep into my bones and my leg muscles were extremely stiff. In addition, my right leg was very swollen from and including the knee downwards and my ankles were very puffy. I began easy jogging a week or so after the race on the advice of the late Dr Lee, the former R.R.C. President, but the swelling did not go down completely till about three weeks after the run and even after a month or so had gone by I had black bruises on both ankles. After every race since then, I have always suffered from sore feet and stiff leg muscles but this has become much less acute, the more races I have completed, and I am able to resume easy running after three days or so. My body seems to have adapted itself to the stresses these races impose upon it.

If I run very hard in the later stages of a 24 hour race, as one has to on occasion to stay in front of, or catch a strong opponent, or to cover a good distance, this may involve running hard right up to the time when the gun goes off to signal the end of the race; if I then stop suddenly, the shock can be overwhelming. To offset this, no matter how bad I may be feeling, I always try to walk around for a while to let the body adapt itself more gradually to the inactivity.

I can never eat very much after a hard 24 hour race, though this is not always obvious at the time. Shortly after a very hard race in Scotland I went back to my hotel, and with great anticipation ordered a large meal (I am a hearty eater); imagine my horror when I could hardly touch a thing! I was very hungry, but in my exhausted state did not have sufficient energy remaining to digest a heavy meal. This race was held in cold winter weather. In hot weather, after a race I do not feel hungry, just very thirsty, but drinking is never any problem; beering it up after a race is always just fine.

I always give myself an easy week after a 24 hour run, this enables the body to quickly regain its strength and also avoid colds and possible injury, whilst the body is in a temporarily weakened state.

With regard to the question how often can an athlete race, really race, a 24 hour run in a year, well that will obviously vary with the individual. I can recover in a month, have done so in fact, see above, but that does not mean to say I will get away with it every time. I think that five to six weeks between races is a good minimum; two months may be better, if there are the races available to be able to space them in this way. For me four races per year would probably be ideal, early May, mid July, early September and late October. There would be plenty of time to recover between races and I would have the opportunity to race in a wide range of weather conditions. As a 24 hour specialist I still run other races mainly for training. If I run a marathon or an ultra race I do not taper off my training and try to resume my normal training uninterrupted after the race. This has caused me trouble from time to time, when the ultra has been tougher than I anticipated and I have raced it too close to a megamarathon.

In 1990 Don Ritchie won the IAU International 24 hour Championship and in 1991 he produced the best 24 Hour performance of the year, some fourteen years after setting his first world track best at 50km

PREPARATION FOR 24 HOUR RACES

Prior to 1988 I had not completed any of my 24 hour race attempts in a satisfactory manner. The reasons for this were mixed, ranging from injury, inadequate preparation to over ambition. Initially I tackled the 24 hour races with a background of marathon/50 mile/100km training, which would see me through to 80 miles plus, after which I could hang on to 100 miles plus at a fairly good pace. In addition I set rather ambitious targets, which led me to run a little too quickly in the earlier part of the race. This preparation and strategy combined with, probably an inadequate food intake led to premature exhaustion.

My first completed 24 hour event was the Cagliari to Sassari 254km race on 17th/18th of October 1987. This was primarily to test my left leg following a stress fracture in my tibia in April. If my leg stood up to the test I would initiate planning for a J.O.G.L.E. attempt the following spring. I had a limited preparation but managed to complete the race in 25 hours 28 minutes 51 seconds, having to walk and jog over the last 25 miles or so.

My second completed 24 hour race was the indoor event in the Kelvin Hall in Glasgow on 19th/20th November 1988. Again this was used as a test for my left leg following a fractured patella in June. I planned to run conservatively and try to run or at least jog for the whole time. I managed to do this covering 144 miles 1009 yards. My patella came through this test with no adverse reaction, so I began planning my next J.O.G.L.E. attempt.

Once I had successfully completed the J.O.G.L.E. I could begin thinking of a serious 24 hour attempt. When I learned that the Milton Keynes event on 3rd/4th of February 1990 was to be the I.A.U. Championship, effectively the World Championship, I decided to prepare for this race. As this decision was made in September 1989 my preparation at least mentally began then. I began increasing my weekly mileage from the week beginning on 10th September, so allowing myself a twenty week build up. My training during the week consisted of a morning run to work by an 11.5 mile route which included a couple of hills one of which is a fairly tough three stager over a mile long. At night I ran back by a shorter route of 9.5 miles including two short hills of a couple of minutes duration each.

These were all steady pace runs, with the pace depending on how I felt. On Saturdays I raced over 10km when local races were available or I ran a steady 15 or 21 miles. On Sunday I worked up to a 31 mile run, mainly on quiet side roads, but including a seven mile loop in Monaughty Forest. This loop included one hard hill and one very hard hill which occurs at about 16 miles.

During this 20 week build up period I averaged 131- miles per week with a maximum mileage of 159, and a minimum of 93 miles. Fourteen 31 mile Sunday runs were completed. My racing in this period consisted of three 10km's prior to the Santander 100km on 7th October where I ran 6-51-14. There was then some time before my next race; the North of Scotland Cross Country

Championships on 25th November, in which I finished 20th.

In detail my schedule from then on was as follows:-

18TH DECEMBER 1989

Monday	a.m.	11 m to work
	p.m.	9.5 m back
Tuesday	a.m.	11 m to work
	p.m.	8.5 m back
Wednesday	a.m.	11 m to work
	p.m.	9.5 m back
Thursday	a.m.	11 m to work
	p.m.	9.5 m back
Friday	a.m.	11 m to work
	p.m.	12.5 m back - begin Christmas Holiday
Saturday	p.m.	4.5 m Cross Country race.
Sunday	a.m.	31 m (road and forest)

Total mileage 140 miles

25TH DECEMBER

Monday	a.m.	15 m (beach and forest)
Tuesday	a.m.	22 m (road and forest)
Wednesday	a.m.	27 m"
Thursday	a.m.	22 m"
Friday	a.m.	27 m"
Saturday	a.m.	15 m (beach and forest)
Sunday	a.m.	31 m (road and forest)

Total mileage 159 miles

1ST JANUARY 1990

Monday	a.m.	22 m (road and forest)
Tuesday	a.m.	18.5 m (forest and road)
Wednesday	a.m.	21.5 m "
Thursday	a.m.	22 m "
Friday	a.m.	15 m (beach and forest)

Saturday   a.m.   22 m (road and forest)
Sunday   a.m.   31 m   "
Total mileage 152 miles

8TH JANUARY

Monday   a.m.   11 m to work
             p.m.   9.5 m back
Tuesday   a.m.   11 m to work
             p.m.   9.5 m back
Wednesday   a.m.   11 m to work
             p.m.   9.5 m back
Thursday   a.m.   11 m to work
             p.m.   9.5 m back
Friday   a.m.   15 m before work
Saturday   p.m.   North District Cross Country League Race
                      (18th) 10 miles
Sunday   a.m.   31 m (wood and forest)
Total mileage 138 miles

15TH JANUARY

Monday   a.m.   11 m to work - Chest cold
             p.m.   9.5 m back
Tuesday   a.m.   11 m to work
             p.m.   9.5 m back
Wednesday   a.m.   11 m to work - Bronchitis; Ampicillin prescribed
             p.m.   9.5 m back
Thursday   a.m.   11 m to work
             p.m.   9.5 m back
Friday   a.m.   15 m before work
Saturday   a.m.   15 m
Sunday   a.m.   31 m (road and forest)
Total mileage 143 miles

22ND JANUARY

Monday	a.m.	11 m to work
	p.m.	9.5 m back
Tuesday	a.m.	11 m to work
	p.m.	9.5 m back
Wednesday	a.m.	10.5 m to work
	p.m.	9.5 m back
Thursday	a.m.	10.5 m to work
	p.m.	9.5 m back
Friday	a.m.	15 m before work
Saturday	a.m.	31 m - Throat infection; Sporanox prescribed
Sunday	a.m.	15 m

Total mileage 141 miles

29TH JANUARY

Monday	a.m.	8.5 m to work
	p.m.	8.5 m back
Tuesday	a.m.	8.5 m to work
	p.m.	no run easing down for 24 hour race
Wednesday	a.m.	8.5 m easy to work
	p.m.	8.5 m" back
Thursday		No running cycled to and from work
Friday	"	42.5 miles

Evening travel to London.

| Saturday | 8 p.m. | 24 HOUR INDOOR RACE MILTON KEYNES |
| Sunday | " | |

During this period as indicated above I had some health problems, including Bronchitis two weeks before the race, but five days on antibiotics cured this.

The race went well apart from a nose bleed (a result of the bronchitis) and a lower quads problem in my right leg near the end. I was delighted to win the race in 166 miles 429 yards, 267.543km. John Lamont and Adrian Stott helped me during the event providing food as required. I drank 200 ml of Leppin Enduro Booster every 20 minutes, and ate a banana or a slice of white bread alternately every hour. I am not sure if this was adequate as I became extremely fatigued during the last five hours.

I planned my next 24 hour race to be the A.A.A. Championship on 26th/27th October 1991 in Copthall Stadium. I began my preparations on the 5th of August, and my weekly mileage leading up to the race, with comments, is listed below.

Week No	Mileage	Comment
1	120	
2	153.5 *	Half Marathon in 1-17-01
3	131	Two Bridges 2nd in 3-41-28
4	180 *	
5	181 *	
6	177 *	31 mile Monaughty Forest course

From then on my detailed schedule was as follows:-

Note: each morning at 05.30 Isobel and I ran a 3 mile loop round Lossiemouth.

16TH SEPTEMBER

Monday	a.m.	3 m + 11 m to work
	p.m.	10 .5 m back
Tuesday	a.m.	3 m + 20 m to work
	p.m.	No run - late class
Wednesday	a.m.	3 m + 11 m to work
	p.m.	10 .5 m back
Thursday	a.m.	3 m + 11 m to work
	p.m.	10 .5 m back
Friday	a.m.	3 m + 15 m before work
	p.m.	No run
Saturday	a.m.	3 m + 31 m (road + forest)
Sunday	p.m.	10 m race in Inverness (7th)

Total mileage 158.5 miles

23RD SEPTEMBER

Monday	a.m.3	m + 11 m to work
	p.m.	10 .5 m back
Tuesday	a.m.	3 m + 20 m to work
	p.m.	No run - late class
Wednesday	a.m.	3 m + 11 m to work
	p.m.	10 .5 m back - late class
Thursday	a.m.	3 m + 11 m to work
	p.m.	11 back
Friday	a.m.	3 m + 15 m before work
	p.m.	No run
Saturday	a.m.	3 m + 27 m (road + forest)
	a.m.	3 m + 31 m (" ")

Total mileage 179 miles

30TH SEPTEMBER

Monday	a.m.	3 m + 11 m to work
	p.m.	10 .5 m back
Tuesday	a.m.	3 m + 20 m to work
	p.m.	No run - late class
Wednesday	a.m.	3 m + 4 m before work
	p.m.	No run - easing down for 100km
Thursday	a.m.	3 m
Friday	a.m.	3 m.
	p.m.	Fly to Spain
Saturday	a.m.	100km Race Santander (5th 6-49-13)
Sunday		No run - returning from Spain

Total mileage 123 miles

7TH OCTOBER

Monday	a.m.	3 m + 9.5 m to work
	p.m.	9.5 m back
Tuesday	a.m.	3 m + 9-m to work
	p.m.	No run - late class

Wednesday	a.m.	3 m + 10.5 m to work
	p.m.	10.5m m back - late class
Thursday	a.m.	3 m + 15 m - on strike
Friday	a.m.	3 m + 15 m
	p.m.	No run
Saturday	a.m.	3 m + 4 m
Sunday	p.m.	Half Marathon at Fort William 8th in 1-15-06

Total mileage 114.5 miles

14TH OCTOBER

Monday	a.m.	15.5 m in Glen Nevis - Mid term Holiday
Tuesday	a.m.	15.5 m as yesterday
Wednesday	a.m.	4.5m + 27 m (road and forest)
Thursday	a.m.	3 m + 15 m - sore throat, runny nose
Friday	a.m.	3 m + 15 m
Saturday	a.m.	3 m + 4 m - streaming cold
Sunday	a.m.	3 m " "

Totalmileage 108.5   miles

21ST OCTOBER

Monday	a.m.	3 m + 8-m easy to work
	p.m.	8.5 m easy back
Tuesday	a.m.	3 m + 8.5 m to work
	p.m.	No run - late class
Wednesday	a.m.	3 m - cold a little better
	p.m.	No run - easing down for 24 hr race
Thursday	a.m.	3 m - nose bleed
Friday	a.m.	3 m
	p.m.	Travelling to London
Saturday		24 hour race Copthall
Sunday	a.m.	"
	p.m.	Return to Aberdeen/Lossiemouth

Total mileage 207 miles

28TH OCTOBER

Monday	No run	
Tuesday	a.m.	3 m
Wednesday	a.m	3 m
Thursday	a.m.	3 m
Friday	a.m.	3 m
Saturday	a.m.	Black Isle Marathon 4th (2-45-45)
Sunday	a.m.	3 m

Total mileage 41 miles

In the race I was concerned about the effect my cold might have on my performance and my health, even though it was much improved. I settled into the race and forgot about any possible effects from the cold. My target was 170 miles plus and this appeared possible as I passed a 100 miles in 12-44-28, and 200km in 16-19-16. However, my pace over the last seven hours was rather poor, so although I was delighted to win in 166 miles 1203 yards, 268.251km I was not totally satisfied with my run.

Again I drank 200 ml of Leppin Enduro Booster every 20 minutes, and ate every hour after three hours, alternating a banana with boiled white rice. This may not have been adequate as again I became depleted of glycogen with some several hours remaining. In another 24 hour I would try increasing my food intake to see if this will enable me to maintain a reasonable pace for longer.

Second in the race was my team mate, Mick Francis [155 miles 1107 yds/250.461km]. Mick and I trained together on Saturdays and Sundays so that part of our training was identical. During the week he ran 8 miles before work then 10 miles after work. I provided encouragement and advice as appropriate.

Newton's Law – 24 hours
Mike Newton eventually moved up to the 24 hours and proved one of the most consistent and formidable performers.

However, it took many years to finally admit my best distances were from 100km to 200km. Did I have the capacity to go beyond 200km? This for me was a difficult question to answer. Certainly the trials and tribulations I suffered over the 24 hour race would take volumes but space for this article precludes me from an in depth dissertation. My trouble always began in the final six hours. Let's face it, the last quarter of a 24 hour race is do or die time. This undoubtedly is the Stalingrad of the event.

When I broke the 200km world track record during the Blackburn 24 hour race with 16h. 42m. 31s, it was a freezing cold November night in 1980. So cold in fact that my drinks froze inside their bottles. However, these energy sapping conditions didn't depress my spirit as before the race I had prepared my psyche to stimulate mental and physical capacity to hold a running pace at 7.5mph for almost seventeen hours. After 500 gruelling laps on the Blackburn cinder track I broke the 200km world record. This short lived elation lasted a couple of laps when I literally ran on air. Then I came down to earth with a bump when it dawned on me that I still had seven hours of the race left to go. True I had a lead of over half an hour on the French champion Boussiquet and I knew I had his supporters worried but the concentrated effort of my punishing schedule had taken its toll. Powerless I watched my lead slip like the ebb-tide. Boussiquet with typical French flair went on to break the world 24 hour track record with 164 miles. In 3rd place came Mark Pickard, at twenty, the youngest athlete to better 150 miles in 24 hours.

After the Blackburn race I had a string of 2nd places in the 24 hour events. For several years I had to battle against this jinx. In 1982 the jinx struck again at Preston's Moor Park, when during the night I tripped and fell, gashing my knee, after appearing a certainty to win. I finished as runner up. On the train back to London one of the runners who had been influenced by my career disdainfully rebuked me saying "You should have won but threw it away in the morning." Now I know how a jockey feels about losing on the odds on favourite.

It was not until Milton Keynes in 1984 that I made a winning mark in the 24 hours. The first 24 hour race to be held indoors in the UK this century, it was a magnet for all the top ultra men in the country. The bone hard marble surface of the indoor hyper market didn't suit everybody. I played a waiting game designed to bring me through the field after 10 hours. Previously a separate development beyond my control had lost me a couple of 975 yard laps through a mix up by the time keepers. Despite this unsatisfactory situation I still won the race with 144(r) miles, an amateur world's best.

The following year at the Costello Stadium, a windy Humberside track, I set a new stadium best with 147 miles 1,540 yards. In a contrary way I suppose it was fitting to conclude my career with a 24 hour road race which was run at Feltham in 1991. Now in my fifties I ran with controlled experience to win with over 140 miles.

My career record in eleven 24 hour races is 3 wins, 6 seconds, a 6th and a 12th. I surpassed 150 miles five times and my best was at Barnet in 1981 when I was second (once again) with 158(r) at the Copthall Stadium.

From my training log one salient factor comes to the fore. Once past my peak, to ensure even a reasonable 24 hour total mileage, at the end of my career I was almost training 24 hours without a break for a 24 hour race at only 6mph. Evidently the deterioration is accumulative, doubling every five to seven years, once past the age of 43.

Between the years of '74 - '84 I missed on average 20 days of training a year. The Winter break was from the end of November to the end of February. In this quiet period I would average 80 - 90 miles a week.

Before the Lausanne 24 hour track race 2nd/3rd May 1981 my training looked like this:-

April	2	20 mile run
	3	70 mile L.S.D.
	4	25 mile run
	5	20 mile run
	6	30 mile run
	7	25 hills in one hour
	8	20 mile run
	9	5 miles (slight injury to Anterior Ligament)
	10	(tried out injury with half hour jog, now O.K.)
	11	20 mile run
	12	25 miles - intervals on track
	13	20 miles - intervals on track
	14	50 hills in 2 hours
	15	101 miles L.S.D. - spread over 3 sessions.
	16	20 miles - track work

17	6 miles - easy day
18	125 miles - 24 hour trial spread over six sessions in 18 hours
19	20 miles - track run
20	50 hills in 2 hours
21	track intervals in 2 hours

From the 26th of April to the commencement of the race in early May I did easy work between 5 and 10 miles a day.

Since the advent of the Marathon craze, interest in road running has grown enormously. The commercial side of the sport has expanded beyond belief. Today there is a far greater choice of running shoes which are superior in design and quality. I always raced in the lightest running shoes money could buy. However, the wear and tear on them makes this side of the sport very expensive. I never allowed the heels to wear down below a certain level, if you do, I'm sure it's one of the causes of Achilles tendon strain. Because of the cost I had to learn to repair my own running shoes. I cut the rubber from a worn out pair, then using a G-clamp and superglue I would build up the heels again. When in full training I had this chore every couple of weeks. In contrast to the above, the wear and tear physically, on an athlete is far more complicated. It is critical to realise that to avoid breakdown one must build up gradually.

Remember the old adage? 'An army marches on its stomach.' This also applies to athletes. Plenty of good food improves condition. Some of the best for nutritional value are - liver, cod roe, whole wheat bread, spaghetti (not tinned), apricots and bananas, just to name a few.

Undoubtedly vitamins and minerals come into the scheme of things. It has been proven that one needs iron and B 12 when in full training. Maybe there is a case for high doses of vitamins C and E a week before a race. No doubt there is a psychological boost when taking supplements. Let's face it, any athlete running over a 100 miles a week needs all the help he can get. Not surprisingly, all ultra distance runners have to learn to eat and drink on the run, especially in multi-day events.

Terry Edmondson belongs to that very small elite group of 24 hour performers who have run 150 miles/ 241 km six times or more). Obviously few runners can hope to emulate Terry's speed or strength but the would-be 24 hour runner can get useful insight into the mental and physical strategies he uses from the article below.

Why ultras?

All my life, well from being 13 years old, I've always done some kind of sport. From boxing and weight-lifting, to cycling and race walking, and always at com-petitve levels. I took up running at the age of 18 when I first ran for Blackburn Harriers. I ran a lot of cross country and road races, for about four years but then went on to other sports. I returned to running, to run for Horwich Harriers I ran on the fells this time, I enjoyed it but found I got a lot of injuries and so it was that I was back to road racing again.

You might say "Why not stick to the average road race, like everyone else?" You said it, "like everyone else?" I wanted a greater challenge. I wanted to do something different, harder, something that would feel like an achievement.

After reading articles on Mike Newton and Jean Giles Boussiquet, I thought I'd have a crack at one of these ultra races and searched out a race close to home, the Blackburn 24 hour track race. I knew these ultra men spent a lot of time out and about, putting in mile after mile, so I'd do the same. After my first attempt, you'd think I'd give up, but it did the opposite for me, I can and will do better, that's what keeps me going.

My First 24 Hour race

You learn fast in this game. For my first 24 hour race I did everything wrong. Firstly, I trained on a school grass track; that was my biggest mistake. I worked up my mileage from about 70/75 miles per week to about 150/180 miles. This I knew I had to do, all the other ultra men were doing it. I would do 15 miles a night after work and probably do two tens on a Saturday. Then on a Sunday I would do my long run. Twelve weeks before the race my long run would prob-ably be a marathon. Then every Sunday I would increase it until 5 weeks before the race my long run would now be up to 80 miles. This, like I said, was my first mistake, the 80 miles was done on grass. The rest of the week I'd run on the road, fells for strength and a little cross country for variety. All the road running was done at speed. Five weeks before the race I'd bring my mileage down to 130, 100, 80, 60 and about 45 miles in the week going into the race.

My first race was the Blackburn 24 hour track race in August 1981. Going into this race as a novice was an experience in itself. The questions I kept asking myself were endless. Should I go off fast and see what I'm capable of? Should I take it easy and watch the rest? Should I run for three hours and take a rest? Should I take a rest at all? By the time I got to the line my mind was numb. I set off in what I thought was a safe pace, couldn't slow down, I felt uncomfortable going any slower, (I still do today). I was pleasantly surprised when I found out that I was leading at the 50 mile mark in a time of 7 hours 9 minutes. A great Frenchman, well I admire him, came up to me and said "Edmondson you can win this race." I later found out his name was Gerard Stenger. Little did we know what was yet to come. At 100K I was in second place but still felt O.K. I took time out to eat, something I try not to do today. I sat down for about 20 minutes, when I tried to get up the knees let me down. I won't go into the agony, but it proves one thing, one minute you're feeling on top of the world, the next, you wonder "What the heck am I doing going round and round here time after time". But I was not going to give up. I had to find out if it was possible for me to keep going for twenty four hours without sleep, and so it was that in my first 24 hours I spent a good 12 hours of it walking. And I also learnt not to train on the grass

While walking round I had time to watch the other runners and see how they coped, what sort of rests they took, what they drank and ate. I learnt too that you don't have to be young in this game to win, the old man of the sport won this one, Mr Campbell no less. I'd never met him before, but I kept thinking if this man, who's got to be touching 50 can win a race then there's hope for me yet. So, after my first 24 hours I'd covered 102 miles 292 yards. But I knew if I'd trained right I could have done better. I came 13th out of 15, and was looking forward to my next 24 hour race.

The next one was the following May, I did the same training, but the long run was on the road. Twelve weeks before I started it all over again. I found a little circuit near home, 1.6 miles round and that is where I would park the car, take my drinks, eats and clock. I'd spend Sunday mornings just going round and round.

The May race was at Preston, on the road this time, I'm sure it would suit me better. It was my first meeting with mega ultra runner Mike Newton. To cut a long story short, I came third to John Towers, and Mike was second, I didn't think anyone could have beaten Mike. I covered 137 miles and it was a lot easier. By now I was hooked. I just had to win one of these races, I wasn't going to give up until I had. And the story goes, when you've won one you want to win another. I had to do 150 miles before long, I knew I had it in me.

Getting the mind right

Peaking for a 24 hour race starts for me about 12 weeks before. You know what training you have to do, so you get down to plodding the roads, mile after mile. But it's getting the mind right that's the biggest problem. So I go through stages of hard thinking and concentration when I'm running on my own, weeks before the race. Firstly I think of winning the race, which is the best thing about them. I think of the final mileage I hope I can do and if I'm capable of doing more or if I've anything left in reserve, for the next one. This goes through my mind night after night, winning has got a lot to do with it. From here on I back track and I begin to think about the hardest part of the race, the first 23 hours.

A lot of runners I know split the race up into miles or hours. I'm an hour man. For the first 3 hours I don't want to feel any twinges or discomfort; I want to feel I'm out with the rest of the lads having a run. If you aim for miles you can put yourself under pressure. It's no good saying you want 25 miles in the first 3 hours and you only get 24; you start to worry about it. "Can I catch up?" Then all your plans have gone astray in the first three hours. The next stage for me is 6 hours. I still want to feel good, after all it's just an average Sunday run and the wife's just sent the lad over to my 1.6 mile course to say "dinner's on the table, it's time to come home". Now I look forward to the 8 hour stage, it's a third into the race. I expect to feel the odd twinge about now but hopefully nothing too drastic, but I do hope I've covered a 100K.

It's about two weeks off the race and my thinking into the 10 to 12 hour stage. I expect some pain now, after all I'm not inhuman. I know this is the part of the race where you have to dig deep mentally and physically, tell yourself over and over again you're O.K. you're doing well. You see others around you both suffering and looking good. You plod on and on.

12 hours into the race and you know it should be down hill from here on. You take stock of how you're feeling, your thoughts are slowing down as well as the legs. The concentration becomes harder at this point so, as the wife says, I switch off and go to sleep, not literally but she knows I won't need her for about 4 hours. From 85 miles to 110 I go on automatic pilot and sometimes, I admit I couldn't tell you what was going on around me.

I wake up, usually two thirds into the race, asking myself "What mileage will I finish with? Can I get a 150?" I work it out as I'm running along and then say to myself, "No Terry, its only pressure, just go and enjoy the last stages of the race."

Seven hours left, my toes are usually killing me (I've got dry joints), the legs have done their job, the mind has kept itself in shape and is looking forward to a well earned rest.

The last 4 hours; if I'm winning, which if you remember is the main objective, and I can't be caught, I say well hopefully "It's a 150, I can take it easy and save myself for another day."

Then I go back to what I thought about right at the beginning to winning another one. So for me my mind has to be right. I have to go through stage by stage as I want it to go. I go over it time and time and time again.

My later training

After doing about ten 24 hour races I found I didn't need to plod the roads as much, I had the training behind me. But I still go through the routine of getting my mileage up about 5 weeks before a race and bringing it down gradually. And I still do a long run on Sunday. Not as much as the 80 miles I did, but I will still run for 6 hours at a time. Quite a few people have asked me for my training schedule going into a race. So I've gone back to my diaries to give them one. But like I've told them what was good for me might not be good for them. On looking through my diaries I was quite surprised at how many days down the years I'd had off through injury or illness, so for those who are interested these are the miles I've run and raced.

YEAR	MILES RUN	MILES RACED	DAYS OFF	AV/PER DAY
1985	3946	1012	79	13.7
1986	3614	810	76	12.5
1987	3976	1020	87	14.3
1988	3594	1010	103	13.7

Now follows detailed account of my training; as you may notice I rarely run on Saturday as we as a family spend two hours on a Saturday night playing badminton (competitively!). I don't get up to the high mileages now that I did in my first four years of ultra-running, but almost every day I go out on the roads.

March 1988

Tuesday		1	9 miles	road	easy
Wednesday		2	rest		
Thursday		3	10 miles	road	easy
Friday		4	9 miles	road	undulating

Total for week 55 miles

Saturday		5	rest		
Sunday	am	6	13 miles	road	
	pm		5 miles	road	
Monday		7	10 miles	road	slow
Tuesday	am	8	9 miles	road	
	pm		10 miles	road	
Wednesday		9	6 miles	road	slow
Thursday		10	10 miles in 58 minutes 10 seconds		
Friday		11	7 miles	road	easy

Total for week 70 miles

Saturday	am	12	10 miles	road	easy
	pm		7 miles	road	
Sunday		13	16 miles	undulating in 1 hour 59 minutes	
Monday		14	7 miles	road	easy
Tuesday	am	15	10 miles	road	

	pm	10 miles	road	
Wednesday	16	15 miles	road	easy
Thursday	17	12 miles	road	easy
Friday	18	17 miles	road	easy

Total for week 104 miles

Saturday	19	rest		
Sunday	am 20	10 miles	road	easy
	pm	7 miles	road	
Monday	21	18 miles	road	easy
Tuesday	22	10 miles	road	easy
Wednesday	23	10 miles	road	slow
Thursday	24	17 miles	road	easy
Friday	25	20 miles	road	easy

Total for week 92 miles

Saturday	26	9 miles	road	easy
Sunday	27	27 miles	road	easy
Monday	28	17 miles	road	easy
Tuesday	29	10 miles		fastish - 57 minutes 05 seconds
Wednesday	30	16 miles	road	undulating - 1 hour 55 minutes 30 seconds
Thursday	31	10 miles	road	jogging

April 1988

Friday	am 1	RACED 10 K in 35 minutes 17 seconds		
	pm	10 miles	road	

Total for week 105 miles

Saturday	2	6 miles	road	easy
Sunday	3	30 miles	road	easy
Monday	4	10 miles	road	easy
Tuesday	5	14 miles	road	easy
Wednesday	am 6	RACED 4 miles - 21 minutes 38 seconds		

			5 miles		easy
Thursday	am 7		10 miles	road	
	pm		10 miles	road	
Friday		8	16 miles		undulating - 1 hour 53 minutes

Total for week 105 miles

Saturday		9	rest	
Sunday		10	RACED Half Marathon 1 hour 78 minutes 25 seconds	
			plus 5 miles	easy
Monday		11	rest	
Tuesday	am 12		20 miles	road
	pm		11 miles	
Wednesday		13	18 miles	road easy
Thursday		14	12 miles	road undulating
Friday		15	25 miles	road slow

Total for week 104 miles

Saturday	16	rest		
Sunday	17	16 miles		undulating in record time 1.43.30
Monday	18	26 miles	road	easy
Tuesday	19	24 miles	road	easy
Wednesday	20	18 miles	road	fast - 1 hour 56 minutes 30 seconds
Thursday	21	20 miles	road	easy
Friday	22	20 miles	road	easy

Total for week 124 miles

Saturday	23	rest		
Sunday	24	38 miles	road	easy
Monday	25	22 miles	road	easy
Tuesday	26	10 miles		fast - 57 minutes 26 seconds
Wednesday	27	22 miles	road	easy
Thursday	28	25 miles	road	easy
Friday	29	26 miles	road	easy

Total for week 149 miles

Saturday   30 15 miles   road   easy

May 1988

Sunday   1   38 miles   road   easy
Monday   2   20 miles   road   easy
Tuesday   3   10 miles   slow
Wednesday am 4   4 mile RACE in 21 minutes 25 seconds
           pm   4 miles   road   easy
Thursday   5   24 miles   road   easy
Friday   6   24 miles   road   easy
Total for week 139 miles

Saturday   7   rest
Sunday   8   34 miles   road   easy
Monday   9   16 miles   road   easy
Tuesday   10 10 miles   road   slow
Wednesday am 11   5 mile RACE in 27 minutes 2 seconds
           pm   5 miles   road   easy
Thursday   12 10 miles   road   slow
Friday   13 15 miles   road   easy
Total for week 95 miles

Saturday   14 rest
Sunday   am 15   18 miles   road
              pm   7 miles   road
Monday   16 10 miles   fast
Tuesday   17 5 mile RACE 28 minutes 13 seconds
Wednesday   18 8 miles   road   slow
Thursday   19 10 miles   easy
Friday   20 8 miles   road   easy
Total for week 66 miles

Saturday   21 rest
Sunday   am 22   20 miles on the moors

		pm	6 miles	road	
Monday	23	8 miles	road	easy	
Tuesday	24	10 miles	road	easy	
Wednesday	25	6 miles	road	easy	
Thursday	26	rest			
Friday	27	rest			

Total for week 60 miles

Saturday	28	DONCASTER 24 HOUR RACE
Sunday	29	1st 151.5 miles
Monday	30	rest
Tuesday	31	8 miles easy jogging (no injuries just bodily tired)

June 1988

Wednesday am	1	4 miles RACE		
	pm	2 miles	road	easy
Thursday	2	7 miles	road	easy
Friday	3	5 miles	on the moors	easy

Total for week 177 miles

Saturday	4	Went with a group to try out "Three Peaks Lands End to John O' Groats Relay Record".
Sunday	5	Ran 70 miles approximately
Monday	6	rest
Tuesday	7	8 miles road easy
Wednesday	8	8 miles road easy
Thursday	9	10 miles fast 56 minutes
Friday	10	8 miles road easy

Total for week 104 miles

Saturday	11	rest
Sunday	12	BLACKPOOL MARATHON 26 miles

Monday	13	7 miles	road	easy
Tuesday	14	10 miles	road	easy
Wednesday	15	10 miles	road	easy
Thursday	16	7 miles	road	easy
Friday	17	rest		

Total for week 60 miles

Saturday	18	HULL 24 HOUR RACE		
Sunday	19	1st 131 miles		
Monday	20	rest		
Tuesday	21	6 miles	road	easy
Wednesday	22	4 miles		jogging
Thursday	23	10 miles	road	fast 55 minutes 40 seconds
Friday	24	5 miles	road	easy

Total for week 156 miles

Saturday	25	rest		
Sunday	26	16 miles	on the moors	
Monday	27	rest		
Tuesday	28	7 miles	road	easy
Wednesday	29	8 miles	road	easy
Thursday	30	10 miles	road	easy

July 1988

Friday	1	rest - travelled to Ireland

Total for week 41 miles

Saturday	2	rest
Sunday	3	MULLINGAR 24 HOUR RACE
Monday	4	1st 134 miles

Editor's Note:

In the Mullingar 24 hour race, due to a misunderstanding with the race organiser, Terry arrived 1 hours late for the start. He immediately set off in hot pursuit of the other runners. Malcolm Campbell, who competed in the race , subsequently wrote in the RRC Newsletter, "Terry was magnificent, and worked very hard. When he had done enough to secure victory and with one hour remaining he retired from the race. He had completed 134 miles in 21 hours which indicated that this race would have been another of his 150 mile plus victories."

Editor's Notes:

In Terry's 156.003 mile race at Chorley he reached 100km in 7:54:26, 100 miles in 13:44:08 and 200km in 18:14:29.

In his 155.997 mile race at Preston he ran 50 miles in 6:23:31, 100km in 8:01:42, 100 miles in 13:42:59, 200km in 17:34:07 and 150 miles in 22:14:22.

The 24 Hour event is one of the least predictable of ultras, few runners manage to consistently produce good results. Marianne Savage showed the ability to produce good results in the event, time after time. Her approach to training and racing in such events will be of interest to many.

My first inkling of Ultra Distance came when I and others were suckered into helping with the 1986 Solihull 24 Hour track race. Here was where I made my first mistake. In the euphoria of post race presentations I fleetingly remarked that I wouldn't mind having a go at the following year's race. I was well hooked. Up stepped John Walker with the training programme like a rabbit out of the hat.

Alone I began the long training runs necessary to compete in a 24 hour race. My thoughts during these initial steps were ones of revenge, murder, mayhem and could Attila the Hun give me a few lessons?

The 1987 Solihull 24 Hour arrived with a great deal of trepidation but after completing 208Km/129M I was delighted. Now I was really caught. The pain, swelling and discomfort over the following days didn't dissuade me. My thoughts started straying towards the next 24 hour race. In 1988 the second

Solihull 24 Hour came and went with a distance of 229Km/142M. Now I had the bug.

My training, which has been devised by John Walker follows a matrix system with variables added to give a high degree of training quality, with an end result in performance. However, the basis of the pattern follows:-

Sunday	20 to 25 Miles
Monday	10 and 7
Tuesday	5 and 10
Wednesday	10 and6
Thursday	7 and 10
Friday	10 and 6
Saturday	Rest Day

Each morning a gym workout is undertaken concentrating on flexibility, strength and endurance. Alternating sessions between hard and easy. These are then followed by swimming, sauna and spa bath. On a monthly basis a massage I find is of great benefit.

Three months before a race I will do a 30 mile plus run on one of the Sundays. This is then followed on the following Wednesday by a 20 to 25 mile run. A month before the race I will finish off my long runs with a 40 mile plus hard training run. It is at this time I will also introduce mountain and hill running. For major championships more and longer training runs are undertaken.

This then is where, I believe, the whole foundation of one's Ultra Distance running is made. The long but not necessarily lonely runs must have an air of enjoyment. However, there has to be a fierce will to succeed. To cut corners in effort, or runs by the odd minute here and there only hampers the mental application and attitude at a later date. The body is capable of going to and beyond one's perceived limits. I believe the mental approach, willingness to make sacrifices, concentration on the running and to ignore all around you, is 80 percent of running Ultras.

Each of my races follows a pattern of effort and relaxation. The effort is a sustained period of controlled running at a set timed pace. However, circumstances can dictate that the effort part has some flexibility in terms of lap times or minor periods of extended running. The relaxing period is an area which is just as, if not more important than, the effort period. A walk will allow the body to recover. This is important if longer distances are to be achieved. Right from the start of a 24 hour race or longer I run for twenty five minutes, then take a five minute walk. During that walk I will eat and drink. A constant controlled effort in ultra runs should stave off fatigue rather than long periods of sustained running.

But one must have control, discipline and a belief in one's own capabilities. If one intends to continue running ultras over a long period, a rest year of one in three should be adopted. This then will allow other areas of running to be explored and also allow the body to recover.

Richard and Sandra Brown came into ultras from the Long Distance Walking Association events and consequently have good walking backgrounds. Both are accomplished race walkers but in races of 24 hours and longer they mix walking and running

Most people have to walk sometime during a 100 mile or 24 hour event and the more "ultra" the event the more important walking is likely to become. But how much walking training and practice do most people put in? Not much we suspect. How many plan what the balance between walking and running should be? Again we suspect a lot of people run until they're tired and do not plan a race to get a balance at all. So how early in an event should you put in a few laps of walking? What speed should you aim for and how can you train to achieve that? We will try and tackle these questions in what follows.

First, let us dispel some mythology about speed-walking or race-walking as it is generally known. It is not a strange art which has to be mastered in the suppleness of youth and then requires exaggerated hip movements - the wiggly bottom syndrome. The only purpose in twisting forward the hip of the leading leg is to lengthen the stride by a couple of inches. Do that a few thousand times with a push off from a straight back leg and you will have gained a lot of extra distance and speed. Excessive wiggle is a waste of energy and totally unnecessary. Similarly a high pumping arm action is only important if you are sprinting and then - like sprint running - helps drive the legs and supports some of the weight of the upper part of the body. For ultra events a relaxed economical arm action with elbows into the side should be the aim. But do try to think of a piston rather than a marching action which does not really contribute to forward motion.

In training just try striding as much as you can on a flat bit of road or pavement. Count the number of strides between lamp posts or trees or in relation to the number of paving slabs and try each time to improve the length of stride. To increase your reach stretching exercises of the lower back and hamstring muscles are useful and should form part of a regular stretching schedule which itself will help avoid injury. Once you have the stride then you can perhaps increase the number of paces per minute. But the stride must come first. You really know when you are making progress when you have that feeling of just gliding along with feet only a few millimetres above the road surface.

The previous generation of race-walkers used to build up stamina and power by just walking long distances or doing cross-country strolls. We have old Race Walking Records which show that our top men thought nothing of walking from London to Brighton and back for a training spin stopping at well known breakfast and liquid lunch refreshment stops on route.

Cross country events can still be an important form of stamina training. The Long Distance Walkers Association (LDWA) organise regular walks of 30 miles and above over interesting countryside with regular check points offering food and drink. Nowadays virtually all of these events allow runners to take part. Sandra and I only started race-walking in 1982 and had only ever run one marathon before then. We are sure that one of the main reasons we are able to make an impact on the long-distance walking and running scene was because of the fitness, stamina and sheer determination you build up flogging over hills and mountains on events which have such delightful titles as the Dorset Doddle (not a doddle by any means as it involves 33 miles of cliff walking from Weymouth to Swanage), the Malvern Midsummer Marathon (35 miles over the Malverns and surrounding countryside), the Wealden Waters (100km of Kent mud), Purbeck Plod (25 miles round the Purbeck hills) and Surrey Summits (did you know you can get 7,000 feet of climb in 100km event if you go up and down enough Surrey hills?). The LDWA also organizes longer events and in particular every year there is a 100 mile cross country. When you have run around 11,000 feet of climb and descent on the Snowdonia 100 mile or 12,000 feet in the Yorkshire Dales then a 100 miles on a flat track only holds the problem of boredom!

As well as ultra people training via LDWA events, we are sure there are many LDWA members who could take up our recognized ultra events and perform with distinction. Indeed a greater relationship between long-distance walkers and runners is something which should bring benefit to both sports and even greater interest to the participants.

However not everyone now believes in the merits of cross country training for walking or running. More emphasis is placed on fartlek speed work. It certainly takes less time if you go flat out during fartleks but there is no point in flailing around at the expense of style. For the same reason we would generally recommend that you decide before you go out for a training spin whether you are going to walk or run. Mixing the two can play havoc with attempts to concentrate on and improve speed walking technique. By all means run over to where you intend to start your speed walk training but then stick at speed walking until you decide to come back. It will take patience and you will inevitably get the odd ribald comment from the uninitiated. But what you are doing is too important for your ultra distance performance to let that bother you and you can always express surprise at the ignorance of people and suggest they come and join you!

As for the balance in an event between running and walking, that will very much depend on the individual as will the walking speed to be aimed at. However, simple maths tells you that to run at seven miles an hour for sixteen hours but then walk at only three miles an hour for the remaining eight gives exactly the same result as running more gently at six miles an hour for sixteen hours and then walking at five miles an hour for the remaining eight. Over thirty walkers per year complete the hundred mile Centurian walks in the UK and Netherlands within 24 hours simply through walking at a steady pace. Although we congratulated ourselves in 1986 at Solihull by saying that more people had gone over a hundred miles in that 24 hour event than in any previous 24 hour event in the UK, larger numbers of walkers have regularly been achieving that within the same time constraint.

Neither need total distance be compromised too much if you can maintain a good race-walking speed. The calculation in the paragraph above involving two thirds running and one third walking would give you 136 miles, not a bad performance by any standard. When Sandra in 1984 set her then women's world best 24 hour performance on a road surface of over 131 miles it was her fitness and speed-walking capability which counted more than her running ability. She probably walked for about ten hours but almost certainly sustained at least five miles per hour for all of that time. She could do that because her speed-walking had reached a peak. Indeed earlier that week she had won the silver medals at 5K and 10K in the European Vets Championship (having just reached the ripe old age of 35!)

The distances that walkers can cover were highlighted by two events in 1986. During a 24 hour race-walking track event at Woodford, two British walkers walked over 125 miles and these distances are regularly achieved in the more frequent Continental 24 hour walks. In October 1986 John "Paddy" Dowling walked from Lands End to John O' Groats in just under 12 days 10 hours against the then recognised running record of 12 days 1 hour and Colin Dixon's then current UK running record of 12 days 7 hours. Not bad for someone over 57 years of age!

It is important that the individual decides whether he is primarily a walker who will supplement walking with some laps of running or a runner who will supplement with some laps of walking. We do not believe that it is possible to be top class at both. Top class walking requires technique and training like any other specialist event. In 1985 Richard concentrated on running and was able to complete 136 miles in the first 24 hours of his winning 48 hour event. But his race-walking suffered in the second half of the season. In 1986, by comparison, he concentrated on walking, won the UK Centurions 100 mile race walk in about 18:25 hours but never managed to run as well as in 1985. We think runners should concentrate on running and only aim for an "acceptable" walking style and speed rather than devote too much time to a second string activity. To try and be good at both, at least within one season, could leave you falling between two stools and ending up worse off.

So what speed should you aim for? We think five miles per hour is quite enough. To sustain greater speeds would require substantial speed-walking practice and would compromise running training. The body naturally wants to run at speeds above about 5 miles per hour. It also requires substantial extra physical effort to do something which is slightly artificial. Though in 1986 Richard won the 55 mile Manchester to Blackpool walk at an average speed of 6 1/3 miles per hour, less effort would have been expended running at that speed - especially down the hills! Over an "ultra" distance, economy of effort is important and that certainly suggests limiting race-walking speed.

When should you start walking in a race? If you can maintain five miles per hour walking, then you need have no hesitation about putting in a few laps of walking near the start of a 24 hour event and continue to intersperse running with walking. This will not only enable you to maintain a more consistent pace throughout the event, introducing a discipline which is so often lacking when runners charge off at the start only to regret it later but it also enables different muscles to be used. It may seem strange that different muscle groups are employed but there is no doubt that you can slow the onset of tiredness and retain your running ability for much longer if every hour or so you put in at least half a dozen laps of walking. There is always a temptation only to walk a couple of laps especially when people around you continue to run. But if you are really to alternate your muscle usage and get into a proper striding rhythm during the walking phase, then you need to walk for a sustained period.

Mixing the two also provides a mental and psychological change while it is normally easier to take on food and liquid sustenance and start the digestion process when you are walking rather than bouncing along running. You need have no fears about others in the event. The faster people charge off at the start, the faster they will come back to you later in the race. So consciously put in sustained and relaxed periods of walking early on. If you can plan your race and keep to your plan (something I am afraid Sandra and I never manage to achieve!) then the walking/running combination should consistently see you safely over 120 miles. After all, that is only 5 miles per hour which is what you are aiming for as consistent walking speed.

When others bemoan their jarred knee or ankle joints or clutch their stiffened thighs, you can continue to glide past them and still have a bit of running left. It is also useful to remember that the injury rate from walking is minute compared with that from running because of the jarring motion implicit in both feet leaving the ground. If you set your mind to it you can go as far speed walking interspersed with running as you can run to a standstill and laboriously crawl the rest.

We all learnt to walk before we ran. Isn't it about time you now learnt to walk at speed? You will find it a refreshing and relaxing experience.

Keith Walker was a keen student of 24 hour track performances for many years and undertook a detailed analysis of the lap sheets or other documentation then available for those marks over 155 miles/250km. Although few runners can hope to aspire to such heights his analysis gives a unique insight into how the top runners paced their runs. From this perhaps conclusions can be drawn as to the optimum pace for runners seeking less ambitious targets.

(Based on an article in the RRC Newsletter No 110, May 1983, updated June 1988.)

As 24 hour races become increasingly common, it is perhaps interesting to look in some detail at how the most successful runners actually put together their performances.

Years ago it was possible to do very well in a marathon by making sure that you avoided walking in the latter stages of the race. Then men came along who actually ran hard over the whole distance. Twenty four hour running has reached a comparable standard in that at least three men have proved that they are capable of running for the entire period without greatly slackening their pace.

Let us now consider a set of 24 Hour track performances that have been definitely authenticated (i.e. run on a track with lap times taken) This listing is not complete but it does give a range of marks and strategies:-

miles yards

miles	yards			
176	388	Yiannis Kouros	1985	Montauban
170	974	Dave Dowdle	1982	Gloucester
169	705	Jean-Gilles Boussiquet	1981	Lausanne
164	192	Jean-Gilles Boussiquet	1980	Blackburn
163	1249	Mark Pickard	1981	Barnet
163	377	Yiannis Kouros	1984	New York
163	346	Rune Larsson	1986	Honefoss
161	545	Ron Bentley	1973	Walton

| 159 | 686 | Paul Bream | 1988 | Frechen |
| 159 | 562 | Wally Hayward | 1953 | Motspur Park |

These fine performances were certainly not achieved in the same fashion! Hayward, Bentley, Pickard and Bream all started relatively quickly, running approximately 8 m.p.h. for the first seven hours. Hayward in fact set a 100 mile record, having run more than seven miles in each of the first twelve hours, and Bentley and Pickard also achieved excellent 100 mile times. Bentley, Pickard and Bream gradually slowed after their fast starts, coming below 6 m.p.h. at around the 18 hour mark. Bentley managed virtually seven miles in his 23rd hour, to beat Hayward's twenty year old record, before walking a mere two miles in the last hour, while Pickard continued to the end at around 5 1/2 to 6 m.p.h. Hayward in the first modern 24 hour race stopped completely for some time at 100 miles and then ran on in very laboured fashion at about 5 1/2 m.p.h. for the remainder of the time.

Larsson's performance was gained in a very much steadier manner, as can be judged from his relatively slow 100 mile time (14:11:53). Two other very similar performances may be mentioned at this point. In 1979 Park Barner (USA) and, a year later, Boussiquet (again!) each ran about 162 miles, although no lap times were taken. In each case a slow start (100 miles reached in well over 14 hours) resulted in a pace that was more or less sustained to the very end.

Boussiquet's two listed performances may now be considered. At Blackburn, showing great control throughout the race, he restrained himself from running above 7 3/4 m.p.h. early on, yet did not fall below 6 1/2 m.p.h. until the 21st hour. He did, in fact, fall away in the last two hours, covering only 9 miles when Bentley's world record was clearly in sight.

In his Lausanne run, Boussiquet was, if possible, even more in control, starting slower, but more steadily, to reach 100 miles a little quicker, and maintaining virtually 7 m.p.h. for 17 hours. He then kept his speed above 6 m.p.h. until the end of the race, the first man to do so.

As 'J-G. B' had run the whole distance without faltering, it seemed likely that the only way his performance would be bettered was by duplicating his perseverance at a slightly higher speed, and this Dave Dowdle proceeded to do. Faster at first, he reached 100 miles in around the same time, but he was running appreciably slower than Boussiquet, and had to increase his speed around the 18 hour mark to give himself a chance at the record. This he was able to do and, in fact, covered an excellent 13 1/2 miles in the last two hours as well.

I originally finished the article with these words "It could well be surmised that 'slow and steady' is the correct way to run a 24 hour race. However, it could quite possibly be considered that the most likely way that a new world record would be produced is by a runner hanging grimly on, following a 'blitz' start".

I feel that I should now write "and then came Kouros!"

Of those who have held the record since the Second World War, Hayward, Bentley and Dowdle were ultrarunners who made one supreme attempt with the record in mind, and achieved their goal. Boussiquet was the first man to actually achieve some consistency in 24 hour racing: four times over 158 miles on the track, plus once on the road, he showed that it is possible to completely recover, physically and mentally, from a high class 24 hour run, and produce another, and yet another, outstanding race.

Even the achievements of the great 'J-G. B' however, pale in comparison with those of Yiannis Kouros. Leaving out his outstanding successes at multi-day racing on both road and track, in which he invariably produces an excellent first 24 hour total distance, the simple fact that he has three times run over 176 miles on a measured course, sets him totally apart from any other 24 hour runner. On a one mile road lap in New York he has run 177 miles (1984) and 178 miles (1985), while his track record was set in the course of a 48 hour race, with his two day total also a record, needless to say! In this latter race, Kouros went through 100 miles in the third fastest time ever recorded (only Don Ritchie and Cavin Woodward have run faster), reaching 200km in 15:11:09 more than eighty minutes ahead of Ritchie's two year old record, and was still running at 6 1/2 m.p.h. when, with a full hour to spare and a 180+ total obviously at his mercy, he stepped off the track for a brief respite before the rigours of the second day of the race.

It is very difficult, at present, to conceive how any man (except Kouros himself!) can better this performance.

Performances of over 155 miles in 24 hours

19 performances - 13 different runners. 155 miles - 249.448k

A further breakdown of the splits in these performances can be found in the Appendix on Page 258.

miles	yards	km		
176	388	283.600	Yiannis Kouros	1985 Montauban France
170	974	274.480	Dave Dowdle	1982 Gloucester UK
169	705	272.624	Jean-Giles Boussiquet	1981 Lausanne Switzerland
164	192	264.108	Jean-Giles Boussiquet	1980 Blackburn UK
163	1249	263.466	Mark Pickard	1981 Barnet UK
163	377	262.668	Yiannis Kouros	1984 New York USA
163	346	262.639	Rune Larsson	1986 Honefoss Norway
162	537	261.204	Park Barner	1979 Long Beach USA
161	1548	260.520	Jean-Giles Boussiquet	1980 Coetquidan France
161	545	259.603	Ron Bentley	1973 Walton UK
159	686	256.513	Paul Bream	1988 Frechen Germany
159	562	256.400	Wally Hayward	1953 Motspur Park UK
158	1622	255.760	Mike Newton	1981 Barnet UK
158	980	255.173	Jean-Giles Boussiquet	1983 Vienna Austria
157	1457	254.000	Patrick Macke	1985 Montauban France
157	515	253.138	Mark Pickard	1982 Gloucester UK
156	1388	252.326	Bernd Heinrich	1983 Brunswick USA
156	791	251.781	Mike Newton	1981 Lausanne Switzerland
156	439	251.459	Tom Roden	1977 Crystal Palace UK

Miles covered in each individual hour in performances in 24 hour races
(distances are in miles and decimal fractions of a mile).

Hour	Kouros (Mont)	Dowdle (Glos)	JGB (Laus)	JGB (Bkbn)	Pickard (Barn)	Kouros (N.Y.)	Barner (L.B)	JGB (Coet)
1st	9:69	7:89	7:46	7:79	7:93	9:19	6:75	7:20
2nd	9:44	7:82	7:34	7:73	8:18	9:19	7:12	7:45
3rd	9:19	7:96	7:48	7:57	8:16	8:69	6:79	7:45
4th	8:94	7:91	7:67	7:76	7:87	8:45	6:77	7:45
5th	8:69	7:78	7:52	7:36	8:23	7:45	6:88	6:95
6th	8:45	7:73	7:45	7:31	7:90	8:19	7:16	7:95
7th	8:20	7:69	6:98	7:43	7:91	7:95	6:83	7:20
8th	7:95	7:56	7:23	7:42	7:72	7:45	7:11	7:02
9th	7:70	7:20	7:27	7:11	7:29	6:71	7:18	6:71
10th	7:45	6:71	7:28	6:87	7:51	6:70	7:15	6:95
11th	7:20	6:83	7:29	6:66	6:97	6:71	6:77	6:71
12th	7:45	6:72	7:29	6:82	6:88	6:95	7:00	6:21
13th	7:45	6:80	7:36	6:93	6:92	6:45	6:44	6:21
14th	7:20	6:80	7:42	6:49	6:34	6:71	6:66	6:21
15th	7:20	6:76	7:49	6:45	6:72	6:70	7:22	6:71
16th	6:95	6:97	7:17	6:94	6:42	6:46	7:44	6:46
17th	6:95	7:01	7:11	6:95	5:10	5:46	6:88	6:46
18th	6:71	7:03	6:51	7:09	5:82	4:47	6:66	6:30
19th	6:71	7:32	6:59	6:75	4:50	2:23	6:77	6:55
20th	6:71	6:11	6:16	6:84	5:46	4:47	6:83	6:27
21st	6:46	5:80	6:22	6:39	6:25	7:20	6:58	6:46
22nd	6:46	6:54	6:11	6:23	6:32	6:21	5:81	6:46
23rd	6:46	6:70	6:38	5:39	5:49	6:70	5:43	6:21
24th	-	6:77	6:49	3:73	5:72	6:44	5:97	6:03
Total	176.2	170.5	169.4	164.1	163.7	163.2	162.3	161.7

Miles covered in each individual hour in performances in 24 hour races (distances are in miles and decimal fractions of a mile).

	Bentley	Hay	Bouss	Pick	Newt	Bream	Newt	Macke	Heinrich
1st	8:16	8:21	8:31	7:49	7:45	8:20	8:11	7:66	7:59
2nd	8:13	8:54	8:24	7:57	7:70	7:70	8:08	7:91	7:33

3rd	8:22	8:56	8:26	7:46	7:70	8:45	8:23	7:66	7:45
4th	8:18	8:23	8:17	7:64	7:95	7:70	8:20	7:91	7:59
5th	7:96	7:96	8:05	7:59	7:70	8:20	7:92	7:41	7:48
6th	8:19	7:89	8:12	7:63	7:70	7:45	7:98	7:66	7:54
7th	7:88	7:15	7:65	7:94	7:45	7:20	8:12	6:91	7:26
8th	7:41	7:09	7:85	6:93	7:45	7:45	7:70	6:41	7:34
9th	6:95	7:41	7:69	7:26	7:20	7:20	6:54	6:16	7:32
10th	7:57	7:21	7:63	6:98	7:20	6:95	7:51	7:16	7:17
11th	6:47	6:07	7:37	6:69	7:20	6:95	7:02	6:91	7:15
12th	6:92	7:23	7:00	6:49	6:95	6:95	6:86	6:91	6:67
13th	6:55	4:86	5:60	6:41	6:71	6:95	6:39	6:16	6:54
14th	6:88	6:29	4:04	6:17	6:71	6:21	6:72	6:16	6:46
15th	6:42	3:16	6:28	6:19	6:71	6:21	5:84	6:16	6:34
16th	6:63	6:81	5:46	6:04	6:95	5:71	5:95	6:41	5:96
17th	6:37	6:73	5:40	5:60	6:95	5:71	6:43	6:41	6:24
18th	6:20	5:06	5:57	6:42	5:21	6:21	5:01	6:16	6:18
19th	5:73	6:72	5:57	5:96	6:21	5:21	5:61	5:66	5:10
20th	5:92	4:19	5:31	5:74	6:21	4:97	5:00	5:66	5:66
21st	5:34	6:07	5:75	5:57	5:96	5:21	4:59	3:91	4:90
22nd	4:15	6:31	5:29	5:37	2:73	5:21	4:80	4:16	4:53
23rd	6:98	5:36	4:99	6:34	4:97	5:46	4:17	5:41	4:37
24th	1 97	6:27	5:60	5:33	3:46	4:22	4:41	7:66	6:16
Total	161.3	159.4	159.3	158.9	158.6	157.8	157.3	156.8	156.5

Intermediate times in 24 hour performances

	50 Miles (80.5km)	100kms (62.1m)	100 miles (160.9km)	200kms (124.4m)	150 miles (241.4km)
Kouros (M)	5:29:41	6:56:25	11:52:40	15:11:09	18:57:52
Dowdle	6:22:02	7:57:58	13:30:08	17:00:17	20:55:05
Boussiquet (L)	6:43:46	8:25:09	13:34:56	16:54:40	20:56:23
Boussiquet (B)	6:36:28	8:14:15	13:48:06	17:21:39	21:11:59
Pickard (B)	6:12:39	7:46:11	13:03:51	17:01:47	21:35:40
Kouros (N.Y)	5:49:22	7:27:42	12:59:12	16:48:32	21:56:03

Larsson	6:43:08e	8:21:00	14:11:53	17:58:27	21:57:25e
Barner	7:14:34	8:55:48e	14:29:45	18:01:00	21:51:15
Boussiquet (C)	6:45:46e	8:49:00	14:18:32e	18:03:32e	22:03:37e
Bentley	6:08:11	7:41:43	13:09:52	16:53:00	21:20:27
Bream	6:06:20e	7:44:10	13:33:17	18:00:28	22:31:25e
Hayward	6:06:44	7:41:02e	12:46:34	17:33:25	22:15:02
Newton (B)	6:37:12	8:14:44	13:56:55	17:57:09	22:21:47
Boussiquet (V)	6:31:15	8:07:03	13:32:26	17:04:16	21:57:18e
Macke	6:19:55	7:56:37	13:24:47	17:27:25	22:21:24
Pickard G)	6:10:39	7:43:39	13:10:43	17:05:18	22:19:04
Heinrich	6:43:57	8:37:18	14:29:04	18:30:10	23:06:53e
Newton (L)	6:41:26e	8:20:37	13:51:25	17:46:28	22:55:36e
Roden	5:59:53	7:55:45	13:34:39	17:03:25	22:24:14

e = estimated time

Further 24 hour breakdown stats appear in the Appendix at the back of the book.

And finally an article on the greatest 24 hour performer of alltime – Yiannis Kouros. Following on from Keith Walker's article, in several ways it complements it and explains what came next!

Yiannis Kouros - a Self Made Ultrarunner?
Up until now, Yiannis Kouros' success has been regarded as being almost superhuman, and few people have attempted a serious analysis of the reasons for his success. Working in collaboration with another gifted ultrarunner, Rune Larsson, I have made a study of Yiannis Kouros' strengths, and how other ultrarunners may utilise some of his techniques.

In my opinion, although Yiannis Kouros may have started out with obvious talent as an ultrarunner, he has invested an enormous amount of time, thought and energy into making himself the best ultrarunner he can be. His greatest asset as an ultrarunner may be, in fact, his attention to detail. In many ways Yiannis Kouros is a self made man.

1] Physical Strength

Probably Yiannis Kouros' greatest asset is his physical strength. Kouros is built more like a wrestler than a runner, and although originally he was fairly strongly build, he has indeed changed shape physically during his ultra career, becoming much more solid and muscular.

a] Upper Body

He has worked hard at specifically developing his upper body strength particularly. I suspect he has undertaken specific work on the arm muscles particularly used in running, enable the arms to continue to drive the body forward effectively for much longer. [This training is also advocated by Valmir Nunes, twice winner of the World Challenge] This positive arm movement is particularly in very noticeable in Kouros's action, almost quadrupedal in the sense of all four limbs moving the body forward.

b] Trunk and Back

Running with good form is bio-mechanically efficient which delays the onset of tiredness and lessens its eventual effect. When tired the body tends to become less efficient - the body is held less upright position etc etc. Working on the back and trunk muscles enables the body to maintain its bio-mechanical efficiency for much longer. The body is more streamlined, the lungs are able to work to capacity, the body's normal balance is maintained etc. Rune Larsson, another veteran of the Sydney to Melbourne event, says that his experience in two such races is that supportive muscle, such as gluteus medius, piriformis, etc, are stressed severely due to the shift in biomechanics induced by change in body posture (induced by fatigue). Kouros does apparently have a posture that does not deteriorate and supportive muscle that can cope with such stress.

Rune Larsson and his wife Mary, another highly competitive multi-day performer, a former record holder for the Spartathlon, have found that an indoor rowing machine has been very beneficial in building such supportive muscle. The machine gives strength to legs, buttocks, the entire back, shoulders, and abdominals. In their opinion a muscular surplus is imperative when the distance is greater than 100 miles. Rune Larsson believes such muscularity is not as important at the 100 kilometres, and at the marathon it is a burden. The Larssons believe the rowing machine is the greatest strength and stamina machine available Rune won the Swedish National Championship at 2000 meters in his weight and age division and Mary is ranked in the top 10 in the World in 1-hour rowing.

c] Legs

It is not just Kouros' upper body which has benefited from specific work on muscles. There are reports of him standing in a swimming pool doing specific exercises on muscles that do not get sufficient development from running alone, work on supporting muscles to prevent potential injury. Also apparently he has worked on strengthening the anterior muscles of the shins, in order those muscles to be more resilient against shin splints.

2] Very Efficient running action

Kouros has a very efficient running action. Over the years he has also changed and refined his running style so it has become very efficient with very little wasted action. Such efficiency does not come naturally but is the result of long practice. Moreover races like the 1000km Sydney to Melbourne particularly have probably done much to habitualise this running action.

3] Strong Will and Determination

Yiannis Kouros is very strong willed and determined. Such determination can be developed in an ultra runner. In the words of British ultrarunner Martin Daykin, "The power of the mind is an awesome thing. I always stress that the mind needs conditioning as much as the body. One must cultivate a stubbornness bordering on the foolhardy. This can be achieved as much in a negative fashion as in a positive way - that is, to keep a little back, so that one does not go into will-power when not racing. Willpower seems to accumulate like a battery on charge, provided one does not keep expending that power needlessly"

4] Attention to Detail

Kouros is determined to ensure that the race conditions to suit his particular needs [see 6] and will uses his willpower and status as an `ultra super-star' to ensure that such conditions are in place. He pays painstaking attention to pre-race preparation to ensure that everything during the race will go absolutely smoothly.

5] Mental Association and Music

During long races Kouros associates - goes into the `zone' as one book on sports psychology puts it. He will use music to put himself into this state. In this state he is able to ignore external stimulus, including his own body. On one occasion he had a stomach upset and diarrhoea. He ignored this completely despite the fact he was several hours in the lead. It is no coincidence that his greatest feats have been set on tracks, closed road loops or open highways with limited traffic where he can easily enter this state. He has found trail races, where such a state is impossible due to the unevenness of the terrain, much more difficult.

6] Pace Judgement

Associated with this disassociation, Kouros has developed excellent pace judgement. Kouros runs lap after lap on the track for instance at a constant speed. This is again something that can be learned. He starts at a speed that he can maintain for hour after hour because of the combination of his strength and his ability to disassociate from his surroundings and body.

The percentage of his total distance covered in each of the six hours of each of his 24 Hour track races over 280km are shown below in chronological order. One can see clearly how his efforts became more even pace over the years, in part because his increasing strength over the closing stages, and possibly because his declining speed as he gets older. Moreover the percentages changed over the years as Kouros gained in experience.

	6 hours	12 hours	18 hours	24 Hours
1985 Montauban*	30.8%	26.3%	24.1%	18.6%
1990 Melbourne	30.0%	26.7%	22.3%	20.8%
1995 Coburg	29.5%	25.6%	22.9%	21.9%
1995 Surgeres *	28.5%	25.9%	24.2%	21.1%
1996 Coburg	27.8%	25.8%	22.9%	23.3%
1996 Surgeres*	27.7%	25.9%	24.3%	21.9%
1997 Canberra	27.6%	26.0%	23.7%	22.5%
1997 Adelaide	27.4%	25.7%	23.6%	23.1%

Note: * 48 Hour race. Montauban -stopped for rest after 23 Hours;

What is also significant is the fact that the first 6 hours he seems to have run virtually the same distance each time, within a lap or two.:

Melbourne - 211 laps, Coburg '95 - 209, Surgeres '95 203, Coburg '96 - 205, Surgeres '96 198, Canberra '97 204, Adelaide 208 laps. So thus each time he provided an identical platform on which to build the rest of his race.

At 12 hours it was 399 laps, 390 laps, 389 laps, 395, 383 laps, 395, and 403. [Surgeres '96 is below average in both.]

At 18 hours 556 laps, 552 laps, 562, 564, 557 [Surgeres '96 - coming back on schedule], 571, and 582.

So you can see that he runs to a tight schedule to 6 hours, then around 390 at 12 hours, still on track to 18 hours [560] then in the last six hours he aims to do sufficient to improve the world best if he wishes..

What emerges from this is not the need for awareness of percentages, that can come after the race. A very realistic assessment of one's current state of fitness is what is essential, so one can adjust one's initial pace accordingly.

If one is aiming for 140 miles, then one will need to run X miles in the first six hours, if 150 miles then Y - in both cases one would use the same percentage of the final distance. An alternative is to aim to run the same fixed number of laps in the first six hours, and see how one's body responds

This does provide another reason for Kouros ran a good 24 hour before his Surgeres races, to assess his fitness in a low key event. Thus the prior 24 hour becomes both a test and training for a subsequent race.

7] Pre-set Feeding Strategies

"The body is like a servant, to whom you have to give drinks and food. You have to pay attention to him, otherwise he will not obey. You have a goal and you want to reach the goal, but if you don't take care of him, you won't ever reach your goal." These are Yiannis Kouros' own words.

Kouros has pre-set feeding strategies. He seems to eat from the start of the race, at least by the first hour, and thereafter at regular intervals. At the Basel 24 Hours in 1998 he was drinking water and an energy drink alternately every second lap, i.e. every 5km approximately, and was eating slices of banana frequently in the first two hours. Then between the second and third hour he added some pieces of chocolate to his intake. Later in the race on the non-drinking lap, and sometimes also on the drinking lap, he ate dried fruit, apricots and dates, as well as homemade cookies. He maintained his drinking schedule of drinking an energy drink and water every alternate lap, and at the 10th hour switched to coca-cola as a treat.

The food he receives from his handlers as he passes.

At drinks stations in races with no handlers he takes on board drinks with a smooth economical action without stopping.

8] Year Planning

Kouros plans his year with care. He forces his body to extreme limits in races, but he then gives it ample time to recover. He seems to target just two major ultra races a year. He has normally run one 24 hour race in the early spring, achieving a very good total, then using the training effect from this race to prepare for the next event, which has usually been a 48 hour event a month later The latter is a supreme effort, and following that he allows his body to rest and full recover before building up to the next major event. He has also taken several years out from the sport at one point. In 1998 he used the national 100km event in the same way as preparation for the Basle 24 hour race. He subsequently ran a low key Comrades and walked a 100 miles in 24 hours late in the year.

9] Heat Adaptation

Kouros is heat adapted and consequently has done well in ultra events in the heat when others have wilted badly. He prefers heat to cold, and is actually apprehensive in relatively cold North European summer conditions. The heat adaptation comes from living and training initially in Greece and latterly in Australia.

10] Still Seeking to Improve

Yiannis Kouros is still dedicated to improving and honing his ultra capabilities. Although he seldom walks in his 24 and 48 hour races, on occasion he has been reduced to walking. Perhaps in preparation for future problems, he entered a Centurion 100 mile walking race in Australia in late 1998, without much practice at race walking. During the race he learnt to race walk and covered over 100 miles in 24 hours in this fashion. This, I suspect, is yet another example of the systematic way he has dedicated himself to making himself the strongest and most formidable 24 Hour performer in the world.

Kouros also has two advantages which cannot be acquired by training:

11] Good Basic Speed
He has good basic speed - he is a 2:24 marathon runner, and 6:44 100km runner.

12] Sleep Deprivation
He copes well with sleep deprivation. As a matter of life style he has been known to drive through the night through choice to get to a distant marathon.

Multiday Events

Having tackled the 100km, and the 24 hours some runners seek a longer, more testing event. Here are ideas from those who have moved up to contest the 6 day and even the one thousand mile events.

Dave Cooper, having gained a great deal of experience in running 24 hour events decided to move up to the 48 hour and 6 day events. His scientific background enabled him to analyse the demands of these new challenges.

In the 24 hour race, to cover the maximum distance you must keep moving the whole time, in the six day race you must have substantial rest breaks, which must include adequate amounts of sleep but many runners have found the 48 hour race an enigma, how much rest do you take, if any? A few hardy, reckless souls, have tried to continue throughout the entire duration with little or no sleep and have covered world record distances.

In my only 48 hour race all things considered I had a very successful race. I had decided to run to a carefully planned schedule, to run for 16 hours and hopefully cover 100 miles before taking my first rest. I felt I could reach this point in the race reasonably fresh due to my experience of two 24 hour races. Then after a good rest including a sleep I could carry on, with a planned walking and running mixture. However I had reckoned without the weather, which on the first day consisted of squally rain and high winds. Having covered 50 miles in 8 hours I felt tired enough to stop and rest, I was unable to sleep, however, and returned to the track after 30 minutes. I continued to run for another five hours but then began to feel the need for sleep and as it was 8 am by then, I stopped for an hour and managed to sleep for part of this time. After this I walked for a lap every hour and rested as soon as I felt really tired.

The one and a half hours rest taken at the end of the first day included a shower and a change of clothes. Running heavily clad had made me sweat a great deal and this had induced chafing. It was at this point I hit on the idea of preceding my sleep, with a large meal, a procedure I also adopted at midnight and 6 am. I have found it a good plan to run for 5 to 8 hours, then when tired have quite a substantial meal, this makes me very sleepy and after an hour or so I wake up wanting to go to the toilet, this ploy gets me up on my feet and back in the race. [In six day races I used the same routine; in addition I finish off my meal with a glass of sherry, a great sleep inducer!]

I had wondered before this race whether I would be able to resume running readily after being off the track for a good while. Might I not be too stiff? My fears were unfounded, after a lap or so walking and easy running I was soon running well again. In the afternoon of Sunday in the closing hours of the race it became quite warm and sunny. I felt fine and was extremely pleased to pass 200 miles for an over 40 veteran's world best performance. My only problem was that the soles of my feet had naturally enough become very sore. But I was able to alleviate this and prevent any severe blistering by coming off the track and rubbing my feet with Nivea Cream. More about this later.

I continued with my one lap per hour of walking and ran well for the rest of the duration and finished in very good condition with a total of 218 miles in third place. I felt somewhat better after this race than after my 24 hour races and attributed this to the fact that I had been obliged to include a substantial amount of walking and rest periods including actual sleep, which I had not needed to resort to in the 24 hour races.

Since then I have run several six day races; these are the most enjoyable races of all and the greatest challenge. I have stated earlier that the 24 hour race is the hardest race an athlete can attempt and given cogent reasons for this. However, this statement was perhaps somewhat of an over simplification. To my mind, what makes the Six Day so tough is its complexity and the fact that it goes on so long that it makes overwhelming demands on the athlete's powers of concentration. These races are dreadfully hard and you hurt all the time, in fact I can not sleep too long for the grinding bone deep ache in my legs, hips and my feet is guaranteed to get me out of my sleeping bag and back onto the track. The accumulated stiffness in one's legs defies description. The presence of a masseur at these races is essential to keep the majority of the competitors circling the track. For the incidence of muscular strains during the race is extremely high.

Quite apart from the real pain one has to endure to successfully compete in these races there is also the almost continuous discomfort. Most of the runners live under canvas for the entire duration and the civilised niceties of normal existence are to a great extent dispensed with. Washing, shaving, shampooing our hair, cleaning our teeth, these things we take for granted become luxuries we just do not have time for in our desperate quest for maximum mileage. We eat, sleep, go to the toilet and run! As the days go by our feet become sore and blistered, our skin itchy and sticky especially our hair and chafing develops under our arms and between our legs.

If these races are so horrible, why do we take part? Well you will have to do one yourself to find that out, and then I will probably be preaching to the converted. The atmosphere in these races is incredible. A camaraderie develops between everyone connected with the race, runners, handlers, spectators and officials, "a feeling of the tribe" as the Australian megamarathon runner Joe Record has aptly expressed it. Few ordinary folk can make the sacrifices necessary to climb Mount Everest or sail single handed across the Atlantic. If you are a long distance runner then the megamarathons are a bit like these feats of skill and endurance, especially the six day race. They are, however, within the reach of everyone.

As in the other megamarathons my pace judgement, leg strength, ability to derive sufficient rest from few hours sleep and strong stomach, all these qualities help make the six day race, for me, the most enjoyable one there is. After a six day it takes about a month for my sleep pattern to return to normal. I find myself waking up in the night weeks after the race longing to be back on the track running with my friends.

But so far it is the one race I have not been able to get to grips with. I ran two races and know what is needed, but was unable to 'get it together'. I think the difficulty is maintaining concentration. You need a good handler to attend to your needs and you should try to stay, at all times, as near to the track as possible. This means having your meals brought to you at the track side.

The mind is a funny thing, if you leave the track for a meal or a shower or even to use the toilet you can easily get diverted, sometimes for hours. You want to get back to the track but the simplest of tasks, which would normally take a few minutes, because you are so tired, will take much longer than normal, without you realising it. I have left the track to get a shower, feeling quite strong and alert, come back to the track and happened to ask my lap recorder how long I was off and been amazed to hear an hour and a half, when I thought I had only taken twenty minutes or so.

My race plan for the six day race follows roughly the same form as that outlined for the 24 and 48 hours. Let us assume the race starts at noon. If the conditions are good and I am in good form I will try to run as I would in a 24 hour race until dawn on the second day, hopefully with 100 miles completed, when I would stop and enter my tent for a substantial meal and my first sleep.

Back on the track after a couple of hours, I will continue running till noon, when I stop for a light meal and sit down and relax, for an hour or so. I then run till 6 pm when I have another big meal and a sleep. After two hours or so back on the track and continue to run till dawn then come off again for another meal and a sleep. I have found by trial and error that the best time for me to sleep in these races is 4 to 6 am and 4 to 6 pm. Apparently it is a Medical fact that it is at these times that the body is at the lowest points of its daily energy cycle. I try to keep to this basic pattern throughout the race. So far, however, without the success I had hoped for. I feel that using my distances for 24 and 48 hours as a rough guide, I should be capable of a distance in excess of 500 miles. In 1989 I covered 510 miles/821km.

In the first race I ran well for the first three days then strained a muscle in my right calf which needed several hours treatment. I then ran well till the last day when I sustained a similar injury this time to the thigh of the same leg which kept me off the track for four hours receiving treatment. I decided to quit the race in disgust, however, my wife persuaded me to get back into the race. I soon found I was able to run freely again, and feeling very strong due to my enforced rest finished in fourth place. You must remember that from the outset in this race, I had run using the same tactics I always use in a 24 hours, namely to start steadily in the hope of finishing strongly in the later stages. My plans had been completely thwarted by injury.

In my second race, I decided to employ totally different tactics; in fact to run very hard in the early stages. Two factors made me more determined, firstly the organisers had incorporated into the race a 24 hour race, secondly I wished to have a go at Gerard Stenger's over 50, 48 hour record of 215 miles. It would be far better I thought to hammer it early on and get a good distance in, than to lay back in the early stages only to be sidelined later with an injury.

As luck would have it in the first few days of this race the weather was bad, cold with high winds and heavy rain. I managed 121 miles in the first 24 hours as opposed to 104 the previous year but was extremely exhausted. The next two days were a constant battle with fatigue. By day four, I had amazingly recovered much of my strength and finished again in good condition in third place, with somewhat less mileage than in 1984. I feel now that the first year's tactics were the correct ones and the fact that I had not succeeded with them was a combination of bad luck and inexperience. My second attempt as related above, proved this for me. The third attempt, covering 204km/126 miles on Day 1, 222 miles/358km by Day 2 and 291 miles/469 km by Day 3 was more successful. The second half saw Day 4 with a total of 368 miles/592km, Day 5 with 437 miles/703km and 510 miles/821km at the finish. [The two halves are not even pace – with 291 miles/469km and 218 miles/352km – Ed.]

I sincerely believe, that some runners have too much courage; are too determined. They will carry on driving themselves round the track when ill, injured or totally exhausted. I just do not have the guts of these runners and tend to quit when I am in a bad way for I believe it to be foolish to risk my health. I want to be around for a long time in the sport.

If disaster strikes I will leave the track and live to fight another day. It is part of my philosophy to think of my running as a career which runs parallel to my daily working career. Unlike work, however, I do not, intend to retire from athletics. I will, therefore, continue to train and race in accordance with how I feel but at the same time control my ambitions for good performances.

Note: Dealing with Blisters

You may recall that in my account of the 48 hour race above, I mentioned the fact that I massage my feet with Nivea Cream to alleviate soreness. Many years ago, I suffered a great deal from blisters. I was relating my misfortune to a veteran runner in the bar after the race. A small, wiry, grey haired fellow with very definite opinions, who turned out to be Leslie Griffiths, previous winner on several occasions of the Poly Marathon in the 1940's [who also ran in the Motspur Park 24 hours in the 1950s! Ed.] . To my surprise he was less than sympathetic, "A blister is a sin and a shame and should not be tolerated! Rub in lanolin!", (a greasy product, derived from sheep wool, the basis for skin creams), "Rub it into the skin, especially the soles of the feet and under the toes. Rub it in till it vanishes then rub in more! The grease will cut down friction as oil does to a machine. Cut your toe nails down close, and rub down any hard skin, with sand-paper. Then get to work with the lanolin and you will not get any more blisters!" Since then I have had very few blister problems.

In a megamarathon, especially a Six Day Race, the blister-prone athlete can find himself in bad trouble almost from the start. Do not adopt the "Grin and Bear It" attitude, come off the track immediately you feel the onset of any trouble and get treatment. This also applies to chafing, which may be a fairly minor discomfort in an ultra, but which can force a runner off the track in agony in a longer race. It is hard to leave the track, even for the few minutes needed to attend to these difficulties, especially if you are running well and totally involved in the race. In the light of the above, however, you will appreciate that any time lost in the early stages may be very well worth it in the long run!

Bryan Smith established himself as one of the world's top runners at 24 hours and upwards. He finished second in the fiercely competitive I.A.U. Milton Keynes International 24 Hour Championships, won the Sydney to Melbourne and covered over 1000km in 6 Days.

I started running when I was about 35, my job kept me away up the country away from home 3-4 nights per week and I found the running was a good way to kill some time after work and to get fit. I progressed from running a few kilometres each night to running marathons. After running about 35 marathons and unable to get below my P.B. of 2 hrs. 46 min. I decided to venture into ultra running, my first one being a 50 miler. From there it was into 24 hr. runs and I found that I preferred these races to the shorter ones so as you can see building up to multiday races for me was a fairly lengthy process - firstly marathons, the 50 milers, 100 km runs followed by 24 hr + 48 hr runs and finally multi days like Sydney - Melbourne and Colac 6 days. It was only after my first 48 hour run in 1988 that I gained the confidence to enter the annual Sydney - Melbourne race and was fortunate enough to finish 4th, the first Australian.

That was a great experience because there was a record number of runners (45) and the field that year was the best of the four that I have run in. There were a lot of international runners competing, runners like Yiannis Kouros, Dick Tout, Don Mitchell, Patrick Macke, Dusan Mravlje, Eleanor Adams, Marty Sprengelmayer, David Standeven, Maurice Taylor etc.

I have never been a heavy trainer compared to a lot of ultra runners I have spoken to or competed against over the last 4 - 5 years. Although I do try to train nearly all year round so that my fitness level does not drop too much, that way I find it easier to train up to a run. I like to run 6-7 ultras a year and freshen up between events over a 6-7 week period. A typical year's racing for me over the last 4 years would have been something like this:

TRAINING

A typical training period for 6 weeks between races for me would be to run 80 km week (1) and just build up 10 km each week to a maximum of 140 km per week. I find this sufficient for races of up to 24 hrs duration. Earlier on in my ultra training I would do quite a few longer runs of up to 35 - 40 km but now prefer to do shorter training runs but more of them.

MULTIDAY TRAINING

I just vary my training by running three times every second day. I have never had a coach so I just devised this schedule and I find it suits me e.g.:-

Day	Morning	Noon	Night
1	15 km	10 km	10 km
2	15		
3	15	10	10
4	15		
5	15	10	10
6	15		

For multi day racing I usually try to do some gym work, 2 - 3 times per week working with light weights to build up some strength and I find it is a nice change to offset the running.

TACTICS

I guess the best tactic of all during 24hr runs and up to six days is to be able to stay on the track as long as possible and to keep circulating, but also to realise when it's time you need a break especially in multiday racing. This is where the crew is so vital, to monitor your drinks and food and to advise you on sleep breaks and rests and to watch for any signs of serious fatigue. I have been most fortunate to have really terrific crews, looking after me and my wife Janet has always been on call in the runs when I have done well. It is so important to have the right crew, people who know how to vary the food and drinks and to have clothing or shoes and medical supplies that could be needed. The crew on runs like the Sydney Melbourne must be able to get on well with each other and have a good sense of humour because they are working in a slow moving van with limited space to cook, move around in and sleep etc and they naturally end up very tired themselves being on call virtually 24 hrs a day for up to 6 days in a row. Sleeping for them is very difficult being in a slow moving van with flashing lights going on all the time, and trucks and cars roaring past constantly makes it a pretty noisy environment. When you have efficient, caring crews such as I have had, it makes a lot of difference to your running. All you have to do is just concentrate on the running and focus on finishing, the crew is in complete control of any situation that might arise.

ITEMS NEEDED FOR MULTI DAY RACING

A really good medical kit which should include plenty of second skin if you are prone to blisters. A good variety of foods and drinks both for the runner and crew (coming up with new ideas for food variety for the runner can be a real problem for the crew). I try to avoid spicy foods and stick to a lot of basic carbohydrates such as potatoes, pumpkin, vegetables, breads, cereals, pastas with some ice-cream, rice and pancakes etc. Naturally plenty of fluids should be taken. I find water is the best with some high energy drinks such as sustagon as well (about 120 litres of fluid is right for 6 days). Plenty of running clothing should be taken to cater for all types of weather because washing and drying clothes on the move can be a problem. As well as taking my normal size shoes I take two extra pairs of one size larger to allow for swelling of the feet after a couple of days, even then the toes usually end up being cut out of the shoes. I like running to music so a Walkman is an essential item for me. In multi day racing I find music is a good motivator and it helps pass those long hours in the time between midnight and dawn.

Although winning a tough race like the Sydney to Melbourne with handicaps included and the never ending hills and extreme weather conditions to contend with was a terrific result for me and my crew, the race I am most proud of is running over 1000 km at Colac in 1989. We had lots of rain that year and the grass track cut up so badly the mud was ankle deep for two days. The organisers finally put down sawdust but this was still difficult to run on. So I rate that particular multiday as my best so far.

I would like to continue ultra running as long as possible. It's a great sport and we have met so many lovely people and made a lot of good friends from competing and travelling to various races. Ultra runners always seem willing to help each other and have a special bond so I hope the sport continues to grow as it deserves to. Ultra running has been good for me and I hope it is for you in the future.

Dick Tout emerged as a major force in Australasian ultra-running, and in the Sydney to Melbourne 1000km, showedhe could compete with the best multi-day runners in the world. Despite pb's ranging from 7:07 for 100km, through 12:52 for 100 miles to a road 6-day best of around 590 miles/948km, he really came to world attention in 1989, when he ran a 24 hour best of 163 miles/ 262km indoors at Milton Keynes. Dick Tout was not just a runner. He coached Sandra Barwick and his own ideas on training can also be seen in her schedules below.

I started running in 1980 with no running background, just to get fit to participate in a 10km fun run "Around the Bays", enjoyed by 70,000 Aucklanders each year, and got smitten by the bug. I have found the best way to train for ultras is by running with a local Harrier club, Takapuna Harriers, and after an ultramarathon, going back to the basics of running, starting off with Club races, 5km to 10km and then up to half marathons and marathons. Then after 8 weeks, 80km or 100km. I find I can build up quickly and enjoy the company of other runners. I also find a bit of track work helps to get speed back in the legs.

800m x 2

400m x 4

200m x 8

or 4 x 1000m on road

I find it takes two to three months to recover from a very hard multi-day ultra and then I am not 100 percent fit but can race. If I don't run a multi-day race I can run two or three ultras very close together and then go back to the basics. My training is based on Arthur Lydiard's schedule, long slow, short fast, etc with hills and speed work.

MONDAY	a.m.	6 miles road - easy
	p.m.	Track or road reps
TUESDAY	a.m.	16 miles on grass
	p.m.	10 miles road - flat
WEDNESDAY	a.m.	6 miles road - easy
	p.m.	8 miles road - fast
THURSDAY	a.m.	19 miles on grass
	p.m.	10 miles road - flat
FRIDAY	a.m.	6 miles road - easy
	p.m.	10 miles - fast
SATURDAY	a.m.	16 miles road - hills and steps
	p.m.	Club Race or 10km or cross-country
SUNDAY	a.m.	20 - 30 miles

ADDITIONAL TRAINING: Aerobics twice a week and weight training twice a week. Aerobics and gym work are essential to maintain and prepare the whole body. Upper body strength is very important in multi-day races so that you can hold your arms up. If you can hold your arms up you can get longer length in your stride.

ONE YEAR OF RACING - 1987-88

24th January 1987   100km Track Race

	50 miles in 5 hours 34 minutes	first	
	100km in 7 hours 7 minutes	first	
26th March 1987	Sydney to Melbourne	third	
	1060 km (658.6 miles)		
	6 days 22 hours		

Day One	222.1km (138 miles)
Day Two	167.8km (104.3 miles)
Day Three	141.6km (88 miles)
Day Four	118.1km (73.4 miles)
Day Five	133.1km (82.7 miles)
Day Six	137.1km (85.2 miles)
Day Seven	132.9km (82.6 miles)
	(22 hours)

31st May 1987   N.Z. "Tree to Sea"   first

80km (49.7 miles) 5 hours 49 minutes

22nd August 1987   Auckland 24 hour track race   - did not finish

104km (64.6 miles) in 8 hours

6th September 1987   Sydney/Woollongong   first

82.8km (51.5 miles) in 5 hours 49 minutes

10th October 1987   "Bay of Islands"   first

70km (43.5 miles) in 4 hours 28 minutes 7th

November 1987   "Round the Mountain"   first

100 miles in 12 hours 57 minutes

22nd November 1987   Auckland Wiri Marathon

2 hours 38 minutes

17th March 1988   Sydney to Melbourne   second

1016km (631.3 miles)

6 days 11 hours 18 minutes

Day One	248.5km (154.4 miles) in 24 hours
Day Two	408.1km (253.5 miles) in 48 hours
Six Days	948.6km (589.4 miles)

5th June 1988   N.Z. 50 miles "Tree to Sea"   fourth

5 hours 50 minutes
Oops! First time beaten in N.Z.
Must be getting old!!

Sandra Barwick set world records at 6 days and 1000 miles on the road. Her exhausting training schedule reveals the dedication involved to produce these kinds of performances.

Note the way she incorporates aerobics into her training, thus strengthening her core strength and ensuring she can sustain a good running posture even when very tired.

I started running after watching a large marathon in New Zealand. I did about 40 miles a week in training and ran around 3:36 for that marathon. After 13 marathons I wanted to try something different so some of the ultrarunners from my club gave me a training programme for a 24 hours. In that race I broke four New Zealand records and the Australasian 24 hour record. Then I ran a 70km and a hilly 100 mile race as training for the Westfields Sydney to Melbourne race. In that race I was the second woman in 8 days 4 hours. Two months later I became the first woman to run under 15 days for the 1000 miles.

I just love to run; my enjoyment makes my training a pleasure rather than an onerous task. Training has to be fitted into everyday life, and because of my divided loyalties of being a mother and a housewife I usually start my day around 4.30 am. I really love this time of the day, being away from the traffic and the fumes, and the opportunity to watch the sunrise. I cover most of my long miles in the morning, anything from 16 miles up, then at lunchtime I take in a daily weight session essential for keeping my upper body strong to cope with my multi-day running (light weights, at most 10lbs/5.5kg) and then to an aerobic class which gives me compulsory stretching. I like to do a late afternoon run between 6 - 8 miles at a faster speed. In between all of this of course there are the general duties around the house and my favourite pastime of baking. I daren't sit down as I would fall asleep. This is all good training for multi-day racing.

Initially my running was a lot of fun but I didn't know where I was going and I was desperate to do an ultra. Ever since my first ultra everything changed.

There was a real challenge now, the will to win and to see how far I could push my reluctant body at times in a multi-day event, but I did not want to lose the undiminished enthusiasm I have for doing ultras.

A typical week's training would be:-

	Morning	Lunchtime	Evening
Monday	15 miles	Gym (circuit)	6 miles
Tuesday	20 - 26 miles	Gym (aerobics)	
Wednesday	15 miles	Gym (circuit)	4 miles speed
Thursday	20 - 26 miles	Gym (aerobics)	
Friday	10 miles (3km time trial)	Gym (circuit)	
Saturday	20 miles	Gym (aerobics)	
Sunday		30 - 40 miles	

Total 130 - 152 miles

Before a multi-day event (at least six weeks before) I do a three day build-up which includes 100km, 80km and 80km on successive days.

For the three weeks between my Sydney to Melbourne run and the 1000 miler my training was:-

Monday	6 miles AM/ 10 miles PM
Tuesday	15 miles AM/ 6 miles PM
Wednesday	16 miles
Thursday	15 miles AM/ 6 miles PM
Friday	6 miles AM/ 5 miles PM
Saturday	10 miles AM/ 6 miles PM
Sunday	20 miles

Total 121 miles

Dick Tout had advised me that I would get fitter as the 1000 mile race progressed, and this would carry me through. In the race, most of the time I would run for 4 - 4 1/2 hours (30 miles) with a 10 - 15 minute walking break every 2 hours to take in food. This consisted of rice cakes or fruit (water melon) and a non-sugar drink called Polycose which was made up for me every 24 hours. At 4 - 4 1/2 hour intervals a half hour break was taken, hopefully around meal-time. Main meals consisted of rice, vegetables, pasta, sweet potato, and fattening deserts like rice pudding. Breakfasts consisted of cereals (cornflakes) with fresh strawberries, but mainly I stuck to carbohydrates, French toast and peanut butter.

My mental attitude is as important as my physical training. I prepare myself to have faith in my ability to keep going over many days. I guess a pretty determined outlook, and maybe being a little stubborn helps a long way.

Self-hypnosis, which I had learned prior to my first 24 hour race, proved invaluable in keeping me calm and very relaxed, when stressful moments were near in both the Sydney to Melbourne and the 1000 mile World Championship races.

My diet is generally the same as when I am running multi-day events:-
Breakfast: Muesli, Cornflakes, Yoghurt, Fruit
Dinner: Vegetables, Salad, Fruit
I eat a lot of fruit during the day as well.

What do I get out of multi-day running? Simply the feeling of exhilarating motion, smoothly unfolding over distances, which prove the beauty and efficiency of the human system once it is properly directed.

Mike Newton pioneered the 6 day race in Britain, bringing the modern world best to a degree of respectability.

The opportunity to pioneer the six day race and the 48 hour races at Nottingham was a challenge I couldn't resist. Certainly there were many anxieties to be overcome, what sort of training should I do? Two weeks before the six day event I used my Windsor/Dachet route, (I called it the Castle Run.) From Streatham I ran to Putney bridge and then along the tow path, following the Thames on the way to Windsor Castle. With no traffic to worry about and plenty of water holes en-route, this was ideal preparation. For a change of scene I came back through Windsor Great Park and Virginia Waters. Those idyllic surroundings could always be relied upon to take my mind off tired legs and to lift flagging spirits. I supplemented my day runs with short evening sessions. In seven days I covered 450 miles. Compared to previous training the immensity of a six day race was mind blowing.

Before the start, at the Harvey Haddon Stadium, there was an air of uncertainty about the whole thing. It gave me a weird feeling to follow in the footsteps of Littlewood and Rowell, professional runners and master exponents of the six day races in the 1880's.

On the first day the organisation was, to say the least, somewhat spartan. Once the media (always on the lookout for a new angle) took an amused interest and when TV and radio crews arrived at trackside, an amazing transformation took place. Overnight the race had gained a sponsor, the Nottingham Building Society. Libby's supplied the food for the competitors. Advertisements miraculously appeared around the stadium. National newspapers sent reporters from London. Suddenly we were a band of glorious eccentrics personifying the human spirit over the adversary of attempting to run for six days and six nights.

Everybody connected with the race was inspired; we were all part of the revitalisation of an almost forgotten Victorian sporting era. Obviously I haven't the space for a personal history of the race in this article. The good, the bad and the bizarre is a story for the future. Nevertheless I finished with 505 miles, a new amateur world's best. I could have done more but this seemed sufficient at the time as I had broken the previous record by 30 miles.

The climax of the six day race was a fantastic experience. In a way we were all winners. The ultra runners had formed a camaraderie which would be hard to find in any other sport.

'Nothing succeeds like success.' So the adage goes. Accordingly the triumph we achieved in the six day race at Nottingham was a spur for the Nottingham Building Society to promote several ultra track events at the Harvey Haddon Stadium.

The following year they put on what I think is the toughest race of all the ultras. the 48 hours! Devising a training programme was difficult. One couldn't justify attempting to run the duration in training, the diminishing returns of such a schedule would probably cripple or burn out the athlete before the race started. I treated the race as two halves. While fresh I went for 130 miles in 24 hours. Then quality running with short rests for the second 24 hours. Disappointingly it didn't work out like this. After 36 hours my pace dropped dramatically to around 5 mph. I was in such a bad state that I was advised by my handlers to leave the track for a meal and a bed in a local hotel. In the meantime Gerard Stenger, a top French ultra distance runner, had moved to within a few miles of me. Someone phoned the hotel and told us the situation. I returned still much the worse for wear. Eventually I got running again but had to push myself hard to win with 227 miles in 48 hours which was then a world's best. It was the nearest thing to personal physical abuse I know!

A couple of years later the six day race was to be the centre piece of the British Festival of Sport at Trentham Gardens near Stoke on Trent. Prize money was to be awarded to the first six, so the race attracted top runners from home and overseas. Before the race I averaged 210 miles a week for ten weeks, and ten days before the race I did a spread over week - 24 sessions in 7 days - Total mileage 475.

During the first part of the race we had continuous rain. I suffered from sore feet and a long drawn out battle with the American Don Choi. In the end I won by 26 miles, with 516 miles a world's best on the road.

Tom O'Reilly ran one of the most controlled 6 days to set a new world best. Unfortunately injury and other commitments restricted his ultra racing and he never reached that level of performance again.

My preparation for the 1982 Nottingham 6 Day Race began on Sunday 8th November 1981 with a 20 mile run from Birmingham along the A453 to Mearsham. A car driven by Howard Neville took us to the Harvey Hadden Stadium. Further visits on the Wednesday and Friday evenings of that week convinced me that I wanted, if possible, to take part in the next race. That week I ran 112 miles and in the weeks through Christmas averaged 99 miles including 7th place in the Barnsley Marathon (2:26:57).

January saw an increase in mileage, weeks of 113, 109, 129,150. The 150 mile week (24th Jan) began with a 32 mile run to Stratford-on-Avon at 7:17 pace, followed by a 9 mile race at 6:40 pace. Most runs were around 7:20-30 pace.

As an example, the week beginning 31st January:-

Sun	9.35 am	17.5 miles	2hr 02m			
Mon	7.00	9.8	73m35s	5.05 pm	10.2	72m30s
(To and from school)						
Tues	7.00	9.8	73:15	6.00	10.2	75:30
Wed	4.35	10.3	73:35			
Thurs	7.00	9.8	73:30	6.00	10.2	75:45
Fri	7.10	9.8	73:45	6.10	10.2	75:00
Sat	7.30	11.3	83:00			
	9.20	5.0	-	12.55 pm	6.5	48:50

13th Feb 8.10 am 33.6 miles to Leicester in 4 hr (7:09 pace).

February mileages 131, 152,114 and 125.

March mileages 121, 134, 90, including 26.6 miles in 3 hr 10 m (7:09 pace) and 140. 28th
March, Wolverhampton Marathon, 20th in 2:29:42. Set up for a steady run , 5 mile splits 29:30, 28:30, 28:40 and 28:25; last 6.2 miles 34:37 (5:35 pace).

April mileages 117, 132, 81 (camping holiday), and 100.
18th April Finchley 20, 38th in 1:51:22, 5 mile splits 27:19, 27:35,28:09 and 28:19.

May mileages 90, 54 (9th in London Marathon 40th in 2:21:08, best since 1977), 74, 126 and 140.

June mileages 98 (5th June, Oulu, Finland, 50 miles 3rd in 5:38:02 (10 mile splits 61, 60:45, 69:15, 80 and 67.02), 137.7, 37.7 miles in 12 short runs. 12th June, Ewhurst 100 miles in 13:10:20 (10 mile splits 79, 74:07, 70:22, 81:42, 79:11, 82:20, 80:18, 80:55 and 80:07).

Diary Notes after 100 mile race:
Ran to 30 miles, stopped for about 5 minutes, had apricots and coffee. At 50

miles, stopped for 6 minutes for rice, apricots and coffee. Brief stops at 35, 45, 55, 60, 65, 70, 75, 80, 85, 90 and 95 to sponge legs and face (drank XLI at '5' miles and coffee and a Mars Bar at each '10'). Went into the lead at 67 miles when Martin Daykin dropped out. Hardest part was 80-85 miles. The dog -leg for 0.8-3.3 miles made each lap mentally difficult.

Generally a good run, calves and rest of body fine, thighs sore from relatively early (before 40 miles) but didn't really get any worse.

Weather good, generally mild, some rain, very heavy at 28 miles and a few warm spells. Pre-race plan was to run sub-18 hours, so quite pleasing. Didn't realize 10-30 miles was fast until worked out lap times at 30 miles. Had planned short walking spells from 30 miles at 5 mile, 7 mile, 10 mile points on each lap to drink, maximum of about 1 minute, except 35 miles which was about 5 minutes.

The next week was 49 miles in 23 short runs, then a week of 129 miles leading to 5th and last in the 150km race at Hirtenburg, Austria in 15hr 29m on 25th/26th of June (almost 15 min mile average); a mentally shattering run.

The following week 106 miles included 32.4 miles in 3hr 56m (7:17 pace)

Sun	7.45am	17.1 miles	2h 4m00s			
Mon	7.00	10.0	76:20	6.00pm	11.8 miles	86m10s
(To and from School)						
Tues	6.55	10.2	76:00	6.25	12.0	88:00
Wed	7.05	9.8	72:55	6.50	10.3	75:30
Thurs	6.55	10.1	71:55	6.55	10.1	72:00
Fri	6.30	10.2	77:00	6.20	9.8	72:00

Sat   8.00100km Track 1st Trent Poly, Nottingham, just under 8 hours. 184 miles for week.

Sun 11th July

  7.30am   7.4 miles   60m30s

  9.00am Sandwell Marathon 261st in 3hr 24m 16s.

  (5 mile splits, 41 (including 90 seconds to start),

  37:30, 38:50, 39:20 and (last 6.2 miles) 47:36. Week 120 miles.

Week 18th - 24th July (on holiday)

Sun	8.45am	11.1 miles	82m20s	1.35pm	11.1 miles	84m15s
Mon	8.25	40.7	5h 3:30 (excluding 25 min stop at 32 miles,			

drank 1.25 litres lemonade - humid day)

Tues	8.50	11.8	86:35	2.30	12.7	96:10
Wed	8.15	60.38:	23:10 (including 4 drink stops)			
Thurs	6.30	10.2	80.00	7.55	9.8	75:10
	8.35	5.9	44:25	9.25	5.9	44:55
Fri	9.35	10.1	75:40	8.55	11.3	84:15
Sat	10.25	37.2	4:42:25			

Week 246.4 miles in 31 hrs 39mins 45secs average 7:43 min/miles.

Week to 31st July 170 miles including 34 miles in 4hrs 25 mins 45 secs (7:49 pace) 28th July.

Week to 7th August 151 miles including 34 miles in 4 hrs 19 mins 15 secs (7:48 pace)

Week to 14th August 106 miles.

Week to 21st August 64 miles in 11 runs, felt very tired and jaded.

Week 22nd - 28th August 6 days - 576 miles 675 yards 1st Nottingham.

I never felt really tired at any time during the six days. Running was a habit; I trained by running to and from work and during the race restricted my running sessions to 2 - 4 hours, when I retired to my trailer to relax for perhaps half an hour, and thought about something else.

This tactic, combined with 4 - 5 hours sleep each night, proved successful. I feel that the distance I covered in the six days could be considerably improved. I aimed for 600 miles and was a little disappointed in not reaching this distance, but to do this, I would have had to push myself during the final night. Leading the race by the margin I had, there was no incentive to do this. I knew that if I were to have any chance of winning the race, I would have to plan the following carefully: time spent on the track, rest intervals, sleep, food, shoes and my support team.

I had prepared well, averaging over 120 miles a week during 1982 with a peak of 246 miles four weeks before the race. I had found from experience that I could run 2 - 3 hours continuously without undue fatigue. Could I manage an interval session of 6 x 2 hours running with about half-hour rests?

I found it easy to relax into rhythmic running. It was important to ignore what the other competitors were doing, especially when I found myself in about 9th place after 24 hours.

I had anticipated that 550 miles would win the race, and certainly felt capable of doing that distance. Optimistically I thought I might reach 600 miles. The thought of non-stop running for hours on end didn't seem to me to be productive; hence the idea of regular breaks.

These shorter breaks enabled me to go to the toilet, change kit and shoes, eat and drink, use ice packs on my legs and rest. I took sleep intervals at approximately the time I would normally sleep.

Food was mainly carbohydrate, small amounts being eaten regularly. I consumed vast quantities of natural mountain spring water and apple juice.

I started the race in very tight shoes, but used shoes with more padding as the race developed. The second half of the race was completed in air-sole shoes.

Probably the most important aspect of the whole race was the unstinting support of my wife Mary and our children, and my regular helper Howard Neville. Howard had the knack of knowing what I needed before I did.

I was fortunate not to suffer from blisters, but did have some achilles tendon strain and ankle trouble during the last 41 hours. This may have been caused by spending about two thirds of the race running in one direction.

The presence of the other competitors was a constant source of pleasure and inspiration. Their good-humour and persistence kept me going for many a mile.

Copyright Tom O'Reilly 1986 (with acknowledgements to the editor)

Dan Coffey has been an ultra runner for many decades. Gradually over the years he moved upwards to greater and greater distances. He became a regular competitor in multi-day races and completed a number of 1000 mile events, the longest of the standard ultras.

As I am approaching the end of my ultra running days, I would be happy to put down on paper a number of random thoughts concerning the preparation, psychology and actual experiences felt during such an arduous event.

If at the end the reader/runner has not been put off then like the carcass said as one of Mickey Mouse's characters entered Death Valley. "Don't say you haven't been warned!"

Preparation. There are three aspects of preparation that I wish to comment on:-

(a) Physical. (b) practical. (c) mental.

    (a)   **Physical**

    (b)   For the reader there very often is a thought when considering such an undertaking that the level of training required must be of an unattainable level; this simply is not true. I found out that by increasing mileage to a level that I was not accustomed to became so arduous that I quickly changed it to a more sensible level and looked for ways in which I could gain confidence.

At my peak my daily schedule for a two week period prior to an event allowing for one week's recovery was as follows; A.M. 15 or 18 miles steady running in woods and heathland. Before lunch a run of 8 miles on roads at steady speed, followed by a run of 10 miles on the roads of about 10 miles at a pleasant pace depending on how the body felt; this could vary from day to day. Very often this would degenerate into a battle of survival to maintain a pace that looked respectable to any observer, however I always honestly thought that I was shuffling like a tortoise; how little did I realise that 1000 miles racing left a runner thinking along the same lines. Would it ever be possible to run at a speed greater than 4.5 miles per hour ever again and that was with really trying to maintain the pace?

This is one of the preparations that the runner cannot get used to in a 1000 mile race. Prior to this period, of to me, intensive training, my daily mileage never exceeded 20 miles nor dropped below 10 miles and always had Sundays off to recover and go to Church to pray for strength to survive the following week!

In terms of mileage only twice did I exceed 120 miles in a week, most of the time it was in the region of 75 to 95 miles, often a hard week followed by two weeks of lesser mileage. At this time a full teaching schedule at School was being maintained. After my first 1000 miles excursion I changed my training strategy to include weight training, with the emphasis being placed on upper body strengthening; which I had found in earlier ultra distance events to be severely weak. Circuit training and the use of an exercise bicycle. Although tempted, I could never include swimming as chlorine in swimming baths affected my eyes too badly and left my muscles like bags of jelly.

Running surfaces for me depend on race needs. If it is to be a road race then training is concentrated on the roads, for a synthetic track I will spend most of the time on woodland paths. I hope that these notes on training will be useful to someone but do urge that although this system works for me it may not do so for others.

All the training undertaken will be useless if in the early stages of a race the runner sustains an injury so may I comment on one or two aspects of multi-day racing. Never consider the whole race but break it down into acceptable portions, a day at a time, a number of sessions, mornings, afternoons, evenings, even changes of direction that most races include.

Settle into a routine and if it is working maintain it. If this is a first multi-day race then use it to gain experience and write down your observations as quickly as possible.

Road surfaces create joint problems; all weather surfaces create muscle injuries therefore consider carefully the choice of shoes and cushioning; this is as important as the actual technique of running. When a runner becomes tired then the problem in a sense disappears because a very low leg lift will quickly be adopted.

Joe Record advocates the use of deep breathing and striding along the back straight occasionally, this lets other groups of muscles come into play after continuous repetitive pace of the same nature; not attempted on bends as injuries may occur to the inside leg.

Some ultra distance runners are happy purists who will never walk, but my experience is that occasional walking before tiredness allows some rest to the body. This is very useful at the beginning and end of a running session acting similarly to warming down and up.

If you need sleep then be like Malcolm Campbell and treat multi-day racing like a job of work with regular breaks.

Never worry about any other runner, a few hours can vastly alter the fortunes of everybody in the race; you can in fact go off, have a hot shower, come back and be running better than ever!

(c)   **Practical.**

The following thoughts are related to various factors that make for an easier time during racing.

Kit; Socks. If like me you wear socks then check the elastication at the tops before racing, as feet swell considerably during these events the elastic often gives the impression of Tendonitis occurring! Therefore I cut the elastic threads beforehand. Turn socks inside out so seams don't rub.

T-shirts. Make sure that these are really loose ones and well worn, it is better to wear them inside-out which prevents chafing from the seams.

In very hot conditions vests would be worn but in strong sunlight a loose light long sleeved top is preferable allowing the use of T-shirts during the night.

Even in the summer months extra cold weather gear is useful, this is because the body does reach such a state of exhaustion on occasions that a slight summer breeze feels like an Arctic blast in Scotland in February. Well that is how it feels to this soft Southern Briton!

The same applies to wet weather gear, often one imagines that a light showerproof cagoule is adequate but if you want to stay out in the rain, you will soon get very wet and cold. The philosophy of taking a break during rain does not really work; you will find yourself lying in a sleeping bag listening to the rain and putting off the evil moment longer and longer. When you finally emerge and see how many miles that you have lost and other runners looking quite comfortable in full wet weather gear; a feeling of being totally dispirited will descend on you as once again you try to warm up the body and gain lost ground.

Head Gear. Again this is a matter for the individual runner, but it does afford some protection from hot sunshine, particularly if you are a little thin on top, and often can be quite comfortable during the night, I might add at this point that a pair of sunglasses is very useful. They cut down the glare of sunlight and reflected light from road and some track surfaces. Tired eyes have a very debilitating effect on your physical performance.

Footwear. This item has been left to the end of Kit preparation because it really is the most important item that you must consider; the following thoughts from my experience may help. The shoes used must have already been broken in and trusted. Consider also the following point; you are going to be on your feet for very long unaccustomed periods of time, so the feet will swell gradually. Therefore another pair at least must be taken that are at least one size too big. Do not use them at the outset otherwise you may experience blistering from these shoes. However, as the race progresses you will use them more and more because the other shoes will not fit. If possible take two pairs of oversize running shoes so that they can be used alternately. If you do this then you might find that one pair would have been enough and wondered whether I was getting commission for the promotion of shoes sales but you could also discover to your cost that what I have advised should have been heeded! Only run in shoes that you know are comfortable to you and ignore any advice given that this is the type of shoe that is the best for such an event.

Finally pay great care to lacing of the shoes, I use the lacing system of cross over and vertical lacing as this allows a lot more width to the tongue of the shoes and prevents bruising of the tendons on the front of my feet.

Finance. Arrange beforehand to pay all outstanding bills that will occur whilst you are away. It is quite amazing how these issues become so important to you as you become mentally more and more tired. I make a list of what I have paid and take it with me; this is a useful way of knowing what has been done. Of course this action may not be necessary to you but for me it helps to know that the house, literally, has been left in order.

Diet. If you are in the habit of taking vitamin supplements and/or iron make sure that you take an adequate supply with you and inform the race organisers what you are taking, this stops the suspicious looks that may happen when you pop a pill in your mouth. Also with regard to favourite foods, if possible take some with you or ascertain whether you can get them locally. They become immensely important to you during the event if you cannot get hold off them, almost to the point of an obsession that you must have them. U.S. laws on the importation of nutritious foodstuffs are very strict so do check these up in advance if proposing to race in the States.

    (d)   **Mental Preparation.**

    (e)   Regard what you are about to attempt as a straightforward job of work that has got to be tackled in a practical manner. You have completed your apprenticeship in the long period of training that you have undertaken.

Do not think about what is in front of you too much otherwise you may become terrified, rather think of it as an exercise to see how much distance that you can cover whilst still being in good condition!

Plan a course of action, how long do you intend to run in one session? Write up three schedules from the easiest to get you round to the one that you consider would give you a very good distance.

I found from experience that by using the top schedule for the first few days, it gave me great confidence to move to my middle schedule as I had so many miles in hand.

Give very careful consideration as to how long you will sleep, this will depend on how much sleep that you normally need. If a lot then plan for it; if you can get away with less then good luck; but do not allow yourself to get into sleep deprivation, this creates problems from which you cannot recover during the race.

In my first attempt at the distance I thought that if I ran a good 6 day race then I would have plenty of time for the remainder. It did not work out like that, I retired sick. You are running a 1000 mile race and that must always be to the forefront of your mind.

Plan to divide your day into a number of sessions. As I have a very simple mind I always divided my day into two sessions, A.M. and P.M. and put my two rest breaks one in each session. This allowed me to see how much I needed to do in the second session to maintain my target!

Psychological Factors. Adopt a positive approach to the race. For instance when you have taken your first running stride in the event, it will no longer be a four number race, you are already in the 900's! The further you go the less distance is left to be covered. Each step that you take will never have to be repeated. This is the culmination of all your training and now you will show all those doubters.

Do not look for bad days to arrive during the race, many runners get very concerned after they have been running for 8 or 9 days that they have not had a bad day yet; surely that was why they did all the training. A bad day can occur for the silliest of reasons or no reason at all, it may be blisters, an upset stomach, an injury, or dehydration. In any of these situations get treatment, put it right, salvage what you can of your schedule and come out smiling the next day to take up the challenge again.

Be prepared to run with other runners for a chat and be ready to leave them if they are running too fast or too slow for you, this after all is your race.

I mentioned using a similar circuit when back at home training, the advantage is that you can in your mind return home and have a run round your own circuit. In fact you can often in your mind run on some of your favourite training courses and feel the rain and the wind of the winter!

Keep a check on what time it is back home, who would be doing what and where. Be it a football team or cricket or tennis or a hundred and one other things, another mile has passed and you never even noticed it. See it does work!

If the time zone is different from that back home wear a watch with your own time on it for a few days until accustomed. This will help to explain to you why you feel so tired at 8 P.M. in New York! Again I use two watches so that I also know what time it is where I am. Try not to worry about positions in the race, someone in front may be coming back to you, there is plenty of time to catch them and if you are passed do not panic, the next day may see a complete reversal. Remember that when you are suffering so is everybody else, even though it is not always obvious at the time.

Towards the end of the race try and visualise races that you have been in at home; one year over the last 100kms I ran in my mind a 100km race, the London to Brighton, the Woodford to Southend, the SLH 30 and the London Marathon; I became quite confused at one stage which race I was actually supposed to be in but delighted to discover that I now had less than 15 real miles to run to complete the thousand.

The final thing to do is to walk for a lap or so after the finish and ask your lap scorer to note down the time taken, this is a lap for Martin Daykin who set a World Best for 200kms only to find afterwards that he was a lap short. Thus NO RECORD!

A few words about experiences I have had during such races. There are highs and lows, times when I felt that I was floating along effortlessly and times when I felt that I could not even reach the end of the lap.

Attempting to sleep with the roar of jets taking off, I always seemed to choose rush hour for sleeping. There was one runner with a radio on the head and all communication was impossible unless by hand signal. Later I found out it was to block the noise of jets, so next time I took earplugs with me - very useful when I could remember where I had put them down last.

One year I watched a young bird learn how to fly, I became quite attached to that little family and they never knew.

Occasionally I found a runner in great distress, at such times all thoughts of competition disappear and you attempt to help. These races can have a great emotional effect on runners.

Another problem that occurred was believing that leader boards were not up to date, this often was the result of a tired mind already marking down the next mile when you were still running it.

Once I asked for a massage as my thighs were so tight. The masseur started, then stopped and refused to do any more work on them until I had gone out and drunk as much water as I could manage, tiredness of the mind had allowed me to forget the simple basics of survival.

The highlights of my races always happened at night when I found that I could run more freely, less heat, no glare, other mortals had sensibly gone to bed and I was gaining on them. But there were also times when it was very difficult not to fall asleep when I would pop into the conveniences and just close my eyes to rest them for a moment.

Sometimes runners have attempted long multiday journey runs for charity. Don Ritchie ran from John of Groats to Lands End. His preparation makes

interesting reading however his sheer determination to continue despite bronchitis and intestinal bleeding is definitely not recommended!

PREPARATIONS FOR J.O.G.L.E.

My preparations for my John O'Groats to Lands End run began, in a sense several years earlier as I had run many thousands of miles in training over the years. Also I had gained considerable experience in many ultra distance races since 1977. Additionally I was a member of the Aberdeen A.A.C. 8 man J.O.G.L.E. relay teams of 1972 and 1982 so I had some idea of what was involved in the project.

Though my first attempt ended with a stress fracture near the end of day three, I learned quite a lot about what not to do, if I made another attempt, so this can also be regarded as preparation. Another aspect of preparation is securing sponsorship to enable the project to go ahead, organise a back up team, transport, food, equipment, plan routes and schedules, charity fund raising, etc.

My physical and mental preparation began over twenty weeks prior to the event. During this period I maintained an average weekly mileage of 128 miles, and often included back to back long runs, such as 27 miles on Saturday and 31 miles on Sunday. These used to begin at 7 am in an effort to minimise their impact on family life. All my training in this period was steady running, but included three races which provided faster pace running, and some variety. Also in this period I prepared mentally for the challenge I had set myself. Below is a list of the individual weekly mileages in my preparation period.

Week number	Mileage	Comments.
1	132	
2	113	
3	113	
4	111	
5	120	
6	112	
7	114	
8	111	

9	120	
10	112	includes North District C.C. League race (10th)
11	143	
12	144	
13	117	includes Scottish Vets C.C. Champs (18th)
14	160	
15	148	
16	159	
17	164	
18	122	
19	127	includes Inverness Half Marathon (14th in 72-31)
20	121	

Begin J.O.G.L.E.

The schedule for running the J.O.G.L.E. would be three three hour sessions, followed by two by two hours, plus whatever was necessary to complete the daily target. During the breaks I would eat, change kit, have a massage and stretch. The first half day brought extremely steep hills and vicious head winds but 65 miles were covered.

I slept badly and woke with a feverish cold! Despite fierce winds and sleet 84.7 miles were achieved on the second day. Day three, 81.8 miles were covered. The next day my cold had progressed to bronchitis, accompanied by nose bleeding. There was also evidence of intestinal bleeding! However, the end of that day saw 80.6 miles added to the total.

I then developed stomach trouble, which seemed to be aggravated by bread and jam, so I eliminated sugar from my diet. I ate dry wholemeal bread, with electrolyte and banana every hour and within a day my stomach pains disappeared and there was no evidence of intestinal bleeding. Another 81 miles were on the clock after the finish of that day.

The next day I felt extremely tired and weak and planned as a result, to run just 72.4 miles

I felt slightly fresher the next day, but during the afternoon I had a nose bleed and this became a regular happening through the run. 73.1 miles for the day confirmed the adjustment of my plan. I would now run at least 70 miles a day to the finish, instead of 80 plus, as the latter was proving too stressful and I wished to avoid a breakdown.

Days of 73.6, 71.8 and 74.2 miles followed, despite chest pains on the ninth day.

On the final day headwinds and rain followed, rapidly turning to gales and torrential rain. The rain eased, but the wind was fierce from Bodmin down to Hayle, but the final stretch was peaceful. The longest run of my life was over. 846.4 miles in 10 days 15 hours 25 minutes.

I think I may have lost about 14 lbs on the run, reducing me to around 9 stone. The aftermath of the run was unpredictable. I was not injured but extremely weak. Bronchitis continued and it took several courses of antibiotics and decongestants and a good five months to totally recover.

I had regarded it vitally important to receive massage and a stretching sequence after each running session of the J.O.G.L.E. The massage would help maintain muscle efficiency by removing accumulated waste products, and this allied to stretching should reduce the risk of possible muscle injury. Malcolm Morgan, the Head of the Physiotherapy Department at Dr Gray's Hospital, who had accompanied me on my first attempt, gave a demonstration of the technique to be used, and provided instruction to my helpers Mick Francis and Donald Gunn. My wife Isobel recorded the session on video tape for future study.

The massage session would start with my quads then calf muscles, hamstrings, then finishing off with the quads again. This was followed by stretching of these muscle groups. Between fifteen and twenty minutes was devoted to such sessions.

To try to minimise stress I decided to limit running sessions to a maximum of three hours, so a typical day would involve three times three hour sessions, then two times two hour sessions. Consequently I received five massage and stretching sessions in one day.

Donald Gunn performed the massages, and initially olive oil was used as the medium between Donald's hands and my legs. Once this was exhausted,

Baby oil was used but this proved unsatisfactory as hairs were being pulled out during the massage. This resulted in a crop of boils on both legs which made subsequent massages unpleasant. Crisp-n-dry cooking oil was then used as an olive oil substitute and worked well. One unforeseen side effect of this was the sickly odour it developed after a day or two, which permeated our kit, towels and clothes. The air bed used for the massages still has that characteristic smell.

The multiday events flourished in the nineteenth century and until now details of the training of the professional 6 day runners of that period, who achieved distances that have only been matched by a very few modern runners, was unknown. A recently discovered book from 1889 included articles written by some of the top ultra runners from this period giving fascinating insights into their training regimes.

The British runner George Cartwright was one of the faster distance runners to tackle 6 days, capable of running 27.5 miles/ 44.2km as a 3 hour split. He set a 50 mile track record of 5:55:04.5 in 1887, a mark that was not to be surpassed for over sixty years. He was less successful at the 6 day event.

Everyone knows how to walk, at least all except those who have lost the use of their limbs. In walking matches, and especially long-distance races, the thing to know how to do successfully is to get into condition for the race and then how to keep in the race. I have raced at all distances, and am certain the most important part of a race is the preparation. In a race where endurance is required, like in one of the six-day races, a long and careful preparation is necessary. I believe in a strict course of training, and attribute my successes in races to this. Hard work, too, is necessary to get into condition for a long contest. I begin about six weeks before the race is to take place and at once settle down to work.

Long runs and dry rubs in the early morning are the first things to start. This is to get off all superfluous flesh, and so not carry in the race any more weight than necessary. The first runs should be taken with heavy flannels on, which will help very much to pull down the weight. When you have reached the proper weight, work has to be taken to strengthen the muscles. This is done by taking good, brisk exercise—long runs in the morning in proper running clothes and good, long walks later in the day. The runs should be about thirty to forty miles a day and the walks from ten to fifteen miles. When training for a race I eat sparingly, only taking just what I absolutely want. In the way of meats I eat beef, lamb or mutton, chicken and steaks.

The meats must not be cooked too much, or the strengthening properties in them will be destroyed. I never eat any fat while training. Bread at least a day old is the best, and vegetables and fruits should be eaten sparingly. To drink I take good old ale and sometimes weak tea. In racing a long distance the feet are a source of trouble to a great many. Great care must be taken to have shoes that fit well. They must not be too large or too small, but must fit all the foot exactly. To prevent cold while training it is a good thing to rub alcohol into the pores of the skin after a good run or walk.

Gus Guerrero from California ran 2:43:45 for 25 miles in 1887 and was one of the faster runners at this shorter distance. He adapted well to the 6 day event, running 949,512km/590 miles indoors at the Madison Square Gardens the following year.

Hard work is what I believe in to get ready for a long race, such as a six days' contest. I like to start in the race in the pink of condition and without an ounce of superfluous flesh on my bones. To get to this condition requires hard work and perseverance. Some men cannot work of their own will, and to such I would suggest that they employ a trainer to make them. I always have a trainer, and he makes me get up with the sun. Then I have to do a run of from fifteen miles up. When the run is finished I have a rub down, and alcohol is rubbed into the skin to keep me from catching cold. After this I take a short rest and then eat breakfast. Rare meat and with vegetables and fruits I believe in. After breakfast I take a little walk to begin exercise until about noon, when I have dinner. This is the best meal of the day.

I eat whatever I fancy and drink ale or tea. The meat I eat is never over-cooked and is always lean. Of course I don't take anything that is likely to affect my digestion or hurt me on account of its richness. Good plain food will not hurt anybody. In the afternoon, after a good rest, I take walking exercise, moving at about four and a half or five miles an hour for two or two and a half hours, and then when cool again eat supper. When training plenty of rest and sleep is needed and I always retire early.

A little tobacco smoke, although not a good thing, won't do much harm. When racing I only eat and drink what will strengthen me and what is easily digested.

James Albert Cathcart, who ran under the name of James Albert, was the first man to cover 1000km/621.3 miles in 6 days, setting a world record of 621 miles 1320 yards/1000.609km.

I attribute all my success in the race in which I beat the record of 610 miles made by Fitzgerald to the fact that when I train I am a total abstainer and do not smoke or chew. Intoxicants of any kind are not good to train on. The habitual use of them undermines the constitution and when used to train on they only help for awhile and after their effect has worn off those who use them feel worse than they did before taking them. To train for a long race like these six-day contests one has to be very careful.

Six weeks to two months should be taken to get into condition before the race commences, and when I begin to train I am careful that I am in good health. Exercise should be taken slowly at first. To get all the muscles pliable I take exercise both with the dumb-bells and Indian clubs. Two weeks devoted to this work, and at the same time taking short, brisk walks or short runs, will get me into shape for hard work.

Then I commence to train in earnest. First, I begin with taking a run of ten or fifteen miles with a sweater on. This distance I gradually increase every day until after two weeks I go thirty to thirty-five miles a day, and in addition to this take walking exercise. Two weeks before the race I put in the hardest work of the training season, which consists of long spins every day. The last week I only take easy exercise, just to keep my muscles limber.

I don't diet myself much and eat any thing that is wholesome and not injurious. Milk, custard, beef, mutton, and some kinds of poultry easy of digestion I eat a great deal of.

One of the most versatile and talented ultra performers of the 1880s was the Sheffield athlete, George Littlewood. An excellent walker as well as runner, his 6 day walking record still stands from 1880 at 531 miles/855km. He was also capable of over 27 miles in 3 hours, set a world record at 50 miles and was the first to cover the 100km distance in less than 8 hours. More remarkably Littlewood was not only the only man to go over 600 miles twice, he also produced the greatest distance seen at 6 days with a record of 623 miles 1320 yards/1003.828 km, a distance that he might have extended further if he had not wished to keep the record accessible for a later profitable attempt. Regrettably that never happened and the record was to last for ninety-six years!

Walking is one of the most severe of all the athletic exercises. All the muscles in the whole body are brought into play in walking and if there is a weak spot anywhere it will be found out in the race.

For a walking race of from one to five miles, speed is the chief thing to obtain and to do this a very severe course of training has to be gone through. A man must be in prime condition, and must be able to move quickly for a short race. The strain on the walker is very severe, and in walking a short distance the body, arms and legs are all used to help the pedestrian along. To walk well the body should be kept in an upright position, the shoulders squared and the head thrown back. The arms should be kept well to the sides, and by using them with each stride they will greatly aid the walker. The stride should be of ordinary length, and should be taken firmly and with the heel well down. To learn to walk fairly is the first thing to learn and then speed can be acquired afterwards. For a long-distance race endurance is what is most wanted.

The man who can jog round the track hour after hour at an easy gait will accomplish much more than the man who runs a few miles at a rapid pace and then takes a long rest. A long and careful training is necessary to be able to compete successfully in a six days' race. First of all, the contestant must be in good health. Then he must get off all unnecessary flesh and then good exercise must be taken to develop all the muscles. I take exercise as much as possible in the open air, but when the weather is cool or wet the work should all be done under cover. For food I take almost everything that is nourishing, carefully avoiding anything that I find is hard to digest. For drinks old ale and tea are the best. During the race I live on such light things as chicken, custard, jellies and beef tea. I do all my training early in the morning, rising with the sun, and retiring soon after it has set.

These articles first appeared in ***Brawn and Brain: Considered by Noted Athletes and Thinkers Compiled by Arthur F. Aldridge 1889***

A modern day multiday performer, William Sichel has studied the details of the training above.

He felt the key points seem to be:

1. Easy week before races
2. Slim down before races - they nearly all mention this - no putting on weight beforehand.
3. The importance of walk training

To expand on one of these:

Increased weight = greater energy output required to transport that increased weight over distance, which is an ongoing drain on fuel reserves and on strength.

My own view is that the diet is also interesting - stale bread was probably one of the most convenient form of carbohydrate at that time. The extra water in bread apparently dilutes the concentration of energy and other nutrients. Stale bread is drier, has a lower water content and therefore has more concentrated energy and other nutrients. The pedestrians were maximising the benefits from the most readily available source of carbohydrate.

The modern alternative of pasta etc would not be readily available. High protein intake would help to re-build muscles of course.

Trail Running

With growing restrictions on ultra road races, many more events are being held on trails. The articles below give ideas on training schedules and strategies are relevant to all runners, both trail/fell and road, seeking to cover extended distances of 100 miles and beyond.

Mike Cudahy was well known for his multi-day fell/trail runs, perhaps most notable of which was his 270 mile Pennine Way feat, accomplished in under three days. His detailed advice for would be ultra fell/trail runners, and his account of his training, preparation and strategies for some of his epic runs will be of interest to many.

INTRODUCTION
Safety and Hill-Running

As with any branch of athletics, training for hill-running requires long periods of physical conditioning. With physical conditioning comes mental toughness. But for ultra hill-running this is not enough. In order to safely enjoy the experiences 'off-road' certain techniques and skills must also be acquired. Unlike the usually well clad and equipped mountaineer, all that may stand between a hill runner and an uncomfortable (or even fatal) bout of hypothermia is fitness, ability to navigate and sound judgement based on experience.

The level of competence required obviously depends on the nature of the run being attempted. Short distance, low-level runs on well marked paths require no special skills. On the other hand such ventures as traversing rough Scottish mountains, journeying at night and running in true winter conditions requires more than ordinary skill. When you begin, as you may, to put these three things together, you can perhaps understand both the exciting challenges and the demands of hill-running.

Apart from a high degree of specific hill-fitness, what is at a premium is ability to navigate. For the hill-runner this ability involves not merely precision but also speed. Attempting to cover long distances lightly clad and equipped means minimal time poring over the map and no time making costly mistakes. Like physical and mental toughness navigational skills are only gained through hard work. Experience and practice are the key words. You can only learn to navigate by doing it. How can you do this?Here are three suggestions:

  a) get out on familiar ground with map and compass,

  b) join an orienteering club,

  c) take a Fell Runners' Association course in navigation.

Once the basics are acquired the rest will follow providing you keep practicing.

Sound navigation is the most important skill which the hill runner must acquire. Through experience other knowledge develops which also reflects on the runner's safety.

Here are my suggested guidelines:-

  1) Become a competent navigator in all mountain conditions

  2) Learn skills from the experts (e.g. join a specialist club)

  3) Plan your hill runs with particular regard to:

  a) the season

  b) the specific weather (and forecast)

  c) terrain (particularly height)

  d) length/duration of run.

(all these factors will reflect on what clothing/food you will need)

  4) Carry sufficient food and some reserve supply.

  5) Be aware of the causes and symptoms of hypothermia

  6) Build experience gradually.

CLOTHING: When fine, warm weather cannot be guaranteed, the hill runner who is out for a long day should carry complete body cover. This may be light, thermal material (e.g. Helly Hansen 'Lifa' wear) but when backed up with a suitable wind/waterproof outer 'shell' will keep a runner sufficiently warm, providing that it is possible to maintain a high work output. Thermal or wool hat, gloves and scarf are remarkably efficient in maintaining body heat. In cold conditions the principle is to minimise heat loss by keeping extremities covered and to safeguard core body temperatures by preventing wind penetration.

Thus, a light windproof over a couple of thin thermal layers is better than bulky layers of non-wind proof clothing.

Also try to avoid becoming saturated with sweat. Even in summer, the rapid evaporation of sweat from the skin can lead to uncomfortable and even dangerous reductions in temperature, if too rapid. Remove excess clothing when working hard uphill but do not underestimate the chilling effects of the wind. The runner will rarely be troubled by low temperature alone; wind and rain are the enemy

FOOTWEAR: There is no perfect shoe for long distance hill-running. However, there are shoes which should be avoided. In general any shoe with thick midsoles, particularly under the heel, will be unstable on rough ground. Heel stability in all directions is of the utmost importance. On rocky ground and well graded trails good, not excessive, cushioning is helpful. A deep tread pattern is needed on soft ground and on steep, rough ground strong studs in low profile shoes are best. I prefer to use specialist fell shoes with pyramid type studs on rough ground (e.g. Walsh; ETA)* and on mixed terrain I compromise by having a bar and stud sole (Walsh 'Raid') fitted to a suitable pair of road or trail shoes. I like may training shoes tight(ish) for foot stability and my 'attempt' shoes bigger to allow for foot swelling and extra insoles or socks.

*Also Reebok Fellrunner series

TYPES OF HILL-RUNNING

Although there are general categories of 'ultra' hill-running, the divisions are not always distinct. My remarks below are neither definitive nor exhaustive but will, I hope, serve as a useful guide. Apart from the sport of fell-running, which is not relevant to this article, I would suggest the following

1) LONG DISTANCE FOOTPATHS (L.D.P's)

L.D.P's have certainly been a 'growth area' over the past decade. The 1993 Rambler's Association Yearbook lists 48 long distance routes covering all the British Isles. The shortest is 30 miles and the longest over 500 miles. The majority are between 70 and 130 miles and so provide plenty of scope for the ultra-runner. By far the most popular with the latter has been the Pennine Way - probably because it was the first national path and passed through areas where hill running has always had strong traditions. It is 250-270 miles in length (depending who you believe) and the current record is 2 days 17 hours 20 mins (M.Hartley 1990). The West Highland Way (Glasgow to Fort William, 95 miles) has an annual (or biannual) race over its largely 'trail-type' surface but it appears to be exceptional in this respect. Other L.D.P's which have received the attention of ultra-hill runners are Wainwright's 'Coast to Coast (190 miles); Southern Uplands Way, (Scotland, 212 miles); and Offa's Dyke (Wales, 170 miles). The terrain covered by L.D.P's is of course, enormously varied, everything from metalled road through to soggy moorland and true mountain going. There is, however, a certain amount of way marking and, quite frequently, official maps and guides. The usual style of record attempts is; firstly to carefully reconnoitre the route, then to run/walk it as continuously as possible. Fellow runners often provide company and guidance. Food and other support are usually possible at road crossings. (Note: all sleep/rest time is part of the total completion time.)

2) ORGANISED LONG DISTANCE HILL RACES

There may be problems of definition here (how long is 'long'?) and there must be races of which I am not aware. However, I will include a few I do know about and which I consider may fall into the category 'hill' rather than 'trail' races. Some races started as 'challenge walks' and though they may remain as such, also increasingly cater for the out and out runner.

One of the most famous of these is the 'Fellsman Hike'. This is a tough, hilly circuit of 60 miles with about 12,500 ft of climbing. It traverses two of the Yorkshire 'Three Peaks' and much rougher ground besides. Winning times are rather weather dependent but between 10 and 11 hours is 'good'.

Rather shorter but equally arduous is the 'High Peak Marathon' in the Peak District. It is for teams of four who must stay together. It takes place in winter and it starts at night. Only 40 miles in length, a time of 9-10 hours will place you among the winners.

I know of no other race along L.D.P's other than that previously mentioned along the West Highland Way. There are, however, a number of relay events (again, the Pennine Way seems most popular,) which are suitably arduous.

Among the 'challenge walks' which cater for runners are the 100 mile events organised by the Long Distance Walkers Association (L.D.W.A.). These well organised events with support points follow what, for the most part, can be described as 'trail' terrain with perhaps 15 - 25% metalled surfaces.

In Sept 1992, the first multi-day mountain marathon was held down the length of Wales. The route followed (in the main) the walk 'Snowdonia to the Gower' (John Gillham) and was named as the 'Dragon's Back Race'. It consisted of 5 days of between 30 to 45 miles per day with an emphasis on hilly terrain and the need to navigate. With the exception of a pair of top-class American Trail runners, who were 5th, the first 6 places were taken by British fell runners.

Other specialised fell events exist in the form of two-day mountain marathons. Here, the 'expert' classes cover about 50 miles carrying all the necessary gear for an overnight camp. Navigational skills are at a premium and entrants at the higher levels are vetted for experience.

3) HILL CIRCUITS

These are usually based on a 24 hour time period and there are three general approaches. For the majority the aim is to complete the circuit in the 24 hours. At about 60 miles and 27,000 ft per circuit this is not an easy task. For the elite the aim may be to lower the time taken to complete the circuit or extend its difficulty by ascending more hills within the 24 hour period. At the time of writing, the relevant statistics for the most popular circuit (The 'Bob Graham' in the Lake District with 42 summits, 60 miles, 27,000 ft) are: fastest completion; Billy Bland 1982, 13 hours 53 mins; most peaks; Mark Hartell 1997- 77 peaks in 23h47m, The two other 24 hour hill circuits are the 'Welsh Classic' or Paddy Buckley's round in Snowdonia (47 summits, 61 miles, 27,700 ft and the Ramsay Round in Ben Nevis area of Scotland, (24 'Munro' summits, 60 miles, 28,000 ft.) Both the Welsh and the Scottish rounds have been extended. In 1988 Jon Broxap climbed 28 'Munros' (well defined mountains over 3,000 ft) in the Cluanie and Affric areas of Scotland. He covered 78 miles and climbed 33,000 ft in 23 hrs 20 mins. In 2009 Tim Higginbottom completed the Welsh Classical round in a time of 17 hrs 42 minutes.

However, the most remarkable achievement to date is that of Mike Hartley. In 1990 Mike completed the 3 basic 24 hr rounds (B. Graham, P. Buckley and

Ramsay rounds) in the amazing time of 3 days 14 hrs 20 mins. This includes two 4 hour car journeys. He covered around 182 miles; climbed 83,000 ft and failed to get under 24 hours for the final round only.

4) *PERSONAL VENTURES:*

With fitness and the hard won experience gained in fast, safe travel over arduous mountain country comes personal initiatives. Exploits may involve extensive support teams with a sophisticated back-up or simply a lone runner, independent, self-sufficient, pitting himself against his own limitations and those which nature will try to enforce. As a first example perhaps I might cite a hill journey I undertook in 1989. I called it the 'Scottish Cardinals'. It followed a cross-country route between the southernmost, westernmost, easternmost and northernmost Munros. I also included all the 4,000 ft peaks and as many other Monros as I could squeeze into my 10 day 'holiday'. As near as I can reckon I ran about 400 miles and climbed 100,000 ft (I also cycled 120 miles on the road because in this kind of venture you make your own 'rules')

Elite ultra distance fell runner and joint winner of the 'Dragon's Back Race', Martin Stone has specialised in solo ventures. In 1986 he completed the 81 mile route over the Scottish 4,000 ft peaks in only 21 hrs 39 mins. He also completed the Bob Graham round in true winter conditions in under 24 hours, running solo! - a remarkable achievement. Colin Donnelly and Pete Simpson, on separate occasions, have made long solo journeys in the almost forsaken Southern Uplands of Scotland. Colin ran 380 miles in 11 days over 130 peaks of 2,000 ft or over. The Pennine Way has, almost inevitably, served to inspire the lone runner.

Following the lead of Geoff Bell, the original pioneer, Robin Price ran the length of the P.W. solo, carrying every item of gear and food for the journey (except water) in 4 days 7 hours 58 mins - he then ran back again! (supported this time). Back in the Lake District the legendary Joss Naylor covered all the major (and most of the minor) peaks in an epic week long adventure. Joss ran about 390 miles over 214 'tops' climbing approximately 121,000 ft. But perhaps the most spectacular hill run to date is that achieved by Hugh Symonds. In 1990 Hugh ran over all 277 Munros in Scotland (including all the ground between them) then continued, still on foot, into England where he climbed the four 3,000 ft peaks; Wales for the 14 peaks of 3,000 ft and finally onto Ireland (temporarily swapping legs for a ferry) where he finished his journey over the seven Irish 3,000 ft peaks. Altogether, Hugh ran 2,048 miles, ascended 303 mountains over 3,000 ft and climbed around 500,000 ft, in 97 days. (He also raised a large amount of money for charity.) The charitable aspects of this run made it desirable to achieve a fairly high public profile. However, I suspect every season there are unheralded runners taking their fitness and skills into the hills and achieving not only impressive physical feats but also great personal satisfaction and fulfilment.

TRAINING FOR ULTRA HILL-RUNNING

It would, in my view, be foolish to attempt to produce a definitive programme for 'hill-running'. Both the type of hill running which is envisaged and the individual runner will determine the nature of the programme. There are, of course, important guidelines which are universally applicable. One of the most important of these is the 'specificity principle'.

SPECIFICITY

The physical demands placed on the runner by any particular hill run are unique to that event. It follows that training should, where possible, reflect those demands. The ability to move quickly and economically over rough and variable ground is a skill and it must be acquired through specific practice. Not only must particular skills of 'rough running' develop through practice on rough ground but muscles must be conditioned to cope with the demands made by such ground. In my view, the body responds more readily to running over variable terrain as a more complete range of movement is required. Road running tends to both narrow and therefore intensify the demands over a limited range of movement.

Naturally off-road terrain is infinitely variable. It is therefore not a good idea to train for an attempt on an L.D.P. by running exclusively over steep, rough ground. The best way of conditioning the body for any particular hill event is by spending plenty of time on it. Where this cannot be done then the course should be analysed and similar terrain should be found which is available for training.

TRAINING SPEEDS AND DISTANCES

While the specificity principle is a good one it can be overdone. For instance, while specific terrain training is good for a particular event, it is likely that the runner will want to run a variety of events. In this case highly specific training can be overdone. It is notoriously difficult to be both ultra-distance fit and ultra-climbing fit. But perhaps the major deviation from the specificity principle occurs with respect to training speeds and training distances.

With the longer events, say over 100 miles, the actual speed at which the runner may have to travel is quite low, expressed as an average (e.g. for the Pennine Way at 270 miles the record speed works out at 4.1 m.p.h.). If a runner spends long periods only running slowly he/she is likely to become a slow runner. Not only that, but if training speeds are low they are likely to be relatively undemanding and therefore vast mileages and unreasonable amounts of time will be needed to produce a real training effect. Furthermore, the P.W. contains a good deal of difficult and slow terrain, some which is covered at night. To produce a 4.1 average therefore, the runner must be able to cruise economically at much higher speeds.

In practice, 'endurance speed' can be developed in the 'off' (Winter) season using good running surfaces (road, rock, trail) and specific hill skills and hill fitness developed in the Spring and early Summer. I would further advise that neither aspect should be completely neglected at any time. An intelligent balance between them should be the aim of an essentially flexible programme.

PLANNING HILL RUNS

Whether training, competing or attempting a record, the longer hill runs can each form a little adventure in its own right. Let me say that hill running has plenty of scope not only for adventure but also epics. If your principal goals are to do with running and not epic adventure you must learn to plan carefully.

It is of course necessary to be able to navigate while out on the run, but it will also be useful to sit down with the appropriate map beforehand and plan the route. Not only direction but time and distance estimates should be made. Weather, clothing and food requirements also need consideration for the longer runs. All this might sound like extra hassle but you will find it is not. The planning engages the mind and gives expression to your motivation. Your dreams of distance will find form in planning and achieve reality in execution. But doubtless, sooner or later you will join the ubiquitous 'Hellarewe Club' and in winter's dusk, will be down the wrong valley, minus torch and with one Polo mint remaining. Don't worry, this is what is known as 'essential experience'.

PLANNING THE PROGRAMME - PRE-SEASON
Naturally enough, most long distance hill running takes place in the four summer months MAY - AUG. After a hard season most runners plan a period of rest (active or otherwise). Pre-season therefore, would cover say, NOV - MARCH. Short daylight and inclement weather will confine hill running so this is the time to build 'speed-endurance'. I have identified two basic approaches:

a) Steady mileage systems. Here, a total mileage for the week is set and this is reached by dividing the number of sessions per week into roughly equal parts. Perhaps more usually, sessions are unequal in length so that some runs are shorter and faster, others longer and slower. In either case there is a gradual increase in weekly mileage. This is a very standard approach and the only real difference for the hill runner is that it may be well to plan the week around a long hill session at the weekend. In winter a hill run of only 25 - 35 miles might occupy 5 - 8 hours. It can also be sufficiently demanding to need to ease down before and afterwards.

If more hill running is undertaken it may become difficult to estimate weekly mileages accurately. In this case the runner needs to rely more than usual on subjective assessments of fatigue. When contemplating challenges such as 200 or more miles continuous running over tough terrain it is natural to think that weekly mileages can never be too high. They can of course. When the runner begins to go deeper and deeper into fatigue it is time to ease back. This is where the next system may be helpful.

b) Overload - systems. This system recognises the need to both take the body to its limit (and a little beyond) then allow it time to recover and strengthen. A system I favour is based on a four week cycle. The first week is based on or a little below the previous cycle's 'high point', the next week sees a slight 'easing-off', the third is the 'hard' week setting a new high and the fourth week is 'active rest'. Here is an example: WEEK 1; 80 miles. WEEK 2; 60 miles. WEEK 3; 100 miles. WEEK 4; 40 miles. The second cycle might then go: WEEK 1; 90. WEEK 2; 70. WEEK 3; 110. But WEEK 4 to stay at 40. Mileage is only one way of adjusting the load, speed and time spent running also need consideration. In practice I have found this system almost impossible to maintain. This has usually been due to interference from things like races, extremely long (and thus fatiguing) Winter walks and weeks or weekends away on mountaineering trips. Other factors which disrupt this system more than the 'steady' state system are illnesses and injuries.

CONCLUSIONS:

1. Plan to maintain a steady progression.
2. Include some 'rough' terrain running in the programme.
3. Spend time maintaining 'high' cruising speeds.
4. Include at least one 'long' run per week (usually over hills).
5. Plan rest and recovery into the programme.

EXAMPLES OF MY OWN TRAINING

In 1984 I became the first person to run the Pennine Way under 3 days. Readers may be interested to compare my training for the P.W. with that of Mike Hartley, the current record holder.

I began preparation specifically with the P.W. in mind in Nov 1983. From then until March 1984 I averaged 95 miles per week for my 'training' weeks and 40 m.p.w. for 5 'rest' weeks (usually race 'ease-down', recovery or mountaineering trips). My highest weekly mileage was 128 and lowest, 27. Below is a typical week's training:

PRE-SEASON (NOV-MARCH)

SUN	20 - 30 MILES (3 - 7 hrs). hill running (sometimes hard walking).
MON	a.m.	3 - 6 miles	easy	(7 min mile pace).
	p.m.	5 - 10 miles		@ approx 6m.30sec pace.

TUES	a.m.	3 - 10 miles	easy.	
	p.m.	10 - 15 miles		@ 6.30 pace.
WED	a.m.	3 - 6 miles	easy.	
	p.m.	10 - 20 miles		@ 6.00 - 7.00 min mile pace.
THURS	a.m.	3 - 6 miles	easy.	
	pm	5 - 10 miles		@ 6.30 pace
FRI	a.m.	3 - 6 miles	easy.	
	p.m.	5 - 10 miles		@ 6.30 pace

SAT: EITHER – 1 ½- 2 ½ hours easy hill running to ease the legs from the road work.

OR - all day hill walk. OR - rest.

Because of my job a number of Wednesdays and whole weekends would be devoted to mountaineering instruction. Thus mileage would need to be increased on the other days in order to maintain the average mileage.

SPECIFIC TRAINING FOR THE RECORD (APRIL - MID MAY)

March ended with a week of Winter mountaineering in Scotland. When I returned I changed the nature of may training completely, now the emphasis was on running over terrain similar to that of the P.W. Distances of individual runs were much longer and speeds much slower.

APRIL. WEEK 1:   a) 9 ½ - 10 hours (approx 45 miles), hills and tracks

b) 3 hours (16 miles)mainly hills

c) 18 hour walking trip - the fourteen 3,000 ft summits of N. Wales (in snow).

[N.B. 1 - 2 days complete rest between each effort]

WEEK 2:   a) 5 hours (27 miles) hills + tracks (hills usually walked)

b) 5 ½ hours (30 miles)   "   "   "

c) 5 hours (26 miles)   "   "   "

d) 5 ½ hours (30 miles)   "   "   "

These training sessions took place on consecutive days leaving 2 days rest before:

WEEK 3   a) 11 hours (50-55 miles) hill and tracks as above.

        b) 9 ½ hours (40-45 miles)   "

        REST DAY

        c) 10 ½ hours (45-50 miles) "

        d) 10 ½ hours (45-50 miles) "

        TWO DAYS REST

WEEK 4 THIS TRAINING TOOK PLACE ON THE P.W. ITSELF

        a) 13 ½ hours (12 hours actually moving, 1 ½ hours on

        stops for food, footwear etc.) (60 miles)

        b) as above (60 miles)

        REST DAY

        c) 14 ½ hours (13 actually running) (60 miles)

        d) as above (60 miles)

MILEAGE TOTALS + TIMES

WEEK 1:	31 hours	approx	85-90 miles.
WEEK 2:	21 hours	"	113 miles
WEEK 3:	41 ½ hours	"	195 miles
WEEK 4:	50 hours	"	240 miles

After these four week blocks of training I took a week's rest (jogging only) then my final preparation was as follows:

WEEK 5:	REST (a little jogging)
WEEK 6:	Record attempt (successful) on my own 'Tan Hill to the Cat + Fiddle' record.
	120 miles, mainly moorland
WEEK 7:	REST (complete)
WEEK 8:	Active rest - about 35 miles.
WEEK 9:	Active rest ""
WEEK 10:	Successful attempt on a sub-three day Pennine Way (270 miles; 2 days 21 hours 54 minutes.)

CONCLUSIONS:

Had I been able to plan the record attempt for late June instead of the last week-end of May I could have interspersed weeks 2, 3 and 4 with a week of active rest. Intense motivation disguised a fatigue build up which the rest week, number 5, did not dispel. Consequently the record attempt of week 6 completely exhausted me. It should have been part of the build-up, not a trial of strength. The actual running part of my training was good, I feel, but the programme overall lacked sufficient recovery periods.

It is interesting to compare my record with the current record of Mike Hartley. Our average running speeds were the same but Mike had astonishingly few stops. I ran through 3 nights (with a 3 hour stop on night 2) whereas Mike went for 2 nights out. He took the chance of having to finish in the dark going into night 3 but of course avoided this with his great performance. Mike endured a heatwave and hard, 'fast' but painful ground. I had cool, even cold conditions and was occasionally up to the knees in mud over the last 30 miles of the Cheviots. It is necessary to prepare for a whole range of conditions. With his approach of minimal stops Mike pointed the way forward. Along with superb physical conditioning he brought a relentless mental disipline which had never been so rigorously applied to a run of this length.

TRAINING FOR THE COAST TO COAST RECORD

PRE-SEASON (NOV - MARCH) This was similar to that of 1984 with perhaps less mileage mid-week and a slightly larger weekend mileage on the hills.

SPECIFIC TRAINING (APRIL_- MID JUNE)

With the attempt scheduled for the end of June I was able to test my theory that longer rest periods between the blocks of training would be beneficial.

The Spring of 1985 was extremely wet and often cold and windy. Motivation was constantly tested and total mileage was less than it might have been otherwise.

WEEK 1:	3 x 6 hours (25 - 35 miles) Hills + tracks
	(alternate days of rest)
WEEK 2:	4 hours (20 miles) Hill + track
	9 ¼ (45 miles)
	12 ½ (50")
	6 (25")
Totals:	32 hrs 140 miles

(alternate days of rest)

| WEEK 3: | 12 hours (55 miles) Hill + track |
| | 6 ½ (30) |

TRAINING CURTAILED - BAD WEATHER

WEEK 4:	11 ½ hours (46) Hill + track}
	10 (40) CONSECUTIVE REST DAY
	8 (40) Hill + tracks} CONSECUTIVE
	11 ½ (50)
Totals:	41 hrs 176 miles
WEEK 5:	THIS TRAINING WAS ALSO A RECONNAISANCE
	OF THE COAST TO COAST ROUTE
	9 ½ hours (43 miles)
	10 (47)
	REST DAY
	11 (48)
	12 (50)
Totals:	42 (188)
	LEAD-UP TO THE ATTEMPT
WEEK 6:	ACTIVE REST
WEEK 7:	1 x 11 hours 45 - 50 miles) PLUS ACTIVE REST
WEEK 8:	RECORD ATTEMPT
	(as last year, 'Tan Hill to Cat & Fiddle' 120 miles of
	moorland.) Successful, 26 hrs 35 mins.
WEEK 9:	ACTIVE REST (JOGGING)
WEEK10:	RACE, 100 miles (Hills + tracks) 1st, 21hrs 45 mins
WEEK11:	EASY HILL WALKING + RUNNING
WEEK12:	ACTIVE REST (JOGGING)

WEEK12:   RECORD ATTEMPT, COAST TO COAST;
                           SUCCESSFUL,
                           Totals: 190 miles, 46 hrs 50 mins.

CONCLUSIONS: The 1985 programme spread the training load over a longer period allowing better recovery from and adaptation to the regime. Most training took place in poor weather. The 100 and 120 mile runs took place in very heavy underfoot conditions - near gale force head-on winds and heavy rain for the first 100 miles and heavy mud thereafter. These forced me into a 2 night scenario instead of two long days and just one night as originally planned. I can only conclude that my preparation had been good and in retrospect this must remain one of my strongest runs.

REFLECTIONS AND DEVELOPMENTS

It is a matter of debate whether running, say, 100 miles as a training run for a longer attempt, is better than doing 2 x 50 miles. There is no doubt in my mind that 100 miles at a fairly intensive pace needs more recovery time than 2 x 50. On the other hand if the body is ready to absorb the longer distance then it should, in theory at least, recover and grow even stronger. Psychologically, it may be essential to explore what is involved in runs of 24 hours and longer. Perhaps once the ultra runner is experienced in runs of 28 - 48 hours, or 100 plus miles there is no necessity to attempt them as training efforts. On a practical basis it is probably more enjoyable (and therefore more motivating) to have one or two seasonal sub-goals of around 100 miles on the way to the season's main goal which may be longer than that.

Perhaps because of the relatively slow nature of much of my training, and certainly because of the onslaught of anno-domini, I have noticed a slowing of pace. Not particularly basic speed (at 50 plus I can still go under 27 secs for 200m) but in 'cruising speed' over distance. In an effort to offset this inevitable slowing I have introduced two changes into my training. With hind sight I feel they would have been valuable earlier, therefore I recommend them to you.

a) Interval running on the track: Keeping the long run on the Sunday I introduced a track session on Tues and Thurs. So now my Winter preparation looks like this:

SUN:	Long Hill Run (as previous)
MON:	Easy Run 5 - 8 miles
TUES:	Run 3 miles to track. Intervals. Run back 3 miles.
WED:	10 - 15 miles steady running
THURS:	As for Tues
FRI:	Fartlek in local park 1 – 1 ½ hours
SAT:	Hill walk or rest.

You will notice this programme reflects retirement from the 'sharp end' of competitive running.

Here is an interval session from towards the end of the Winter preparation period:

Jog to track (3 miles)
Warm up with stretching and strides 1 mile

4 x 200m	(32 - 33 secs)	200m	jog recovery
4 x 400m	(73 - 76 secs)	"	"
2 x 800m	(2m 45s - 2m 48s)	400m	"
4 x 200m	(34 secs)	200m	"
4 x 400m	(76 - 78 secs)	"	"
2 x 800m	(2m 50s)	400m	"

Warm down and stagger back 3 miles.

SPRING TIME PREPARATION

To some extent the central problem of training for ultra hill running is how to combine endurance with speed. I began to run my usual hill/track routes of 20 - 30 miles on a time-interval basis. What seemed to suit me best was a period of 20 mins 'effort' followed by 10 mins 'easy' (jog and walk).

I made the following observations: the system encouraged me to re-develop faster downhill running; it induced an even greater focus of attention towards 'effort' and bodily 'output'; it encouraged powerful uphill rhythms (not necessarily running) rather than using uphill as 'recovery'; the easy or rest phase was when the subjective feeling of fatigue was greatest; I re-learnt to plan necessary pauses (for change of clothes, food, drink etc.) during the recovery phase, (planning ahead on a run is an essential discipline). I found the sessions stimulating.

TRAINING DOSE: I regard these sessions as quite intensive and suggest two per week. The system is infinitely flexible along the parameters of time, speed, distance and terrain. It is necessary to go out and experiment. I would guess that at least 4 'efforts' (of around 15 - 25 mins) are needed for an overall training effect for a fit runner. I found that after about four weeks I could manage 6 - 8 efforts which, with recoveries, gave about 2 - 4 hours, 20 - 25 miles.

EFFORT - SPEED: I would suggest that the speed (or the intensity) of the effort should relate to the event speed at a factor of about 1.5 to 1; thus, if you plan to run a 100 miler at 5 mph you should run the efforts at 7 mph. This may assume a level of pace judgement you have not got. Until you acquire it I suggest as a rule of thumb: 4 x 20 min efforts with 10 min recoveries. You should be able to maintain the speed throughout. You may need to do some experimentation with measured distances and stop watch in order to achieve the right training dose for your own needs.

Using this interval system I would recommend the following schedule for the early (spring) season:

1. LONG RUN   (8 - 12 hours)   30 - 50 miles
2. ACTIVE REST
3. INTERVAL SESSION   (2 ½ - 4 ½ hours)   15 - 30 miles
4. MEDIUM LENGTH RUN (5 - 7 hours)   20 - 30 miles
5. INTERVAL SESSION   (as above)
6. ACTIVE REST
7. MEDIUM LENGTH RUN (as above)

Such a schedule would give between 110 - 180 mpw. Particularly at the latter workload, it would be advisable to introduce a rest week, say, every third week. At this level of training individual differences assume paramount importance. I have assumed my remarks are addressed to expert or elite runners.

Final word: The host of variables in hill running make it difficult to estimate what are your theoretical limitations in any venture; when theoretical limitations are removed anything becomes possible.

Mike Hartley was well known as one of the top British ultra fell/trail runners, with wins in the 62 mile Fellmans, the West Highland Way, the South Downs 80 miler, and set a new record for the 270 mile Pennine Way run. In 1992 he was chosen to represent Britain in the European 100km Championships at Winschoten where he ran a controlled 6:54. Mike ran 6:37:45 for fourth place in the 1993 IAU European Championship, running negative splits (3:20 at 50km!). His experience in preparing for such contrasting ultra events will be of interest to many ultra runners.)

The idea of an attempt on the record first occurred to me during the Snowdonia 100 in 1988. I ran most of the course in the company of Mike Cudahy the previous record holder. His time of 2 days 21 hours 54 minutes set in 1984 was the first time the 270 mile route had been completed in under three days. In record breaking terms Mike raised the game somewhat by taking less sleep than anyone before him (about 1 hour 40 minutes).

I was in no doubt that I would need to train, plan and prepare very carefully if I was to make a serious attempt on this formidable time.

My plan for the following two years was to check the route at weekends, complete a long (100 miles) and a very long (200 miles plus) run in 1988, then put maximum effort into training for the attempt in 1989. It was important to me to start the Pennine Way with the knowledge that I had trained and planned to the best of my ability. I didn't want my conscience pricked by doubts about the quality of my preparation. The route checking was enjoyable and informative, usually running long out and backs. The White Peak 100 in May 1988 went very well, 17 hours 58 minutes felt quite comfortable. Two months later the 212 mile Southern Uplands Way did not go well. To say I found the route tough would be a gross understatement. Plain old blisters were of no consequence, compared with extreme stiffness, swollen legs and septic toe nails. My elapsed time of 55 hours 55 minutes equated to a time 1 hour 30 minutes slower than the existing Pennine Way record. and that was assuming I could cover the additional 58 miles at the same pace. The way I felt at the finish I couldn't have run another 58 miles at any pace.

Despite this difficult and slightly disappointing run, my enthusiasm hadn't been dampened and I had learned a lot. I now knew I could go through two nights without sleep, this being a crucial factor. Also, I knew I would need to be a lot fitter. At least I knew where I stood, I could evaluate my position. There were six main areas to pay attention to during the following twelve months and during the attempt itself.

Fitness

As with all types of athletics it is vital to train specifically for the event. In terms of the Pennine Way, I needed to be very strong and resilient both physically and mentally. A high mileage, off road programme over the final nine months including several long runs provided the necessary stamina. My highest training week was followed by a five week taper to a long fast run four weeks prior to the attempt. The programme went according to plan, so during the last four weeks I could do nothing to improve my chances except rest and easy running.

Route Knowledge

It was essential to know the route if the record was to be broken. A wrong turn, especially at night could have degenerated into a cross-country trespass. Route knowledge also meant that I could spend energy at an economical level, Knowing when to 'save a bit' or when to 'open it up'. At the same time road support points were checked for accessibility and parking and the maps then marked accordingly.

A Realistic Schedule

A carefully planned schedule allowed the road support crew to be ready with the food and drink, (there's nothing worse than running up to the car in the middle of the night only to find everyone fast asleep). When writing the schedule I used data from my other long runs with adjustments for length, terrain and the time of year. This coupled with an appreciation of my 'pace reduction rate' formed the basis of my scheduling. I planned for 2 days 15 hours 40 minutes (4© mph) including stops with a pace reduction factor of © mph every 27 miles. This eliminated chances of being 4 or 5 hours up at the halfway point, only to lose it over the second half.

My split times were passed on by telephone to my co-ordinator, who kept follow up pacers informed of progress. This allowed all concerned to be in touch with the event and therefore be in the right place at the right time.

Pacing and Road Support

The help of friends who knew the route at least as well as I did was good insurance in safety and route finding. An experienced pacer picked a comfortable even speed to suit my physical condition, or even my mood at any one time, he or she fed information back to me if I unwittingly slowed down or sped up. This did not necessarily force me to stick to a metronome like pace but it allowed me to monitor myself more easily. Extreme heat (90+) on the weekend of my run ensured my pacers were kept busy carrying and passing drinks at 10 minute intervals.

My road support crew were also very experienced. For me to know that they would without doubt be at the appointed place was a major worry that I could forget. My wife had supported many times and knew what I was likely to need. On reaching the car I found an array of food, drink, clothing and foot aid. Everything organised and to hand.

Food and Nutrition

During the final nine months preparation I had experimented with various foods and drinks. With an intake of 8000 calories per day during peak training I had plenty of scope for experimentation.

A list of food in order of eatability was useful for the road support crew. I worked my way down, saving food at the bottom for when everything else seemed unpalatable. The list looked something like this: buns, cakes, bread rolls, doughnuts, Eccles cakes, honey, bananas, rice pudding, condensed milk, various tinned fruits, and fresh melon. At night pasta and/or soup were always acceptable. I didn't find any advantages with sports drinks whilst training, (quite the opposite with some brands!) so I only took water on the run, with sweet tea or coffee at night and early morning. Opinion suggests that sufficient levels of vitamins and minerals can be gained from a normal diet. A high mileage training programme followed by a three day continuous run couldn't be considered a normal lifestyle, so I decided to play safe and include the following in my diet.

During training
Dolomite (Calcium and Magnesium)
Multivit tablets
Vitamin C
Vitamin B12 (to aid the absorption of carbohydrates)
Desiccated liver (to aid recovery after a hard run)

During the attempt
Dolomite
Vitamin B12
Milk of Magnesia (to help with digestion)

I did carbo load for 5 days prior to the attempt but unlike a marathon or even a 100K I don't consider it to be vital. On a long ultra it is much more important to eat and drink regularly right from the start, and maintain your appetite.

Final nine Months Training
An average weekly mileage of 78 over the 2 years prior to the attempt, minus injury and holidays gave me a good stamina background. Long runs from home ranged from 20 to 45 miles, perhaps one per fortnight. Specific events or races were less frequent, my idea was to work hard on the weekly training for longish periods, and ease off a bit then make a good job of a long race or record attempt. Normal training being resumed after little or no recovery time.

I started training in earnest in September 1988, ready for an attempt in July 1989. A typical day would be to run 7 miles to work, walk about 7 hours carrying out my job as a meter reader, then run 7 miles back. As my schedule progressed I would double up first the morning and eventually the evening run. While injured or easing down I would cycle.

The following is a breakdown of the final 9 months.

September Weekly average 106 miles

Long runs   1 x 40   1 x 45

October Weekly average 100

Long runs   1 x 23   2 x 30

Cycling 30

November Weekly average 25 (injured)

Long runs   1 x 20   1 x 40

Cycling 290

December Weekly average 100

Long runs   1 x 23   1 x 27   1 x 32   1 x 45

Cycling 30

January Weekly average 100 miles

Long runs   1 x 20   1 x 30   1 x 35   1 x 40

Cycling 106

February Weekly average 87

Long runs   1 x 25

1 x 50 muddy cross country   (7 hours 36 minutes)

Cycling 86

March Weekly average 78

Long runs   2 x 20

1 x 81 muddy cross country   (13 hours 34 minutes)

(Dales Way footpath)

Cycling 135

April Weekly average 90

Long runs   1 x 23   1 x 62

1 x 92 muddy cross country   (16 hours 10 minutes)

(Staffs Way footpath)

Cycling 93

May Weekly average 125

Long runs   2 x 20   1 x 28   2 x 30

1 x 62 11500 ft ascent (10 hours 32 minutes)

(Fellsman Hike)

The heaviest 7 day period during May was 170 miles, part of a total 306 miles in 12 days.

June Weekly average 52

Long runs   1 x 20   1 x 23

1 x 95 (West Highland Way)   (15 hours 32 minutes)

Cycling 125

July Weekly average 28

Long runs270 miles Pennine Way, 2 days 17 hours 20 minutes

Cycling 120

After Thoughts

Prior knowledge of the route, expert supporters and the ability to run through two nights without sleep all proved to be crucial to success. Approximately one hour of my 3 hours 37 minutes stopping time was spent treating blisters caused by the unusually dry hard ground. The remainder having been spent eating. My basic training of two runs per day plus several hours walking was certainly conducive to a high level of stamina. A long, off road run every two weeks followed by a rest day may have been more beneficial than a long run every two or three weeks with no rest days.

A Comparison With The 100K

Before my first serious attempt at the 100K (European Championships) I had completed 25 runs of between 60 and 270 miles, 8 of these being over 100 miles. To move down to the 100K was an unusual if not unique position to be in. I did not need to overcome the psychological barriers that a marathon runner must have to. I knew I could run 100K. My problem would be maintaining a brisk unrelenting pace without blowing up or sustaining injuries.

Having completed the race in a very pleasing 6.54, I am of the opinion that a 100K road race is more stressful both physically and mentally than the equivalent distance off road. A whole range of special techniques are required to be successful off road. These can only be learned with practice. Apart from those mentioned earlier there is map reading, compass work and on long ultras carrying a small rucksack or bum bag. Crossing boggy or bouldery ground especially in mist or darkness, requires a fleetness of foot only developed from years of running. Injuries or blisters seem a bit easier to handle when the terrain is constantly changing. We all have a 'bad run' from time to time, when that happens off road there's always the scenery, birds, animals and the route finding to take your mind off the pain.

The 100K road race is so much more intense, injuries and blisters caused by the constant unvaried pace could terminate your run. Attention to detail on your body preparation, e.g. tapes, vaseline, clothing and pre-race food need to be right first time. A three and a half minute stop to make alterations, gives the opposition a half mile advantage. Course side support needs to be organised in passing food and drink. On a multi loop course to shout a code word then pick up the necessary item on the next lap seems to work well.

Specialisation is again the key word in training. Only having seven weeks to prepare for the European Championships, everything had to be relevant and useful. An average of 80 miles per week, a highest week of 120 and a longest run of 40 miles was all time would allow. The long runs were made up of three loops from home, ideal for picking up drinks etc., but sometimes requiring a mental effort to start the last loop, (good training in itself). Short fast time trials and regular track sessions helped keep my pace up.

Experimentation with food and drink on the long runs soon provided a good system. Fifteen grams of Glucose powder mixed with 300 ml of mineral water plus 3 or 4 Jelly Babies every 5 miles worked well in both training and on the day. The race was 10 laps of 10km, at the 10km point my support would pass a 300 ml bottle with sweets attached, at the 5km point I would take plain water, to either drink or tip down my neck, thighs etc..

I believe a higher level of fitness and a greater commitment to quality training is vital if you want to run well on the road. In particular, speed and speed endurance work to develop a high cruising speed.

It would be easier for a road runner to learn off road techniques than for an off road runner to become fitter.

Stephen Moore having written an earlier article on the 'getting started in Ultra distance running and assumed that most will start with shorter distance road races, perhaps one is entitled to ask 'is there an alternative way in?' Stephen started his running on the fells. Here he deals with questions how

trail running and road running relate. Can one switch from long distance fell or trail running to road? Would you want to? If a comparison is being made between Trail Running and Road Running which one would I choose? Does one have to choose?

My background, my 'way in' and my motivation was very definitely the hills and specifically the Lake District hills. As a young and enthusiastic fell walker I had completed the four three thousand peaks trail (from Keswick, over Skiddaw, Scafell, Scafell Pike and Helvelyn and back to Keswick with a total of 11,000 feet of climbing and 46 miles all round) as an 18 year old in 1966, with a time of 15 hours and 23 minutes being recorded. Those long days in the hills, weekends and holidays, were a regular feature whilst living a mere 70 miles away, at Lytham St. Annes. The peace, tranquillity and the beauty of the hills was such that I could not get enough of it - I had to cram as much as possible into a day and over time the only way to cover more ground was to run.

The serious fellrunning, however, started in 1981, with a move to Horwich, near Bolton, Lancashire. The local club Horwich R.M.I. Harriers were pretty strict fellrunners. On a training night, if the leaders so much as set foot on a surfaced road there would be recriminations - this was strictly off road - dirty socks every night and the fell shoes were banned from the washing machine! The fell racing calendar provided ample competition and some very famous races such as the 10 mile Ben Nevis Race, which I completed 3 times (best 1984 - 1 hour 33 minutes) the Coniston Fell Race, the Welsh 1000 Metre Tops Race over 22 miles (twice) the Ennerdale Horsehoe 23 miles (3 times) the Yorkshire Three Peaks (3 times) the Wasdale Horsehoe 20 miles (twice) and the Haworth Hobble 33 miles completed 5 times finishing in the top 3 positions on 4 out of 5 occasions.

Between 1982-7, I was putting in up to 32 fell races per year (including 20-22 mile races on consecutive weekends) and in 1985 finished 8th in the British Fell Running Championships. However, perhaps the most enjoyable events were in 1983 completing the 72 mile, 42 summits, 28,000 feet of climbing Bob Graham Round in 18 hours and 52 minutes (definitely my best ever day out in the Hills!) and in 1987 (21 years after first completing it!)

winning the Four Peaks in 8 hours and 26 minutes. For me, the hills were my first and only choice. At that time I did not really know what a 10k was. There were, however, a few deviations from the fell as when someone, knowing I spent much time running, asked if I had run a marathon and when I said no I had not, his reply was, "So you're just a jogger then?"

I had to respond to the challenge and in 1984 completed my first marathon, the Cumbria Lakes Marathon in 2 hours 36 minutes to finish 4th. London followed in 1986, with 2 hours 28 minutes and in 1987 I was encouraged to run in the Bolton 40 miler as it almost started outside our home. It would suit me - I was told - and it did, as I won it in 4 hours 21 minutes. But I did not choose to leave the hills for the roads. No - in January 1988 a work move was to deny me the regular visits and competition to which I had grown accustomed. I have been restricted to visits once a month to the Lakes ever since but that is very valuable and enjoyable training time. As a new member of Hertford and Ware AC from May 1988, it was a case of 10k's, 10 miles and 1/2 marathons with up to 3 marathons a year capitalising on my new Veteran 40 status. However, after 18 months I was desperately in need of a new challenge. It was then I heard of the 80 mile South Downs Run, and off the road race which should suit me - I hadn't realised they had hills in the South! On my first visit I was very impressed with the scenery and was asked what did I think? My response 'Not bad for the South of England' was something my club colleagues have never allowed me to forget.

The specific training involving longer runs both on and off the road was a notable feature of the South Downs build up. The race was 'committed' at least in my mind 12 months ahead with the mileages and races selected accordingly. During that period I ran over every part of the route at least twice as this was a trail race. Preparation in terms of food and drink was meticulous and was made possible by tremendous support from Kath, my wife, who was, and still is, a fully committed member of 'the team'.

Race Build Up.

(distances over 20 miles only)

1989	30/10	Harlow Marathon	2 hrs 35 mins	(3rd)	
	2/12	St. Albans Marathon	2 hrs 30 mins	(1st)	
1990	25/2	Bury St. Edmunds 20	1 hr 54 mins	(9th)	
	22/4	London Marathon	2 hrs 27 mins	(129th)	
	(all subsequent races)				
	2/5	Welwyn 10k	33 mins 42 s	(1st)	
	17/5	Ware 5 ½ mile	28 mins 12 s	(1st)	
	6/6	Baldock 10k	33 mins	(1st)	
	10/6	Welwyn ½ Marathon	1 hr 11 mins	(4th)	
	20/6	Royston 10k	33 mins 34 s	(1st)	
	23/6	South Downs 80 mile	9 hrs 37 mins	(1st)	(course record)

TRAINING

weekly miles longest run (R = 1 race)

w/e	22/4	100	R	40
	29/4	70	R	11
	6/5	80		17
	13/5	73	R	20
	20/5	85		17
	27/5	104		25
	3/6	51	RR	12
	10/6	89	R	30
	17/6	109	RR	80

Whilst the schedule shows highly variable and sometimes low distances, runs were often in the Lake District or on the South Downs and were undertaken concurrently with an active race programme. In particular, w/e 22/4 started with the London Marathon on a Sunday and ended with a 40 mile run on the South Downs on the Saturday.

Reflecting on the preparation, the training and the races, I used long runs in the hills for strength, endurance and for sheer enjoyment, for when one is enjoying oneself, the miles pass without counting them. One other great advantage in doing distance work in the hills is that there is almost always a constant supply of liquid in the crystal clear streams such that one can mix one's drinks as you go along. On the other hand, speed work is essential and that is best undertaken on the roads - both in training (reps - intense and sustained training) or in one of my preferences, 10k & 10 mile races. The faster one is over 10k, the faster one will be over 100k provided the stamina is also there.

Having raced off road in June 1990, my next target was on the road, the Bolton 40 in September, when I established a new course record of 4 hours 17 minutes. These performances at 80 miles (I think it may be 2 to 3 miles shorter!) and 40 miles (accurate and hilly) resulted in selection to represent Great Britain in the World 100k Championships on the road in Duluth U.S.A. in October 1990. However, illness caused me to withdraw at 75k. 1991 was plagued with injury (3 1/2 months off) but I completed two 100k's finishing 13th in the World 100k in Italy (7 hours 23 minutes) in May and 6th at Winschoten, Holland (7 hours 3 minutes) in September. After that race I did not run again until 9th November and so thought my chances of running well at Palamos, Spain in the 1992 World Championships were low. However, confidence received a boost when early in January, Carl Barker and I finished joint 1st in the North Downs 54 mile trail race in a time of 7 hours 44 minutes. The overall race and training build up (bearing in mind starting after injury) was as follows:-

Race Build Up.					Training w/e	Weekly miles	Longest run
1991	8/12	6 m cross country		(11th)			
	22/12	10k Epsom	33.07	(5th)	9/11	15	6
1992	1/1	10k Hyde Park 33.03		(4th)	16/11	62	12
	5/1	54m North Downs 7.44		(1st)	24/11	71	15
	26/1	6 mile X Cnty			1/2	80	13
	2/2	Watford ½ M 1.11		(12th)	8/12	107 R	28
	16/2	100k Palamos 6hr 43m		(7th)	15/12	71	12
					22/12	107 R	29
					29/12	60 R	11

5/1	96 R	54
12/1	82	14
14/1	70	23
26/1	75 R	13
2/2	97 R	13
9/2	57 R	23

Again, a volatile training pattern, but, it is up to the individual to find his/her own mixture of speed, endurance, fitness and enjoyment. Upon reflection, comparing my training for the South Downs with that for Palamos there is very little difference - my background is in the hills and I guess it has been easier for me to switch from the hills to road than it would be the other way round - access to the hills for regular training helps to put the hills in your legs which can be very useful in any race providing you have the speed training as well. The result at Palamos, 7th overall in 6 hours 43 minutes 52 seconds and a mere second outside the English senior men's record but an English, British and Commonwealth 0/40 record, set me up well for the rest of 1992 which included 9 races of marathon distance or above (eight being on the road) and brought into question, for me, recovery time. Palamos occurred after recovering from a long lay off. Should one race less frequently?

In September I had a bad run in the European 100k Championships finishing 22nd in 7 hours 33 minutes. The London to Brighton Race (55 miles) was in a mere three weeks time and I needed a good run but was it too soon? Preparation was not ideal. On the Friday evening it was Kath's 40th birthday and I arranged a surprise party in Blackpool . . . . As she stepped onto a tram on the seafront, she was more than surprised to find party poppers flying, champagne bubbling and thirty guests en route for a tour of the illuminations, a trip to the top of the Blackpool Tower and dinner. It was a heavy night (and an early morning!) with champagne coming out of my ears (who said you don't get a hangover with champagne!) The drive South on Saturday was subdued and interrupted many times. When the alarm went off at 4.30 a.m. on the Sunday morning, I turned over and said I was not going - Kath said the party was not over yet and told me to get up! I got up.

Halfway to London I tried to turn back but Kath said I had I had rested my legs and I should forget my head! It was not until the 30 mile mark that I seemed to come round. Hill training certainly seemed to come in handy up Ditchling Beacon as I pulled away from Russell Crawford to finish 1st in a time of 6 hours 1 minute. The point for me was that perhaps three weeks is adequate recovery time from an ultra but remember that everyone is different - one thing I would not recommend for anyone is carbo-loading on champagne - even if it did work for me!

After a number of ultras on the road, 1993 started back on the trails with the 54 mile North Downs Way Race and a new course record of 7 hours 11 minutes 46 seconds before the Barry 40 miles, a track event in March. Rather than introduce track into the debate, how does road compare with trail? It seems to me, that trail and fell racing is more healthy and enjoyable, but less competitive and perhaps more dangerous than road racing. It avoids car fumes, is probably easier on the joints and can have scenic advantages. It can, however, be dangerous on high ground in bad weather, there are risks of ankle injuries particularly when descending and don't forget that dirty kit!

On the other hand, road racing is more competitive, faster and more satisfying in terms of ability to measure speed. But does one have to choose between the two? Some will have no choice having no easy access to the hills or better known trails. For those that do, relative success at each may well be an influencing factor. For my part, and considered to be perhaps over the hill, it is the roads which now provide the greatest competitive satisfaction but the hills and trails remain the real favourites to which I return as often as possible for training but, most important of all, for enjoyment. And if I do get lost when out training on the hills I just end up doing a bit more!

Ultra Training for Women

Although training regimes for men can be easily tailored to women, women do face some specific issues which hopefully some of the articles below will address. But first an article I wrote which suggests that women may be bettered adapted to Ultrarunning than men!

Is the female of the Ultra Species tougher than the male?

One of the most interesting developments in Ultrarunning in recent years is the number of times that women have won races outright. This phenomenon seems to be more common in ultras; generally at 10km and the marathon men reign supreme. This prompted me to attempt an analysis of the possible reasons for the female successes.

Way back in 1971 American Natalie Cullimore amazed the totally male dominated ultra world by clocking 16:11 for 100 miles, finishing second in the race, and producing the fourth fastest time ever by an American, male or female. This performance, allied to the perception that many elite women runners still looked fresh at the finish of marathons and ultramarathons, prompted Dr Joan Ullyot and Dr Ernst van Aaken to suggest that women were innately better suited to long distance running than men. The theory was that women were better at metabolising fat than men, after their glycogen stores were depleted, and moreover also carried greater fat stores than men. In other words women had a better engine and a bigger fuel tank than men. However in 1979 David Costill showed that in fact women's ability to metabolise fat was actually inferior to men's. Other studies have shown that women's greater fat stores can count against them. On average women are fatter with less total muscle mass than men of equal body mass. So why do the women keep on winning ultra races outright?

First let's look at the type of race women are winning. They generally range from 12 hours to 6 days, with the 24 hour event being the main focus. Thus it is the more extended endurance events, those not dominated by sheer speed, in which women excel vis a vis men. Yet, if one looks at the world bests for these events, the differences between men and women are generally greater than the 9 to 11% which is the norm for events from the sprints to the marathon. (This greater difference is probably due to the fact that women have only been running such events competitively for less than twenty years.)

Thus for women to win these ultra events, their elite male opposition have to produce sub-standard performances. In other words in these events women are better COMPETITIVELY than their male opposition. Why?

One key to the success of women is their better tactics - they pace their races better. Dr Karl Lennartz has commented that in ultra races most male runners start too fast. Women generally run their races differently, in 100km for instance the difference in pace between the first and last 10km is minimal. There are even female ultrarunners who run faster during the second half of the race. Intellectually male ultrarunners know that even pace is the best strategy, so why don't they use it? The answer can perhaps be found by looking at the 24 hour race worldwide. In 1990 amongst the most successful 24 hour performers were two 50 year olds (162 miles), a 55 year old (155 miles) and a 60 year old (149 miles). Why should much older male runners be so successful, beating younger men who on physical tests would almost certainly be faster and stronger? Perhaps the question we should be asking is what such older runners have in common with female ultrarunners?

The answer possibly is, that compared with the average male ultrarunner of 35-45, they have lower levels of testosterone, the male sex hormone. The higher testosterone levels in the younger male ultrarunners makes for more aggressive, more competitive behaviour - just about the most counter-productive attitude in any long ultra. Perhaps it is much easier for women and older men to start a race at a sensible speed, they don't have chemicals in their blood forcing the pace.

Pacing the race better is one strand, but I suspect that women have other advantages as well. Van Aaken and Ullyot's idea of better fat metabolism and greater fat reserves is worth looking at again. Women may not be able to use their fat more efficiently than men, but in long races of 6 days or more their relatively greater stores would seem to give them a built in advantage!

In 1991 Hilary Walker ran from Lhasa (Tibet) to Kathmandu (Nepal) in the Himalayas, 590 miles/ 950km in 14 days 9 hours 36 minutes. The run was made at an average altitude of 42000 metres/13780 ft. Due to the altitude she had little appetite. In the course of the run she lost 14 pounds in weight out of a total body weight of 112 pounds - 12 % of her total body weight. Much of this was subcutaneous fat, but there was some muscle loss as well. It is interesting to speculate whether a man, with a lower proportion of body fat, and thus proportionally lower fat reserves, could have run the distance and in such a time with a similar low food intake.

The larger reserve of subcutaneous fat that women have has a further advantage - it gives them better insulation. The longer the ultra the greater the likelihood that there will be big variations in temperature and climate generally. Women are better protected against such variations than men. A classic example of this was in the Blackpool 48 hours held in November 1988. A field of top British male 24 and 48 hour performers faced a group of top women. On the first night the temperature dropped to -2ÃC, on the second night to 0ÃC. (It is probably no coincidence that James Zarei, perhaps the male with the least subcutaneous fat, who is very susceptible to cold, was the first to retire within the first 10 hours.) In that race women finished 1st, 3rd, 4th, 6th and 7th. The leading lady Hilary Walker, ran 227 miles for a new 48 hour women's world best performance.*

Cold is just one of a host of variables that may have to be faced in the course of a long ultra. Although speed, strength and running endurance are still important factors, another major asset is the ability to handle prolonged stress, both physical and mental. Many studies have shown that women cope better with stress than men. (Classic extreme examples of this are the Donner Party Wagon Train in the nineteenth century and the Siege of Leningrad in the last war.) Possibly this ability comes in part from the female's need to cope with the prolonged stress of childbirth. In past centuries women unable to cope with such stress would not have survived, nor in all probability would their offspring. Thus evolution over generations has discriminated in favour of stress-resistant women.

Studies of mental and psychological stress have also shown that women cope better than men. In my experience in long ultras men are more likely to quit if things go wrong, whereas women just keep going.

Having hopefully made a case that women's success in ultrarunning is due to better tactics, better insulation and a greater ability to deal with prolonged stress, there is also another reason why women win ultras outright. Often the woman runner is the class athlete in the race, she is not opposed by a male athlete of equivalent ability. Eleanor Robinson, Ann Trason, Hilary Walker, Sandra Barwick and Marianne Savage among several other women have all won ultra races outright. All of them at one time or another have set women's world bests.

Men depressed by finishing second to the fair sex should be philosophical. In the greatest ultra of them all - Life - women consistently achieve greater performances, outliving their male peers. Basically they are just tougher!

* Interestingly in another long distance sport, where fat insulation could well be an important factor, women are also very competitive with men. The current absolute records at the time of writing for swimming the English and Irish Channels were both held by women

The late Hilary Johnson was a mature, experienced international ultra runner who also managed the British women's ultra teams. A formidable performer in her own right – she won ultra races outright, beating the men - she had a down to earth attitude to the challenges faced by women seeking to enter the world of ultrarunning.

The shape you're in.

Why is it that any fella who puts on a tracksuit and T-shirt over whatever passes for his body gets rounds of applause? He's giving it a go, having a try, just doing it. His torso may make a jelly look rigid, his footfall may register on the Richter scale but all credit to the good old boy, he cares about his health and wants to see his kids grow old. Just let "Er indoors", the missus, the partner, better half or girlfriend emerge in shorts and a T-shirt in daylight and there are problems. "You're not going out in that! You'll get black eyes! Those tights show your bum up." Even when you finally manage to escape it's - "Will you be back in time to cook dinner? Don't go too far, you'll get lost, mugged, raped, molested!"

The attitude of men in a man's world is certainly improving, but slowly. For these females who are breaking new ground in family or career tradition, it is still very much an uphill struggle. Disapproval of partners who are left with children, household chores, silence, an exhausted lover, is a strong deterrent.

Is the whole thing worth the hassle? The answer has got to be an enormous YES. A woman seeking equality in time, value, opportunity, and ability to follow her own interests will be a much more relaxed, contented, fulfilled and whole individual. If her interests are athletic, then the extra bonus is that she will look good, feel great and have loads of energy for living the life she wants. If there are children involved they also benefit from their mother's positive, lively attitude and zest for life. It may take some harsh words and brave actions to begin, but after the initial "slings and arrows" the running lifestyle becomes the "norm" and raises less and less comment. Be happy with what you are doing and if your shape is not as you would like, then imagine it is, until it is.

As your shape changes you may find that you do not lose weight so much as lose inches. Muscle mass is heavier than fat but much more compact, so you can be thinner but weigh the same as you did. Care must be taken, especially with younger women, that this weight loss is not taken to extremes and anorexia allowed to develop. Women who exercise need an adequate diet or they cannot continue. They should ensure that they take in all essential nutrients in proper quantities for their height and build. I will talk about obsessions later.

As distance, endurance and speed improve people find that the odd five miles round the block is no longer adequate. They need to push themselves harder, faster, further to obtain fulfilment. There may be a problem here for a female erstwhile jogger, turning into a serious athlete and expecting to compete at weekends, formerly family time. Time management and an understanding and knowledgeable family and friends are necessary. Marathons and shorter races can be accomplished in half a day but ultras take ages so parking the kids with a neighbour for a couple of hours is not on. Your weekend schedule needs careful planning so you feel relaxed and all those concerned know your needs and you know and have catered for, theirs. If your family are coming out as your support crew they will need appropriate feeding, watering and toilet facilities, as you will. Plan these well in advance and they will not sap your immediate pre race energies. If they are staying home they will still need feeding, so take early appropriate action to see that they are happy and you are not fretting over their welfare. The people to whom you return after your run need to be aware of your probable condition which could last several days. You will be immobile, tired, sore and very short tempered!! Warn them in advance!

An increasingly advanced level of fitness will gradually contrive to change the shape of the female body. Fat will be used up and the body will become more slender and less soft than previously. In fact many female ultra athletes resemble a youth in their shape. I always take it as a compliment when other athletes mistake me for a fella from the rear! What may upset some female ultra runners however, is the loss of boobs! There are no big busted ultra runners - sorry! What an "ultra female" should avoid is becoming so slender that she has used up all her body fat. Her periods will cease at this stage and this is a danger signal. Osteoporosis begins to weaken the bones, the female hormone levels fall and skin, hair and nails are badly affected. Ultra females need some fat on their bodies. This is what feeds you during a long run, you can't succeed without it.

Kit to cope.

Wear what you feel good in. If you feel you are "uncontrolled" in any body area then wear garments that will pin you down to your own satisfaction. If you need an enveloping tent then wear a big T-shirt, and baggy shorts or bottoms. You must feel good about your image or you will never get out of the door. You may feel improvements can be made, but wear what you are happy with at the time. As a woman, do not feel that you should be invisible to avoid comment or censure. This is not a ploy to get bystanders to encourage you, but you should always make your presence obvious by clothing or personal acknowledgement at many stages in your training run. Should, God forbid, anything happen to you, then the more people who have seen you pass and remembered that, the better your chances. This is not an offhand comment but most important.

There is now lots of kit to cater for people who want to run, beginners through to International athletes. Talk to people whom you trust and who know what is on offer. Don't expect the new "all in one" will dramatically improve your Tuesday 5 miler or the latest leotard will increase your aerobics mobility. Wear what suits you and what you feel comfortable in.

For ultra races, choose clothes that fit properly to start with, avoiding cheap vests or shorts with exposed stitching against your skin. Some women find a stretch nylon vest gives all the support they need, plus a cotton T-shirt to prevent chaffing. Always wear a bra or lycra short top even if you don't really need to, otherwise nipples will rub on a sweaty top and, believe me, it is very painful. You have blood running down the front of your T shirt and you can't shower in comfort for a week! Don't wear a T Shirt or top which flaps on arms or body. After several hours running, the part being hit by the garment will bruise and become increasingly painful.

Your feet are the most important part of you during a long run and take quite a hammering. Make sure they are well vaselined and your socks fit exactly with no wrinkles or seams to rub or blister. Smaller footed females may need to look at children's socks for an exact fit, big foots like me are adequately catered for. Make sure toenails are cut short and square - you can't see nail varnish in trainers! Try different sock combinations. Some women dislike wearing socks at all - including me, others wear one or two thick or thin pairs. Find out what suits you during training. Mistakes whilst racing are extremely painful. There is enough written about shoes to fill an encyclopaedia. Just make sure you buy shoes that you can wear for hours and not necessarily the ones with the best hype. Shoes, like feet, are all different. Try lots until you are happy, then stick! Try and get two or three pairs of shoes you can run in and remember that ultra running kills shoes quickly. Even though as a female you are lighter than the target zone male athlete so your shoes will last longer than average, check them regularly for wear and loss of shape. Try to keep two or three pairs on the go during training. A regular change eases your feet and you may feel better with a change during an ultra race, many athletes do this.

By experimenting with different clothes in training during different weather conditions you will discover where those clothes chafe. Put vaseline on any vulnerable spots. Other points to grease are the under side of each upper arm, and where the upper fat pads of the thighs rub together. [Ensure these areas stay lubricated.]

The crotch seam of tights often chafe. Using scissors cut the seam right along each side of the stitching of an old pair for about six inches. This will give you additional freedom, and most nylon and lycra tights will stand up to the washing machine even after this treatment. Ordinary running shorts worn over the tights provide modesty, warmth and protect against leg chaffing. They also enable quick, less revealing pit stops.

Women should not feel inhibited over pitstops however. Most male athletes stop when the need arises unconcerned about onlookers. Continental females are totally unabashed at taking a public pee when needed. "Athlete" is a non sexist noun so feel free to do what is necessary when it's necessary without embarrassment. I have found that this is totally accepted by all athletes in an ultra race.

Running and Periods.

We can't escape - we're stuck with them. Some women cruise through every month without bother; others put on 1/2 a stone and feel like Michelin Man who has been shot through the abdomen. Most are in between these two. It has been proven that the greatest period problems are eased by exercise. The pains and the fainting bouts can be better controlled by a fitter woman, as the body can more readily regulate what it can accept. It has already been asked to regulate its heart, lungs, intestines etc when running. The old ideas of things you cannot do during a period are pretty much thrown out now.

Moreover a surprising number of women still think they should not exercise, swim, do aerobics etc. during a period. This is not so. The only thing that should stop you doing whatever you want to do on any day of the month is your own choice. You may not perform as well during a period as you do normally, you may have to take your exercise a little easier for a day or two, but there is no need to stop totally. If there are problems with loss amount, then you must be confident that the methods you employ to counter this do work. You may have to double up on protection while you exercise to start with, but as you get fitter these problems should ease as the body adapts. When you reach a time when your races matter a great deal and dates clash with period times your doctor can supply a course of pills which will delay your period a few days without any damage to the body.

It makes sense to have available supplies of tampons or pads with you to an ultra event of extended duration, just in case. Periods have been known to start during such races! A tendency for unexpected periods to start during or immediately following an ultra race has been noted by female ultrarunners. Blood seems more turgid than sweat and can cause major chafing problems, so vaseline is also a necessary supply. Try to make sure your back up team has everything you may require. Baby wipes are good as a clean-up. If you have no supporters then carry supplies in a light, well fitting bum bag.

Running and Pregnancy.

Pregnancy is a natural part of being a woman. It is not a time to suddenly take up exercise but you should be able to continue your training throughout pregnancy. There are stages during pregnancy when training is difficult. The first three months are very tiring even though your body shape has hardly changed. Internal changes can make you exhausted and severely limit your physical energy. Listen to your body and don't push yourself at this time. I know several people, myself included, who only knew they were pregnant because their race times worsened even though they were putting in 100% effort. If this happens, even though you have stopped having periods because of low body fat, if you could be pregnant then do have a test quickly to avoid flogging yourself unnecessarily.

The second three months are usually uncomplicated if you are lucky. Of course your doctor will monitor your progress and you must abide by his/ her wishes. You should also make him/her aware that your lifestyle includes exercise and you are not willing to sacrifice this without good cause. Increased weight means stronger, more supportive shoes may be needed. Also your centre of gravity changes so you may have to run on more level ground, if you normally enjoy cross country running, to avoid trips and falls.

The third three months is a containment exercise! The discomfort of movement can be totally inhibiting. As soon as you attempt a jog you need to rush to the loo. You feel like a beached whale with indigestion. If you can stand the initial horrors these feelings will go and your abdominal muscles will tighten and hold you firmly so you can jog in relative comfort. Wear loose kit so you don't feel constricted and have confidence that you are providing oxygen rich blood to your child.

Child birth can possibly cause bladder displacement which is a common cause of stress incontinence - possibly better known as 'down hill dribble' (it is the inappropriate loss of urine due to the jarring of the downhill running). If the bladder is emptied often there is less urine to leak, so a pit stop before a long down hill is a partial remedy. Pelvic floor exercises and specific remedial exercises can be prescribed by your doctor and they do help if practiced regularly. (Another cause of stress incontinence is the loss of tone in the urethra itself due to estrogen loss when ovaries are removed or stop functioning. This oestrogen loss can be remedied by an oestrogen prescription.)

Women still menstruating can experience mid cycle fluid loss during a run because excess secretions during ovulation can overflow. This is not urinary incontinence and can be dealt with as you would a normal period.

Running with a family.

The little perishers take every instant of your time, raise your blood pressure, frazzle your nerves and make keeping your abode neat and smart an impossibility, They take each other apart all day long and have a relay crying team for the night shift which would win the Olympics. They make more washing and ironing than any Rugby team and you want some time to do some running!!?

What you need to do is find some like minded soul. Convert neighbours, find a play school or nursery, use your works' crèche or find a child minder locally. I know this may involve cash but it could be worth it for your peace of mind and health of body. It will also establish the fact that you are a person in your own right, needing your own time with your children and they will be much less likely to take you for granted as resident drudge.

You should appreciate that caring for a family is a full time occupation. If you do this as well as holding down a job then you are using up a fair amount of physical and mental energy. If you then attempt a training programme - no matter how easy, you will become tired. This is no reason to give up however, it is only a point to be acknowledged. Your body will adapt to whatever load you put on it. You should make your family aware of your needs. Let them understand your reasons for indulging in exercise. Make exercise the norm rather an irritating exception.

Finally - try and take the kids with you. Jog round the block with them first and then go and train. Get them to time you, involve them. Take them Orienteering when you can all run at your own pace. Let them share your joy and you share theirs. They will grow up much better balanced adults as a result and will not be afraid of being seen to try their best in their life's tasks.

During an ultra run or race it's really cheering to see and hear your family shouting for you. They can fetch your drinks and snacks and help you change kit or shoes when you are too stiff or sore to move. They can enjoy being a part of an ultra race. When you finish and tell your partner/family that you couldn't have done it without them you can watch the pride shine on their faces.

Running Later on.

Many women have taken to running later in life when their homes and families are secure and they find that their body does not suit the image they would like. By later in life, I do not mean 'old' but not a teenage athlete. The London Marathon inspired so many females to take exercise and some of these are now at International level. Most women can now see that taking exercise on a regular basis does not turn them into a muscle-bound monster, the likes of which we viewed in horror when they competed for Eastern Bloc countries. Instead it means they have more control over themselves - body and mind.

No matter at what age a woman starts running, it has advantages. It helps circulation and skin tone, muscle tone and shape, energy and vitality. Because of increased blood circulation and endomorphin production, it also improves outlook on life and a positive attitude. Far from feeling that life is passing you by, you find there are objectives to achieve, targets to meet and a whole new "raison d'Ôtre" in life. The menopause is more easily accommodated by a fit body. The ensuing thinning of bones is slowed measurably by females who have taken exercise on a regular basis. The waning of muscular strength causing older females to stoop and take on fat where they least want it, is slowed or halted by ensuring muscles are used, are strong and lean, especially across shoulders, down the back and across the abdomen. Heart and digestive problems are relatively rare in running females of any age.

It may be difficult for an older female to start to jog without any background fitness. In New York, USA, the more mature females who feel a need to improve their physical appearance and fitness start off with "power walking". They wear all the modern gear for running but walk rapidly and most energetically - not like a race walker, but just walk as fast as they can with a vigorous arm action and fast legs. This is definitely a wise start for anyone who finds herself suddenly overweight, flabby and short of breath. In England - unless you are in similar company, I think people may snigger (less fit people) but in Central Park, N.Y. there are so many of these females they are the 'norm' and nobody dares comment for fear of being handbagged! The message - do it in company.

Ultra running is a great asset for "late starters". Once basic fitness is established there may not be a liking for sprints and fast track work. The obvious direction for improvement and satisfaction is in greater distance. Many mature females have found that they cannot run quickly but can stick to their pace for hours in fair comfort. There are presently, some excellent ultra runners who disliked PE at school, never set foot on a track and hardly recognise the enthusiastic, energetic person that ultra running has made them.

Having this new found ability or success can lead to obsessive behaviour. This can take several forms. There is no bore like a running bore! Non stop talk about PBs, courses, times, reps, mileages and injuries can send a family to sleep or next door - beware! Runners need good food, an adequate diet, but this doesn't mean you need to convert your family and friends to eat what you eat. Your family may like fish and chips on a pre race Saturday night, you may be the only pasta muncher. If you have more than one sportsperson in your family, as I have, you may have to cater for different diets and training times. In this case a huge pasta pan and rice pan with quick meat or cheese sauces is an advantage. Plan in advance and teach your family to cook - male or female, and be flexible and tolerant.

If your family and friends tell you you are getting too thin, take notice. The onset of anorexia is hardly noticeable but its effects will last a lifetime. You can't run your body without adequate fuel so make sure you take enough calories in your diet to enable you to run the distances you want to. Calorie charts on intake and expenditure are readily available - so use them. Don't make mileage your guru. You are a person and a female first and an athlete second. Keep your life in proportion if you can. Aspects of it can wax and wane. Remember that this is not a practice run but the real final run in. Enjoy it, and you can walk forth as a fulfilled person with all the advantages this brings to you and your family. Ultra running magnifies the strengths possessed by female athletes which can go unrecognised in a male world. These attributes benefit not only family and friends but a raising of female kudos in society which can only be a positive step.

Finally

Women are wonderfully constructed beings. They can endure most things, cope with most things, do without food, drink, care and shelter, smile when they want to cry and cry when they should be smiling, give their all to their offspring, uphold their partner and still manage to be a person with a life of their own. A tall order!

Exercise is not a bolt-on extra, but an essential ingredient for any woman wanting to stay sane in a man's world. It gives a female an inner certainty that they do not need to justify their existence to any other person. That they are here as themselves - not somebody's mother, wife, girlfriend, granny, partner, sister, auntie, or any other relative. They know, recognise and accept their frailties and limitations, just as every man must do, but they also recognise their strengths and abilities, project these and use them.

The neurotic, insecure, indecisive, weak image must be eclipsed by the strong, secure, fit and able woman. This woman must be certain that her physical strength matches her mental strength.

Physical fitness through jogging, running and competing can ensure this physical and mental tenacity and enable a female to enjoy her role of - "Being a Woman".

Eleanor Robinson was the foremost female ultrarunner in the world and has set close to twenty ultra track bests, including four 6 Day marks. On the road she held the woman's course records in the Spartathlon and the Sydney to Melbourne; and also won the London to Brighton. She won ultra races on the Continent, in the U.S.A. and in Australia, competing in events from 50 miles up to 1000 miles. She was a match for all but the very top male ultra runners, particularly in races from 24 hours upwards.

Road running in general and ultra running in particular is the one branch of athletics where men and women compete on equal terms. We all stand on the same starting line, face the same course and weather conditions. Indeed, in some ultra races we even compete on equal terms for the awards. No distinction is made for sex and age. In fact the majority of other runners are in the veteran age group and have built up the necessary strength and endurance after years of training and racing. So if we are to compete alongside the men then our training must follow a similar pattern. Very little has been written about training for ultra distances and training methods seem to be as diverse as the individuals who compete. We have evolved our own training pattern to fit in with our own life-style, preferences etc. For women to be involved in sport at any level is much more difficult than for their male counterparts; this being due to the many differing roles facing modern women and their divided loyalties. For those of us with houses, families and a job it isn't always easy to fit in a demanding training programme too. However, the very fact that it is difficult makes the sense of achievement so much greater.

The key to the problem, for me lies in good organisation. A training programme has to be fitted in to everyday life. Running is only part of life - not the "be all and end all" of it. After a training session or race we are the ones who have to return home to cook the meal, see to the children, prepare for tomorrow etc. So it follows, that training has to be fitted in to suit each individual's needs.

Some athletes profess to train over prodigious mileages. One of my American rivals claims to do daily 30 mile runs. whilst a British girl says she has no training pattern and runs infrequently. Ultra running is essentially endurance and strength based, with little emphasis on speed. Having said that however, the best ultra athletes, both male and female, have very creditable marathon times. There are those however, who have never run faster than a 3hr marathon. Most ultra runners rarely venture into short road races, finding themselves lacking in speed but there are a few, myself included, who like to compete weekly at whatever distance is available. So it is apparent that there is some room in this sport of ours for everyone regardless of their particular strengths, weaknesses, age, sex or lifestyle. It is important to decide what your own aims are and how you can work this into your own life.

I favour in the main the concept of LSD for ultra runners but prefer to call it LONG STEADY DISTANCE as opposed to LONG SLOW DISTANCE. 'Steady' running is a very indecisive term and completely individualistic, i.e. a 'steady' pace for one person could be too fast or too slow for another. I use it to describe a pace of about 7 mins per mile. This is based on my average 10 mile race time of 60 minutes which makes my 'steady' pace 1 minute per mile slower than 10 mile racing pace. For training runs longer than 11 miles the pace will drop slightly but for runs shorter than 10 miles it will be slightly faster. So, I shall be 'pleasantly ' tired but still able to converse with a training partner should one be available.

Ultra running itself brings about a loss of speed. Struggling at the end of an event to achieve 5 mph or even 4 mph, it is no easy matter in the following days to get back to more respectable speeds. If no attempt is made to do this though, then your body gradually becomes incapable of raising the pace at all. As we get older too, then our pace naturally diminishes so I feel we must make a definite effort to counteract this. I include a weekly race as part of my training programme. Not so long ago I used to compete on the track at 800m, 1,500m and 3,000m Now I still find myself competing in 2 mile XC races. Usually I try to find a localmarathon or 10 mile road race.

Perhaps it is sensible to decide how much time is available each day for training and work out a schedule correspondingly. It may be possible to run to and from work or in the lunch hour. I get the first session of the day in at 6 am when the children are all in bed. 100 miles per week is a good base to aim for though there are those who are regularly over or under this distance. With two sessions a day the mileage soon mounts up. I find that because I race frequently at ultras (about 6-7 each year) very long training runs are unnecessary. There is a carry over effect and once you have worked slowly up to a training mileage that suits you then it becomes a question of maintaining the schedule. For those people who aim at one ultra a year - perhaps their local event, then it is a different matter.

So, having determined your available training time next decide what your aims are, both immediate and long term. These factors will dictate the shape of your training schedule. I use my weekly races as an important part of my training. Races involve hard, sustained running, the sort of effort that is impossible to reproduce in solitary training sessions. It also makes a welcome change for me to join a group of perhaps thousands of other like-minded people in a Sunday race, as almost all my training is done on my own.

It may be difficult to run in the early morning or too close to a meal and while this is obviously true it is also worth remembering that ultra races involve being able to run at all hours of the day and night. Races can start at any time between 4am and 8pm and multi-day events go on continuously. You have to be able to eat, drink and even sleep during races so though it may be uncomfortable having to put in a session too close after a meal, or having got straight out of bed it is all useful training.

Having built up your training to the point where you are confident enough to enter a race I have some suggestions which may be of help and if not all are applicable every time, a good number will be. You will learn most by first going along to watch, or better still, to help another competitor, acting as his/her support crew.

Though it is perfectly possible to get by on your own in a race the presence of a reliable handler can be a tremendous help. They will sort out your kit, make and hand out food and drink, keep a check on your pace, schedule and position etc. In this way you can appreciate at first hand just what is involved. Always go to an event expecting the worst. This way you will seldom be disappointed and often pleasantly surprised. Take everything you expect to need with you and extra besides. Even in international events the food and drink you require may not be available, It means that a great deal of thought and preparation is necessary in order to get to the start line well equipped.

For track races most athletes find it best to take their own tent, chairs, working equipment etc and be completely self-sufficient. Then, if the organisers promises are not fulfilled you can still comfortably get by. A hot drink at the end of a race or in the middle of the night can make a tremendous difference yet there are still ultra events where such a basic requirement is ignored. It is essential to eat frequently and most athletes will 'snack' right throughout an event. Few races, even very top class events, make provision for this.

Take everything you need - be warned. It is also worth bearing in mind that race organisers are male and some not even athletes themselves. I have yet to come across a female race organiser. Thus, problems specific to the ladies are often ignored. All events should provide track-side loos (usually the portable type) but even at a recent international 24 hour event the ladies were expected to make a 200m trip to the changing rooms and negotiate two flights of steps! While the men find it of little inconvenience to use the outside of the track, for the ladies it is not so simple, especially if, as often seems to be the case, it is the wrong time of the month! A simple beach wind-break can provide enough shelter if necessary.

Always take clothing for all weathers and several pairs of shoes. Even if you wear the same pair all the race the first thing you will want to do once you finish is to take them off. It is a relief to put a different pair on and in any case you may well find that your feet swell and you can no longer fit your racing shoes. After the 1986 Sydney/Melbourne event I had to borrow a pair of size '9s' for two days until I could get my own on. Sometimes it is sufficient just to remove the insoles. Finally, work out your plan for after the event. Will you have to drive yourself home? This is never a good idea so avoid it if at all possible. Will you have to provide a meal for the family? If so prepare it all beforehand, also anything you need to get ready for the following day. You won't feel up to doing anything once you get home.

I have built up my training gradually over the last 10 years and have held my current level now since 1987. I aim to run 100 - 120 miles (200 km) a week and this is broken down as follows:

Mon - Fri : 18 - 20 miles each day in 1, 2 or 3 sessions depending on work and home commitments. Two of these sessions will be long runs of three hours duration and one session will be a speed-endurance track session
   (e.g. 16 x 400 m, 8 x 800 m, 20 x 300 m or 5 x 1 mile)
   or a hill session.
Sat - Sun : 15 miles + race of ½ marathon or less. or
Sat - Sun : 5 - 10 miles + race marathon.

The weekly race is a very important part of my training schedule. I run it at 100% effort thus putting my body in a competitive situation very frequently. Because I am still successful at the shorter distances it also provides interest, variety, competition and change of pace, I don't ease down at all so my body has to get used to working hard while it is already tired, a very necessary component of ultra distance running.

So my basic plan is designed to enable me to compete at any distance, at any time. I like to put in an ultra event about every 6 weeks and I decide at the beginning of the year which events are to be the main ones. Then I can choose which events I shall use as a build-up to the key events.

For instance:-

Before the 100 km World Championship I would try to run several 100 km races and many marathons.

For a 24 hour race I would aim to run several ultras close together or back to back marathons.

For a multi-day race I would aim to run several 24 hour races and a 48 hour race.

The races chosen as build-up events are however important races in themselves. I never run ultras purely for training. So I would always aim for a world record distance in 24 and 48 hour events or under 8 hours in 100 km. My programme is on going. I never take a break and each race is preparation for the next one.

The other main difference would be in mental approach. Before each race I work out the plan for how I'd like it to go. Multi-day races require a lot of planning and preparation.

So to sum up:-

I have a BASIC training programme to cover the full range of distances

> A SHORT RACE at least every week is very important.
>
> I race an ULTRA about every 6 weeks.

The exact events chosen will depend on what my major targets are.

> EACH RACE IS IMPORTANT IN ITS OWN RIGHT

Whatever training programme you embark upon it will need to be flexible and varied. However well organised you are there is always the unexpected crisis that crops up. It also helps to have as varied a schedule as possible using different routes, distances, speeds and training partners.

If it all seems too much to cope with remember that if you really want to do something then you will always find a way, but if you don't then it isn't hard to find an excuse.

Marie Caldwell took up ultra running at the mature age of 52. Her successes have made her a role model for many women of her generation, and a local folk heroine.

You've heard the saying, 'Life begins at forty', well in my case, it was forty-five. I watched the first London Marathon on T.V., in 1981 and twelve months later, I finally summoned up the courage to start jogging - me a middle aged mother of four! Until then, I had never run a step, except in a dire emergency and apart from playing netball and tennis at teacher training college, in the late fifties, I had never taken part in any kind of sporting activity.

So it was that my life began at the age of forty-five, in the summer of 1982. During the next few years, I entered all kinds of races, winning age category prizes in most of them, simply because there were so few mature women running in those days. In June 1989, in Blackpool, I completed my fourteenth marathon and received the prize for the first lady over fifty. However, I realised that my times weren't improving so as I wasn't able to run faster, I'd try to run further.

I returned to Blackpool to compete in my first "24 Hour Race". It was the weekend of my fifty second birthday, in August the same year. The day of the race, I was numb with fear. What on earth was I doing on the start line with twenty-nine top class ultra runners - some of them record holders! I'd read about this type of event in "Training for Ultras" and realised that I'd need to start slowly, conserving as much energy as possible for the later stages. Food and drink would have to be taken regularly and in my case, often. I consumed vast quantities of rice pudding, bananas, bread and biscuits, all washed down with lemonade, tea, coke and water. I can honestly say that it was one of the best birthdays I have had and when at the end of the race I'd covered eighty-four miles, I was converted and eager to enter another.

I have to admit that I competed in this event after only five weeks of training, during which time, the afore mentioned book became my "Bible". The Blackpool race was a journey into the unknown and certainly intended as a one off, but since then I have taken part in thirteen ultra races. What made me continue in this branch of athletics was the encouragement and advice I received from the other runners and the friendly, relaxed atmosphere. Although there are very few women taking part, I have always been made to feel completely at home - despite being of mature years!

Age can be an advantage in ultra events. I'm far more likely to overtake the young hares than the old tortoises. In my talks to potential joggers, I try to get across that patience and brainwork play a large part in long distance races. Obviously fitness and training are essential too and pre-race planning is of the utmost importance. Unfortunately a lot of women have too many commitments to be able to give the necessary time to training. Over the last couple of years, I have evolved a schedule that works for me but everyone is different and what works for one runner might be totally wrong for the other. One has to be prepared to go back to the drawing board, if the results aren't as good as one had hoped.

From a "ticking over" base of thirty to forty miles per week, I build up gradually over a period of twelve weeks. I try to peak at a one hundred mile week before reducing the mileage again. The last couple of weeks I keep to just a few miles of gentle jogging, completely resting on the last two to three days. My longest run during the twelve week period is about twenty-two miles and the further the distance, the slower my pace. I also train with weights, twice a week, to build upper body strength. Our local leisure centre has a well equipped gym, with special concessions for the over fifties, three mornings a week. I find the rowing machine and the computerised "step" very beneficial. My own exercise bike comes into its own if the footpaths are slippery - a fall on the ice could see me out of running for months! Failure to train for any length of time would have a two-fold effect. Firstly, I would lose fitness and secondly my weight would rocket!

Prior to starting running, I spent my spare time reading cookery books and experimenting with all kinds of recipes; consequently I was forever dieting, as I put on weight very easily. Now I am able to eat what I like because the high mileage compensates for my liking for chocolate, ice cream, puddings etc. Having said that, I do try to stick to a healthy diet as much as possible and I always take a multivitamin tablet each day. At the first hint of a cold I run for the vitamin C and Zinc tablets which I find work for me - or is it psychological? My diet, during the last few days of training for an ultra-race, consists of plenty of bread, potatoes and pasta. Breakfast on race day will be muesli and loads of toast with either marmalade or jam. However, once the race starts, I really begin to enjoy myself; within an hour, I'll be guzzling rice pudding, bread and jam and bananas with plenty of drinks in between. I keep to this regime throughout the race, much to the amazement of some of my fellow competitors! It is quite usual for me to have gained a couple of pounds by the end of the race but if I don't keep eating, I know from experience that I will begin to feel faint and that would mean taking time out of the race to re-fuel.

My training schedule, diet and race strategy are carefully planned in advance but have to be adaptable; sights have to be lowered in unforeseen circumstances, e.g. a sudden deterioration in the weather. Occasionally, I choose to eat something on offer by the organiser and end up "bingeing" on it for the rest of the race. I liken it to having cravings during pregnancy! I start the race with the intention of covering five miles per hour for as long as possible, walking a lap on the hour and the half hour. However, "the best laid plans of mice and men..." and the pace drops to four and a half, then four until, at the best, I'm just about keeping forward momentum. Then I talk to myself, remind myself that I have to face the children when I get home and then consider taking up knitting instead!

I do receive a lot of encouragement from the male runners and their wives are very kind and support me too. I enjoy the friendly banter that goes back and forth. Running is a great leveller, where else could a fifty-five year old mum feel so at ease on her own? It is not unusual to arrive at a race to find I'm the only female but this helps me relax as there isn't the same pressure on me. All I need to do is improve my own performance and I'm quite happy seeing how many men I can beat!

Plodding on in my own sweet way, picking up tips here and there, has brought its rewards. (I owe a lot to Dave Cooper for his advice.) During the last three years, I have achieved British bests in all distances from thirty miles to twenty four hours on track, road and indoors. The question I'm most often asked is, "Don't you get bored running round and round a track?" On the contrary I find it relaxing, interesting, challenging and hopefully at the end, rewarding - boring never! Even competing at the Birmingham Indoor Arena, on a 200 metre track was fun, apart from the severe banking at either end,

For the first time, though, men were aware that women are normally at a disadvantage when it comes to the "calls of Nature". At an indoor event, men have to leave the track, too!! The track did cause me more blisters than usual but the six European records which I set, more than compensated.

I have only taken part in one "100km" race, that being in Nottingham, 1992. Everything was going to plan, despite high temperatures, until the final six miles. The most awful storm arrived and the few other remaining runners took shelter. It was very lonely out there, even the ducks vanished but I knew I had to keep going for the magical sub twelve hours or what would I have told the children? A quick sprint over the line and I'd done it - 11h 58m 40s. I do prefer the duration type of event, though, where everyone finishes together, then I don't keep the officials waiting! My outdoor track event of 1992, was back in Birmingham, with a personal best of 103.5 miles; my last race as an over fifty and twenty miles further than Blackpool race, three years before. Definitely my best year to date, as regards ultras.

Generally speaking, I have suffered a severe personal trauma this same year and I can honestly say that running has been my saviour. Training has helped to relieve the stress and the ensuing success has improved my self image - some kind people tell me I'm looking younger! I live in a small town and have become quite well known for my escapades. In 1990, I was voted Sportswoman of the Year by the Sports Advisory Council. I write a column for the women's page of the local paper and only recently was asked to start an adult beginners' group for Bury Athletic Club. I have just been featured as a "role model" in Age Concern's magazine and the society for retired professional and business men has invited me to speak about my exploits.

I think I am seen as a local curiosity by some. It is not unusual to strike up a conversation, whilst queuing for a bus or waiting to be served at the fish stall on Bury Market. Suddenly I am asked the familiar question, "Aren't you the runner?" Nine times out of ten, this is followed by "Oh, I can't even run for a bus!" or "I tried it once but I got out of breath". The next most popular question is, "Have you always been a runner?" to which I reply, tongue in cheek, "Oh yes, ever since I was forty-five!" Occasionally, I get, "You must be mad!" which I suppose is only to be expected. One or two people actually admit to envying me but a conversation during a dinner only last week, took a rather different course. I was introduced to an elderly, local business man, who knew someone who had run in the New York Marathon. When I said I hadn't been there, he wanted to know why not. "I suppose it's the expense". "Right, you get your name down and I'll pay for you to go". I didn't hear a word of the after dinner speech! Now that I've moved into the over fifty-fives, it seems life may just be beginning - again!

More Ideas for Ultra Training

Every other article in this booklet was written by an experienced ultra runner, all with their own views on training. I am not a runner and therefore have no axe to grind. My international contacts have given me a chance to discover training methods and ideas not mentioned in the previous articles. The ideas came from individuals, letters, books and magazines. As with all the other articles it is up to the reader to assess how valuable a particular idea would be for him or her.

Running Style

It is important to develop as economical a running style as possible. Runners like Derek Clayton and Alberto Salazar developed a short striding shuffle which did much to make up for their relative deficiencies in oxygen uptake etc. Arthur Newton said 'The longer you stride the more you bob up and down, and the sooner you tire. You ought to almost slither your feet over the ground, going as near to touching it without actually doing so'. Jean Lamothe recommends the use of the short stride for another reason. The longer the stride the greater the force necessary to move the legs. Short strides, keeping the weight of the body over the legs as much as possible, are more economical and less tiring in very long races such as the 24 hours.

The Long Run

The benefits of very long runs - over 35 miles - are queried by many people who say they result in overtraining and that adequate rest afterwards is difficult for ordinary runners. [A rest day on Monday, following the week's long run, is an essential part of one top runner's training.] Some people prefer to do the 'long' run in two parts, one perhaps longer than the other, on Saturday and Sunday. Rune Larsson, the top Swedish ultra runner, runs to work and back once a week, 25 miles each way. Jean-Paul Praet has built up his long run up to 65km/40 miles out of a total weekly mileage of 125-150 miles. Bruce Fordyce never runs over 40 miles in training, and probably will only do that once a year.

The rest of his 'long' runs are in the 25-35 mile, and 18-25 mile range. These are tackled in a hard/easy fashion - a longer run one weekend will be followed by a shorter one the following weekend. In 1983 when Bruce won the Brighton he only included two really long runs - 55k/34 miles and 60k/37 miles - in his training with no loss of endurance.

Marathon-type training for ultras

With over 10,000 entrants the Comrades Marathon is the largest ultra in the world. The event is highly regarded in South Africa, attracting most of the top distance runners, sometimes to the detriment of marathon running in that country. Because the Comrades is such a major event there is far more commercial and academic interest in ultras in South Africa than elsewhere. Many of the top runners, like Bruce Fordyce, are also very competent marathon runners, and as a result approach the event basically as they would a marathon. They naturally make adaptations to their training to cope with the hills and length of the 55 mile/90km race.

The top two competitors in the Comrades at the moment are Bruce Fordyce and Bob De La Motte. A summary of a training schedule devised by Bob appears below, reprinted by kind permission of SARunner. I have highlighted the hill training and interval training as being of particular interest. The training suggested is very demanding and should not be used by novices or those not capable of completing the Brighton within 7 hours.

After four weeks of 55-60 miles per week easy running hill runs can be incorporated into one's training as follows:

A hill running session should begin with 1 - 2 miles easy running as a warm up. The chosen hill should not be unreasonably steep and should not be longer than 300 yards. Although a hard effort sprint the 300 yard run should be completed without reducing one to a crawl. Five repetitions, with hard running uphill and relaxed downhill to start with, increasing the number of 'reps' by two a week up to a total of ten. The last repetition should be run at the same speed as the first.

A track session should start with 15 minutes relaxed stretching followed by a warm up of at least two miles including three or four short 50 yard sprints. Such sessions should be incorporated into a training programme only after a good distance base has been established, including a 10 mile run twice a week run at 6 minute mile pace.

The recommended track reps are:-

Week 1 10 x 200m   with 200m recovery jog between each repetition.
Week 2 8 x 400m   "
Week 3 6 x 600m   "
Week 4 4 x 800m   "

Each rep to be run as fast as possible with the last as fast as the first. During the next four weeks the long distance runs are increased - 28 miles, 36 miles, 28 miles 36 miles, the hill and track sessions are suspended and the 10 mile 'fast' run is replaced by a 15 mile easy. Then the Sunday run is cut back to 20 miles and the hill and track are re-introduced. The track sessions should now be on successive weeks - 10 x 400 metres, 8 x 600 metres, 6 x 800 metres and 5 x 1000 metres. The reduced mileage should allow you to concentrate on the quality of your sessions. You should now be ready to cut back the mileage dramatically for the final week prior to your target. Each Monday is taken as a rest day. Such days are an essential part of the training, allowing the body to recover and re-build. The week should be organised so that a hill, track or fast run is followed by an easy run - usually 5 miles.

Bruce Fordyce prefers longer intervals because they more closely simulate the pattern of continuous running combined with surges. He recommends:

1 x 800 metres   with 400 metres jog recovery,
1 x 1000 metres   "
1 x 1200 metres   "
1 x 1000 metres   "

An alternative is 1 x 800 metres, 5 X 1000 metres with 600 metre jog recoveries. This should be followed by an easy 2 mile run. If a track is not available he uses a 'fartlek' session, using lamp posts or trees as markers. Bruce also fits in a midweek 15-18 mile run at ultra race pace. (Bob also suggests a 10 mile run see above).

Tapering training as one approaches a major event is crucial, and it is essential that rest, as opposed to last minute training, is the keynote of the final week prior to the race. It is better to start a race slightly overweight and slightly undertrained than overtrained!

Training the mind

"The power of the mind is an awesome thing and whenever people ask for advice or running, I always stress that it is the mind that needs conditioning as much as the body. One must cultivate a stubbornness bordering on the fool-hardy. This can be achieved as much in a negative fashion as in a positive way - that is, to keep a little back, so that one doesn't go into will-power when not racing. Will power seems to accumulate, like a battery on charge, provided one doesn't keep expending that power needlessly. A few years ago, I ran a string of ultras, one a week during one autumn period [4/9/82 6:32 Amiens 100k; 11/9 6:39 Winschoten 100k; 25/9 6:44 Santander 100k; 16/10 6:41 Hamm 100k; 31/10 6:36 Montlucon 100k - Ed.] The effect was a cycle - deplete and replenish. At the end of the 'season', it was as if I had run for months without racing" - Martin Daykin.

A constant theme in the writings of many experts on long distance training is patience and caution. In training it pays to be patient, the body takes time to adjust to each new level of stress. Mileage should be increased by about 5% a week, or else 10% with that distance held for two weeks. If you have a persistent ache or feel under the weather take the day off. There will not be any great loss in endurance. If, in the course of a long run, you get the first twinges of an injury, stop. Pushing on to the finish will only aggravate the problem. Always err on the conservative side in your training. Don't attempt to do more than you planned to do no matter how fresh you feel at the finish. Don't try anything new on the day of the race. All new equipment and new ideas should be tried out during the months preceding the event. Such cautious behaviour is the cornerstone of the success of Bruce Fordyce, perhaps the canniest of modern ultra runners.

Hard/Easy Training

Some runners advocate the hard-easy training developed by Bill Bowerman and Bill Dillenger. Kenny Moore finished fourth in the 1972 Olympic Marathon training one day hard followed by two easy. (Perhaps Cavin Woodward's frequent racing interspaced with relatively low mileage is a version of this.) Steve Warshawer (7.08 - 100km/ 142 miles - 24H) aims to run about 10 out of every 14 days and will sometimes take two consecutive days off. The theory is that hard training breaks down the muscle tissues and the mitochondria which convert fuel into energy becomes swollen and inefficient. A day's break or a low mileage day gives the body a chance to repair itself, time for waste products to be dispersed and allows the mitochondria content of the muscles to increase. Without the rest some of the damage will remain and the gradual build up of waste may lead to injury. The rest days enable you to train harder or longer than you could otherwise. Thus you can in fact end up with a higher weekly mileage than before with less chance of injury. As American Skip Hamilton says, the secret of successful racing and training is finding the best combination of rest and stress.

One important thing to remember is that your long run should be considered as a hard day, not an easy day, even though the run is tackled at an easy pace. Some people may prefer to organise their training on a hard week/easy week basis.

Overtraining

Overtraining is a problem any runner has to face until they learn how their body reacts to training.

If you take a record of your weight and pulse rate first thing in the morning, and the number of hours you sleep you can tell when a rest day is indicated. Signs are:

1. Your resting pulse rate first thing is increased by 10%.
2. You feel the start of illness such as a cough or sore throat. [Training when you are under the weather is a good way of prolonging any problem]
3. You get 10% less sleep than normal.
4. A sudden weight loss of 3%.
5. You feel extremely tired.
6. You are very thirsty.

Not just running

Non-running training can be useful as an alternative or supplement to traditional high mileage. There is evidence that general conditioning is very important in the longer events. A case in point is Christine Barrett. She is well known for the limited amount of running training she does, sometimes going for four or five days without running at all. Yet in April 1984 she set a world 100 mile road best of 15:07 and in May a 6 Day best of 421.7 miles. The background of these two performances is very interesting. In October 1983 she competed in the Hawaii Ironman Triathlon. Her preparation for that event, and her subsequent training actually involved limited amounts of cycling and little running. In fact her cycling following the Ironman was limited to only one or two short rides a week. She taught aerobics for 4 x 1 hour sessions a week and also took in 4 x * hour sessions of intensive swimming weekly. She did very little running. The aerobic work involved a lot of upper body work, and also did much to strengthen her stomach and back muscles, important in races of 24 hours and longer. She found the swimming greatly improved her breathing and it was obviously good cardio-vascular training. Such success with non-specific training is perhaps due more to talent, mental attitude and fitness than the training itself?

However Christine was not alone in advocating swimming and aerobics as ultra training! (See Erik Seedhouse's article.) Swimming properly forces you to breathe in a rhythmic and controlled way. This is a good habit for an ultra runner to develop. Moreover, since you are horizontal when swimming, your heart has to work harder against gravity - with each contraction your heart is pumping 10 to 20% more blood. Regular swimming also aids general conditioning and building up upper body strength, often lacking in distance runners. Some ultra runners have used swimming as a relaxation (almost massage). When Martin Daykin was running at his peak (see Training the Mind above) he used to swim a mile in approximately 25 minutes twice a week, on a Friday and a Monday. He found that swimming acted like a massage, speeding recovery. Finally swimming is a useful way of keeping fit when injured, and will improve the blood supply to the injured area. It provides gentle exercise for the injured area without forcing it to bear your weight or take the impact of running.

Other ultrarunners have also found aerobics useful. Steve Warshawer went to three or four classes a week which he found has improved his flexibility while building up his overall body strength and muscle tone in muscle groups not normally used in running. Steve's aerobic work was done using Heavy Hands [light hand-held weights - 3-4 pounds], which he also uses occasionally in his running training. (The Human Performance Research Laboratory at Brigham Young University stated that running with such weights results in a rise in oxygen uptake, thus intensifying the training. However training with weights will only improve fitness not speed.)

Bruce Fordyce did gym work three times a week all year round. In his opinion general gym work increases flexibility, improves general body condition which enables a good running action to be maintained longer and it also prevents injuries as a result. In his gym sessions Bruce also used weights. He worked on those leg muscles most affected by downhill running - quadriceps, the calves, the stomach and the back. Jeff Hagen, an American trail runner, advocated working on the hip adductors and on the thigh adductors as well. This is again to combat the effects of downhill running. Lion Caldwell, and Steve Warshawer used nautilus-type training to improve upper body strength; Warshawer, prior to his move over to Heavy Hands aerobics, used low weight/ high repetition Nautilus workouts four or five times a week. Bruce Fordyce also did some upper body and arm work. Nearing a major race he cut back on the weight he lifts and the number of sessions.

Bicycling as an alternative to the long run

Some people advocate extended bike rides as a replacement for part of the long slow training run/s. It provides extended cardio-vascular exercise yet does not involve the stress and fatigue associated in a long run. The suggestion is that the bike ride replaces one third of the long run/s. However when he was forced to use the bike alternative when injury curtailed his long runs prior to the L.A. Olympics John Tuttle (US) found although he was fit enough the bicycling worked on different muscle groups and his running muscles weren't up to the demands of the full marathon distance. So bicycling has its uses and its limitations.

Hiking as training

A feature of the British ultra scene in recent years has been the appearance of members of the Long Distance Walkers Association in road and track ultras. Hill walkers and runners like Hilary Walker and Richard and Sandra Brown have made a big impact on the sport. Interestingly Jean and Francoise Lamothe advocated going off into the mountains and hills, clambering over rocks and boulders, as a good final preparation for a 24 hour race. They believed it improved one's general fitness which was important in such a race. With Francoise capable of covering 114 miles at the age of 64 their theory had good supporting evidence.

Fluid replacement drinks in ultras

Both in South Africa and the United States research has been made into replacement drinks in endurance sports such as ultras. In events lasting longer than two or three hours the body needs water and carbohydrates. Up until recently 'sugar' drinks have slowed the stomach emptying, delaying hydration, and so have been watered down, thus making carbohydrate intake negligible. An answer to this is the use of glucose polymers, and several drinks now include these as the carbohydrate source. Such drinks can be consumed up to a concentration of 7 per cent. Such drinks are very useful up to 100km, beyond which easily assimilated carbohydrate food is needed as well.

Rune Larsson came from a country with little or no tradition of ultrarunning, yet seemed to be a born ultrarunner. His credentials were impressive - a 2:18 marathon runner, a sub seven hour 100km runner and over 163 miles/262km in 24 hours on the track. His greatest successes were in the Spartathlon, a rugged point to point course that, as you will see from the article below, suited the personality of this tough Swede)

First of all, let me tell you a little about my athletic background. How I'm training today may be interesting, but it is just a link in a long chain.

At the age of eight I decided to become a marathoner when I got older. In the meantime I had to satisfy my desire for endurance sports with cross-country skiing and orienteering, but in 1972, when I was 16 years old, an old dream came true, as I ran my first marathon. My time was 3:04:24, and now I needed new dreams to dream. One dream was to run faster and another dream was to run longer.

At that age I ran 10 - 30 kilometres a day at a comfortable pace, and I loved it. Lots of self-proclaimed experts tried to save me from a training they were convinced would break me down, but I was stubborn enough to do what I believed in. The 'experts' wanted me to run lots of intervals and hill repeats. If I had followed their advice, I would not have been a runner today, because I really hated that kind of training.

Luckily, I was blessed with a lack of athletic success all through my first years of competitive athletics. That helped me adopt a very special philosophy about my running and it also made me set my goals straight - I'm doing this for fun. One may say it was a loser's reason to run, but today it feels very good to know that I can start a race and enjoy it without winning it.

At the age of 23 I ran my first ultra-distance race a 51 kilometre trail race, and won it. That was the first real race I had ever won, and the unexpected success inspired me to increase my training to 200 kilometres a week, at a pace of 5mins/kilometre. Earlier I had only averaged 80 - 120 a week. There was no time to train more, because I studied full-time and worked part-time as a security guard.

In 1980, at the age of 24, I got a scholarship for cross-country and track at United States International University in San Diego. For the first (and only) time in my life I had a coach. I ran 160 - 200 kilometres a week and the training consisted mostly of hard steady runs over very hilly terrain. It was during this period I set all my personal bests at shorter distances.

When I came home to Sweden again in 1983, I went back to my beloved training method of 200 kilometres a week at 5 mins/kilometre. That's the way I like it.

Now, let me tell you how I have been training for the last four years. My running year starts in October (after the Spartathlon) with a 6 weeks long recovery period. Recovery means running 50 - 100 kilometres a week. To go into a period of hard training with a worn body and a mind that is not burning with desire to train, is not very likely to give good results.

When I let myself train hard again I do 160 - 240 kilometres a week without feeling any compulsive pressure that I must do it. As soon as the snow comes, I wax my skis. It can be 30 - 50 kilometres a day when the snow is fine. Skiing gives me a break from running and it is as much fun to ski as it is to run. The muscular and cardio-vascular benefits of skiing are good as well, and saves joints and tendons as it gives the body an excellent chance to repair all little damages running may have caused.

When the snow has melted I do most of my training in the woods. No trail can be too hilly, too muddy, or too rough for me. Running in the woods is good for the motorics of the muscle, since one constantly has to adjust the strides to roots, rocks, and other minor obstacles. Since I love nature, the trails can give peace of mind and a certain joy of running that I can't find on the roads or on the sidewalks of a suburban housing estate.

During my summer vacation I do lots of canoeing and kayaking. This is great pleasure and strengthens the abdominal muscles. Strong back and stomach muscles are, I believe, very beneficial for an ultra-runner. If one can't hold the posture when fatigue sets in, the running economy will deteriorate. I kayaked 810 kilometres in 1987.

Every summer and winter I treat myself to adventures on the waters or in the woods. I load my backpack with tent, sleeping bag, maps, compass, and lots of food, and head out or home from somewhere. My longest walk was 750 kilometres in 18 days and 730 kilometres is the longest of my canoe adventures. In the winter I take long trips on ski and sleep under the stars at night. The reason why I do these adventures is for the adventure itself, but they also give me very good endurance training as well as knowledge about how I react under extended periods of physical stress under primitive conditions. The psychological benefits of hard adventures are great. A 24 hour run on tartan, with at the most 200 metres to a handler and food of my own choice seems so undramatic when one remembers three days on ski with 20 kilos on the back and cold mornings in the sleeping bag.

Whenever I have time, I do a long run of 50 kilometres or more. By doing long runs I have explored every trail within 30 kilometres from where I live. When I feel the urge for an adventure and some new scenery I buy a one-way ticket and take the train or bus to somewhere and run home. Those runs can be up to 100 kilometres and they are more adventures than work-outs. I do them just for fun.

I race just a few times every year but then I try to peak. About six weeks prior to the race I take one or two weeks of easy training, so my body will be well rested. Then I run a lot during three weeks, 250 - 350 kilometres a week, and the last week before the race I run just a little every day.

After the race I make sure I don't start training hard again until I'm well recovered. If my resting pulse is still elevated I take that as an indication that the body needs more time to repair itself.

As far as racing goes, I think I could benefit from running lots of marathons at a comfortable but fairly good pace, about 2:33 - 2:40. That would build strength for the 100 kilometres but would not wear me out. Unfortunately, I have neither the time nor money to go to many races. I'm working 7 days a week teaching physical education and preventive medicine Monday to Friday and working as a maintenance man Saturday and Sunday mornings. Rest, this essential component of any training schedule suffers. I do rarely sleep more than six hours a night. Here is another room for improvement.

A good mental attitude about training, competing, and the hardships of extreme races, is very important. After all, it is the brain that tells the body to keep running when every cell is worn and there are many hours to go to the finish line. If the brain is full of negative thoughts and emotions about running with fatigue, cramp, and a stomach that can't hold anything down, one would have a hard time bringing out the best under difficult circumstances.

One important aspect of my training is to build positive feelings about fatigue and other hardship. I would never do any kind of training that would break my mental attitude and destroy my great love for running. Every long run and every adventure in the woods is a kind of mental and motivational training for me.

Russell Prince, the current New Zealand record holder for the 100km, made a major impact on the Ultra World with a powerful run in the 1990 Duluth 100km World Cup where he was second, after leading for much of the race.

He has also run the two fastest 50 miles ever run in New Zealand. This arti-
cle on his training was written by Stuart Payne and appeared in the New
Zealand Ultra Newsletter and is published with their kind permission.

The first thing to keep in mind is that Russell is not just an ultra-runner; he is a multi-sports competitor: running, cycling, canoeing and he is always training across these three disciplines. This enables him to develop overall body strength, stamina and speed without excessive miles of running training.

Russell's philosophy is that constant high mileage training destroys you. "Running knocks you about."

Because in the lead-up period for the 50 miles he is also competing in other priority events, such as the Coast-to Coast Longest Day event, his training obviously has much that is unique about it. Also this year the Brighton 50 was also part of his build-up for the Westfield Sydney-to-Melbourne.

As far as the Brighton 50, in New Zealand goes, though, the targeting for it starts with the Kepler mountain run at the end of the first week in December (a 5 hour race). Soon after this he starts a six week training scheme for the Coast-to-Coast.

The weekly run-down for the 1991 Brighton 50 looks like this.
For 6 weeks to early February and the Coast-to-Coast.
Running: 2 x 3 hour mountain run (23k) at 90% aerobic capacity plus 10k a day on remaining days alternating hard (32 to 34 minutes) and slow (40 minutes).
Cycling; At least an hour a day usually in a low gear, sometimes a 4 hour ride.
Canoeing: Each day.

This regimen totals about 25 hours of training per week which would equal 200 miles+ of pure running. But actual running is only about 100km per week. Russell contends that 200 miles a week would destroy him, 100km as part of multi- event training works better.

Included in this 6 weeks, on Jan 12, was the Wild Challenge multi-sport event of 6/7 hours including a 3 to 4 hour run.

Feb 9 Coast-to-Coast Longest Day, 12 hours of cycle/run/paddle/cycle.
After the Coast-to-Coast.

Running: 20 mile Sunday run plus 5k-10k runs with rest day Friday. This still does not exceed 100km running per week. The rest day reinforces Russell's view that too much mileage is stressful.

Cycling: Each day.

Canoeing: Each day.

4 weeks out from the Brighton 50 for TWO weeks -

Running: Total now upped to 200 to 240km per week on the road. Two runs have 70km time trials targeted at 4 hours to 4 hours 10 mins which equals race pace. (Exceed replacement and Power Bars used on these runs.) Rest of week is long slow and steady, 4 to 5 min/km pace.

Cycling and Canoeing: Continued but with a slight drop in total time.

Two weeks to go. Running drops back to 100km. Cycling & Canoeing.

One week to go. Running down to 40km. Cycling & Canoeing.

Race day - 5 hours 13 minutes 30 seconds for 50 miles.

More philosophy. Cycling maintains leg exercise and strength without the stress of running. Canoeing develops upper body strength which helps in running. In ultra-events the arms get tired first and since the arms set the leg pace it is important to maintain arm strength.

Throughout his training Russell uses food replacement bars (Power Bars), food fluid and electrolyte replacements. He also trains with a heart-rate monitor to control and test effort.

Two tips for leg injuries. Running in water using an aquavest, or running in soft sand; on beach right along the tide mark where it is soft.

A final tip. A lot of runners don't get the best out of themselves in ultras because they don't pay enough attention to food and drink. Getting the right amount of these is one of the keys to improving performance.

Lynn Fitzgerald when she wrote this article was Senior Research fellow Department of Medicine, St. Georges Hospital Medical School, London S.W.17

RRC L.61 Former holder of the Women's 100 mile track record. Published by kind permission of the Observer Newspaper, London, who retain the copyright.

Some of the world's best athletes never win medals because their immune system fails to cope with the rigours of training. Sebastian Coe's brilliant athletic career was punctuated and finally brought to a full stop by illness. The infections he suffered all appear to result from an inability of his immune system to hold them in check. After his best-ever year, 1981, he became ill in 1982 with so-called glandular fever. However, the infection was eventually diagnosed as toxoplasmosis, a parasitic disease normally causing clinical illness only in people whose immune system is depressed. "I didn't feel back to that everyday feeling of well-being, of full fitness, which I had experienced in 1981, until about 1985" he reflects. But in 1988 Coe missed the Seoul qualifying race because of a viral infection. And finally another viral infection stopped him competing in a much-publicised "last race before retirement" 1500 metres at the Commonwealth Games.

Viral infections have ruined the career of many U.K. Track and Field athletes: John Ridgeon, John Gladwin, Dave Moorcroft, Kathryn Binns and Sarah Rowell. Toxoplasma infections caused Diane Edwards and others to miss important competitions. Del Harris and Adrian Moorhouse are examples from other sports who have lost months or years through illness. Intense training is the common factor in all these cases.

But well-publicised cases of famous athletes represent only the tip of the iceberg. You never hear about the hundreds of athletes who don't reach the top because they get sidelined by infection after infection before they get there. What they all seem to have in common, though, is intense training.

Recent research from around the world pinpoints the immune system as the crucial link between illness and elite athletes. This does not mean that intensive training is unhealthy; it does mean that you should learn to recognise the risks of overtraining.

Overtraining. A number of research studies have shown that a single bout of exhaustive exercise reduces the efficiency of the immune system by up to 70%

for 24 hours. Today's elite athletes train harder today than ever before. Whereas in the past a short competition season permitted low-level off-season training, the trend in all sports is for year-round meetings and hence year-round top-level training. The Kenyan athletes are legendary for their apparent ability to resist the infection so frequently afflicting other squads: it should be noted that for several months of each year they maintain fitness but do no specific training. So you must plan your own training to give the body some months to recover. And on a day-to-day basis adopt the hard-easy principle: follow a hard day with a light or rest day. This makes sense to allow the immune system to recover as well as the muscles.

Build your fitness gradually. Build up your training intensity gradually. After illness or injury you'll want to get out there and get back to your old level of fitness. But training too hard too soon is the worst thing you can do. Sarah Rowell admits she trained too hard when coming back after injury. "I thought I was coping physically, but in doing so much so soon after the lay-off and also completing a PhD, I can see now it was too much". You must give your body time to adapt.

Hormones and Chemicals. Exercising intensity induces the release of huge quantities of adrenalin, cortisol and beta-enomorphins: all can have deleterious effects on the immune system. Adrenalin, vital for peak performance, suppresses the actions of the T-lyphphocytes, the most important cells of the immune system. Improved sports performance comes from training schedules which break down and build up muscle, albeit at a microscopic level. Cortisol, a by-product of muscle breakdown, reduces inflammation in the damaged muscles but is potently immunosupressive. Thirdly, pushing yourself hard induces the production of the neuropeptide beta- endomorphin, the so-called "runner's high". But beta-endomorphin drastically reduces the ability of NK (natural killer) cells to recognise and kill virally-infected cells.

Stress management. Research shows that mental stress also has immunosupressive effects. Identical chemicals to those released by physical stress - adrenalin, cortisol and endomorphin - are released in response to stress of any kind.

And the effects are probably additive. Racing and competing are enormously stressful psychologically as well as physically. And when this is combined with major life events, such as changes in personal relationships, taking exams or moving home, the immunosuppressive chemicals can reach catastrophic levels. John Ridgeon now realises this " I see now that my mistake was to think that I could get by on four hours' sleep a night and constant physical and mental stress".

The message is obvious ... avoid multiple stressors. If you seriously want to succeed at your chosen sport, simplify your life. When stressful things do happen, cut back your training or even take a holiday. Listen to your body and help it to cope. Learn and use a stress-reduction technique. I studied Iyengar Yoga for years before I took up running and I know that it helped me cope with the rigours of training 100 miles a week and racing against the best ultra-distance runners in the world (Yoga also reduces the risk of physical injury: you don't need to "warm-up" if your body is already supple).

Diet. Studies from all over the world have shown that most top endurance athletes are malnourished. Intakes of vitamins and minerals essential for proper immune function are generally inadequate. It is well known that endurance training depletes muscle glycogen and that athletes need to eat plenty of carbohydrates to replace this: nevertheless, the studies show that most elite athletes' diets are deficient in carbohydrate. This has indirect immunosuppressive effects, in that lymphocytes depend on muscles to supply glutamine, essential for optimal lymphocyte function. Glycogen-depleted muscles are poor suppliers of glutamine. So the best advice is to eat a hearty healthy high-calorie high-carbohydrate diet and take a multivitamin, multi-mineral supplement each day. Incidentally, never take mega-doses of vitamins or minerals - they can be immunosuppressive themselves! And don't take glutamine as a supplement; it won't help your lymphocytes and can be toxic.

This advice holds particularly true for young female athletes, gymnasts and dancers, many of whom are overly concerned to keep their weight as low as possible. An inadequate diet increases the incidence of menstrual disturbances so common in women training intensely, and this in turn significantly increases the risk of serious osteoporosis (reduction in bone density), with a consequently greater risk of stress fractures. The best way for athletes to protect their bodies is by adopting a diet rich in calories, vitamins and minerals.

Avoid close contact for the first few hours after hard exercise. If you are serious about succeeding, say no to social gatherings just after a really hard training session, when your immune system is particularly vulnerable. Perhaps athletes would be well advised to avoid travelling on the Northern line just after a race!

As you strive for the ultimate in performance, remember that the limiting factor may not be genetic endowment or avoiding injury, but the ability of your immune system to cope with repeated bouts of exhausting exercise and competition. Minor illnesses may be a price worth paying to reach the top, but if you repeatedly ignore the warning signals you may never get there. If, on the on the hand, you plan your training, competing, living and eating sensibly - you should be able to train hard without ever experiencing "runner's low".

Avoid hard exercise during infection. No matter how careful you are you are bound to get viral and other infections from time to time. The really important thing is to cut back your training at these times. Many studies have shown that otherwise mild infections can become serious chronic diseases if hard exercise is continued during the incubation period. So again, listen to your body. Test your resting pulse. If you feel a bit off colour, cut back on your training. You could salvage a great athletic career!

Suzi Thibeault started 16 trail 100-milers, and finished every one of them. In her spare time she put out an excellent quarterly newsletter about trail 100-milers.

The book titled, Eat to Win was probably a success because we would all like to be capable of winning by simply eating certain foods. We are even willing to read about how to train correctly to win, though obviously only a few ultrarunners will ever win an ultra during this life, because it also requires talent. However strange it may seem, the title to this article is not as senseless as it appears. I agree, nobody consciously trains to quit, but my training philosophy is geared towards a finisher's reward, not a winner's award.

My personal achievements in ultrarunning, and those of others I have listened to, prove that the one most important ingredient for completion in an ultra is mental attitude. Not just on race day, or race weekend for a 100-miler, but during training. The SUZI T definition of training may reveal the secret to all my 100-mile finishes, in that I believe LIFE is training for everything. Not that training should be your life, but that your life should count as training. When a 50-mile race turns into a 50-mile hike, I consider it a training session of grand proportion.

Setting goals that you believe are attainable helps, no matter what everybody else thinks. You can finish your chosen event if you honestly deep down trust your ability and your preparation. There are stories after each run about someone doing well who "doesn't" train. Well, what is training?

The components I base my plans on include the facets that everyday life revolve around. First and foremost, to finish, your head has to be on straight, which means emotionally you must be sound. Certainly I act in a less than sane manner at times, but for me that passes for normal. The relationship I have with myself, my husband, my family, my co-workers, my friends and even strangers is reflected in my success possibilities. If you sacrifice your personal relationships for an all-consuming training regimen, your success ratio drops as well as the satisfaction of a finish if it occurs.

Everything you do counts as training and you can reward yourself accordingly. When I walk to the post office instead of driving I feel better mentally, and I count it physically as part of my training. At work in the travel agency I often stand at my desk instead of sitting; the time on my feet is training. When I work in veterinary clinics I consider lifting a big dog "upper body work-out". Sure, I could train more mileage and run faster during races, but what would I sacrifice to find the time and energy? Why give up rock climbing, when you can just count it as strength training? Take your kids for a bike ride, or your dog for a walk; it's life, it's training, and it counts.

Even resting is part of the plan. When I'm injured, or tired, or both, I try not to begrudge the runs I am missing. Instead I do my planning. The strategy I feel is needed to finish includes wardrobe planning, food preparation, equipment modification, and lots of daydreaming. The anticipation is half the enjoyment, and if things go right, it won't be ALL of the enjoyment.

Give yourself credit. Count your life as training. Make your life the best you can manage and your ultra experiences will provide the satisfaction that comes with a completion.

SOME FINAL THOUGHTS

Having waded through the mass of ideas contained in this book, a would be ultra runner could be forgiven for being confused by the sometimes contradictory advice. Your choice of training will depend on many factors - personality and temperament, ability, build and metabolism, resilience, experience, environment, lifestyle and the time you have available to train. Runners should take from the articles those elements that they think they can use, which suit their own personal requirements.

For Ultra training and racing to be effective and successful it must be approached in a systematic, reflective and controlled way. I feel there are certain basic essentials that underlie most of the advice given. Here are a few guidelines which summarise the information given in the preceding articles which the novice ultra runner might use;-

1. It is important to keep a detailed training and racing log book. Record your daily training - strategies, distances, speeds, courses, and how your body responds to each element in that training. Record your race strategies split times etc, how the race went and how long it took to recover. By reflecting later on this information you will be able to discover your strengths and weaknesses, your successes and perhaps more important your mistakes.

2. Allow your body time to recover from training - build rest days into your training schedules. Aim to give your body a 'fallow' period each year, to rest up and recover ready for each new season.

3. Try to integrate necessary daily activities into your training, i.e. decorating the house/digging the garden as upper body work, standing at work as training in being on your feet for extended periods, where appropriate walk instead of taking the car or bus, etc. etc.

4. Never try anything new in a race. Always experiment with new racing techniques, new food or drinks, new clothing in training first. Simulate the race environment in training.

5. Incorporate cross training into your schedule to make it more enjoyable; to develop your upper body strength and for general conditioning. This will enable you to maintain an efficient running body posture longer. Build the various elements of cross training into your week in a planned way. Free exercises such as press-ups, sit-ups, etc., together with a programme of stretching exercises improve strength and mobility and may well condition the body against injury. Weight training, cycling, swimming, ski-ing canoeing and aerobics may all be used as valuable supplements to running training.

6. Select your races carefully. Initially, while a novice, move up in distance slowly. Jumping from marathon to 24 hours can work, but it is very likely to be counter-productive in the long term. Give your body time to adapt to the new demands that are being made upon it. Later, focus on one or two events a year - by all means run other ultra events as part of your build up, but not as highly competitive all-out efforts. RACING ultras frequently without allowing adequate time for adaptation and recovery invites injury and a cycle of declining performances.

7. Plan your race with care. Start at a pace you feel you can maintain to the finish. Have alternative strategies worked out. If, at halfway, you feel strong then you can increase the pace somewhat. However, if the weather conditions are bad and/or you are struggling, have a survival strategy worked out that will enable you to run to the finish.

8. Make a study of your chief rivals in the race. If possible get hold of previous race results, with split times. The rewards of a little homework of this kind can be incredible. You can get valuable information as to how your opponents run their races. Do they blast off and then hang on in the later stages, or move through strongly after a steady start? Do they tend to wilt in the sun or run badly in cold conditions? Work out ways to putting this knowledge to the best

advantage. As well as possibly turning things your way, this will also make the race much more interesting for you.

9. If you think you will need to walk in a race, either because you are making a big move up in distance or because you doubt your ability to run the whole way, build the walking into your race strategy in a systematic and controlled way from the start. DON'T just run until you can't run any more and then plod around slowly to the finish. If you are going to walk, practice walking briskly and effectively in training so it becomes another technique you can rely on.

Now all you need to do is put all of this into practice!
Good Luck, have fun.

Bibliography

Books

Some of the older books, (and newer ones too unfortunately), are out of print but may be obtained through the Inter-Library loan service. I include publisher's addresses for the later books.

Running - Arthur F.H. Newton. Pub. H. F. & G. Witherby, London. 1935. pp. 224.

Running on Three Continents - Arthur F.H. Newton. Pub. H. F. & G Witherby, London. 1940. pp. 187. "Contains accounts of many marathons and ultra races, record breaking performances and training runs, a vivid account of the two Trans-America Races in the '20s. This book also contains a detailed account of Hardy Ballington's record breaking run from Bath to London in 1937" - Dave Cooper.

Commonsense Athletics - Arthur F.H. Newton. Pub. George Berridge, London. 1947. pp. 75.

Races and Training - Arthur F.H. Newton. Pub. George Berridge, London. 1949. pp. 94 These last two books, along with 'Running', contain a mass of advice illustrated with examples from Newton's career. In Tim Noakes' view "they chronicle the first detailed description of ..... the modern training approach to distance running." Newton was first and foremost an ultrarunner, and much of his advice is still applicable today.

Race Walking - Julian Hopkins. Pub. BAAB 1976.

Corbitt - John Chodes. Pub. Tafnews Press, Book Division of Track & Field News, Box 296, Los Altos, California 94022, U.S.A. 1974; 1978. pp. 154. The biography of Ted Corbitt, one of the founding fathers of U.S. ultrarunning, who set national 50 mile, 100 mile and 24 hour marks in R.R.C. events at Walton. Includes an appendix on hot weather running, treatment of injuries and diet supplements.

Ultra-Marathoning - The Next Challenge - Tom Osler & Ed Dodd. Pub. World Publications Inc., Mountain View, California. (The imprint of 'Runners World'. Since taken over by Rodale Press, 33 E. Minor St., Emmaus, PA 18049, U.S.A.). 1979. pp. 300. Part 1 The Great Six Day Races 1874 - 1909. The best account to date of such events, in many ways the origins of modern track ultras. Part 2 Advice on ultra training for events up to Six Days. Advocates combining walking and running for beginners.

Ultramarathon - James E. Shapiro. Pub. Bantam Books, 666, Fifth Avenue, New York, NY 10103, U.S.A. 1980. pp 252. Opens with a chapter on the 1979 Crystal Palace 24 hours in which Jim Shapiro set a new U.S. best. Principally interviews with top ultrarunners around the world. Not a great deal on actual training, but good insights into the psychology of ultrarunners.

The Ghost Runner: The Tragedy of the Man They Couldn't Stop [Paperback] Bill Jones Pub: Mainstream Publishing 2011.pp 352 Detailed autobiography by John Tarrant of his life and training. He set world track bests for 40 miles and 100 miles, the latter in the same race as Ted Corbitt (see above).

Mehr als Marathon (More than Marathon) - Werner Sonntag. Pub. Meyer & Meyer, Am Beyergays 23, D5100 Aachen, Germany. 1985/86. Two volumes - pp. 192 & 176. Written in German. Covers, History, training (programmes for those who seek to cover 100km in 20 - 24 hours, to jog it in 14 - 20 hours, to run it in 9 - 14 hours, and for the elite sub 9 hour runners, including contributions from runners. Also sections on psychological and physiological factors, nutrition, clothing, techniques and tactics, as well as profiles of runners and 100km courses. Price - 24.80 DM per volume.

Tear Along The Dotted Line – Roger W Alcorn Pub. Integrated Business Information Systems 1987 The history of the New Brighton 50 mile road race in New Zealand and many leading New Zealand ultrarunners.

Wild Trails to Far Horizons - Mike Cudahy (contributor). Pub. Unwin Hyman. 1988. Details of Mike Cudahy's training and preparation for his multi-day trail runs over moor, mountain, fell and trail.

Unstoppable – The Sandra Barwick Story – Sandy Barwick with Garth Gilmour, Pub. HarperCollins New Zealand 1993 pp 182 Her running biography with details of her world record races.

Long, At The Top – Richard and Sandra Brown 1982-1993 – collated by Dudley Harris 1994

Racing the Antelope – What Animals Can Teach Us About Running and Life – Bernd Heinrich Pub. Cliff Street Books 2001 pp 292 studies of animal endurance and how they relate to humans.

A Step Beyond: A Definitive Guide to Ultrarunning Edited by Don Allison. U;trarunning Publishers, Weymouth Massachusetts. 2002 pp558 Chapters on Racing and training, Physiology, history of Ultras, Races and Places, Ultra People, Philosophy and finally Humor.

Everyone's Guide to Distance Running Norrie Williamson Publisher Globe Pequot Press, 2004 pp 436 . Norrie Williamson an experienced ultrarunner, has developed a comprehensive book that covers the preparation and training necessary to prepare for events from 10km to the Comrades

Lore of Running - Tim Noakes. Pub. Human Kinetics Publishers (Europe), P.O. Box 1W14, Leeds, LS16 6TR. 2003 pp.932. Paperback £19.95 Hardback £22. Professor Noakes is a noted exercise physiologist and his book is firmly based on the latest research into long distance running. It is by far the most comprehensive book on training for the shorter ultras - up to 100km - yet produced. In addition to chapters on the physiology and biochemistry of running, training theory from Newton to the present day, details of the training of every major Comrades winner since Newton, injuries, nutrition and medical problems, there is also a chapter on racing beyond the marathon. Its limitations are that there is a limited amount on the longer ultras 24 hours and upwards. South Africa is very Comrades orientated. As a result few runners are interested in going beyond 55 miles.

King of the Peds – P S Marshall. Pub. AuthorHouse UK ltd, 500 Avebury Boulevard, Central Milton Keynes MK9 2BE www.authorhouse.co.uk 2008 752pp Paul Marshall provides an exhaustive survey of newspaper reports on 6 days races of the nineteenth century, breakdown of splits in races, brief biographies of the main competitors etc. http://www.kingofthepeds.com/

The Clock Keeps Ticking – Sharon Gayter Pub. Grosvenor House 2010 The story of how Sharon Gayter went from a an extremely shy, skinny withdrawn child, with a difficult childhood to becoming a Commonwealth Ultra Champion. pp272.

North American Ultrarunning – A history – Andy Milroy DP Books 2012. A comprehensive history of the Ultrarunning in North America from its earliest roots.

Appendix

Hour	Kouros (Mont)	Dowdle (Glos)	JGB (Laus)	JGB (Bkbn)	Pickard (Barn)	Kouros (N.Y.)	Barner (L.B)	JGB (Coet)
1	9.69	7.89	7.46	7.79	7.93	9.19	6.75	7.2
2	9.44	7.82	7.34	7.73	8.18	9.19	7.12	7.45
3	9.19	7.96	7.48	7.57	8.16	8.69	6.79	7.45
4	8.94	7.91	7.67	7.76	7.87	8.45	6.77	7.45
5	8.69	7.78	7.52	7.36	8.23	7.45	6.88	6.95
6	8.45	7.73	7.45	7.31	7.9	8.19	7.16	7.95
7	8.2	7.69	6.98	7.43	7.91	7.95	6.83	7.2
8	7.95	7.56	7.23	7.42	7.72	7.45	7.11	7.02
9	7.7	7.2	7.27	7.11	7.29	6.71	7.18	6.71
10	7.45	6.71	7.28	6.87	7.51	6.7	7.15	6.95
11	7.2	6.83	7.29	6.66	6.97	6.71	6.77	6.71
12	7.45	6.72	7.29	6.82	6.88	6.95	7	6.21
13	7.45	6.8	7.36	6.93	6.92	6.45	6.44	6.21
14	7.2	6.8	7.42	6.49	6.34	6.71	6.66	6.21
15	7.2	6.76	7.49	6.45	6.72	6.7	7.22	6.71
16	6.95	6.97	7.17	6.94	6.42	6.46	7.44	6.46
17	6.95	7.01	7.11	6.95	5.1	5.46	6.88	6.46
18	6.71	7.03	6.51	7.09	5.82	4.47	6.66	6.3
19	6.71	7.32	6.59	6.75	4.5	2.23	6.77	6.55
20	6.71	6.11	6.16	6.84	5.46	4.47	6.83	6.27
21	6.46	5.8	6.22	6.39	6.25	7.2	6.58	6.46
22	6.46	6.54	6.11	6.23	6.32	6.21	5.81	6.46
23	6.46	6.7	6.38	5.39	5.49	6.7	5.43	6.21
24	0	6.77	6.49	3.73	5.72	6.44	5.97	6.03
Overall	176.2	170.5	169.4	164.1	163.7	163.2	162.3	161.7

Appendix

Miles covered in each individual hour in performances in 24 hour races

(distances are in miles and decimal fractions of a mile).

Bentley	Hayward	Boussiquet	Pickard	Newton	Bream	Newton	Macke	Heinrich
8.16	8.21	8.31	7.49	7.45	8.2	8.11	7.66	7.59
8.13	8.54	8.24	7.57	7.7	7.7	8.08	7.91	7.33
8.22	8.56	8.26	7.46	7.7	8.45	8.23	7.66	7.45
8.18	8.23	8.17	7.64	7.95	7.7	8.2	7.91	7.59
7.96	7.96	8.05	7.59	7.7	8.2	7.92	7.41	7.48
8.19	7.89	8.12	7.63	7.7	7.45	7.98	7.66	7.54
7.88	7.15	7.65	7.94	7.45	7.2	8.12	6.91	7.26
7.41	7.09	7.85	6.93	7.45	7.45	7.7	6.41	7.34
6.95	7.41	7.69	7.26	7.2	7.2	6.54	6.16	7.32
7.57	7.21	7.63	6.98	7.2	6.95	7.51	7.16	7.17
6.47	6.07	7.37	6.69	7.2	6.95	7.02	6.91	7.15
6.92	7.23	7	6.49	6.95	6.95	6.86	6.91	6.67
6.55	4.86	5.6	6.41	6.71	6.95	6.39	6.16	6.54
6.88	6.29	4.04	6.17	6.71	6.21	6.72	6.16	6.46
6.42	3.16	6.28	6.19	6.71	6.21	5.84	6.16	6.34
6.63	6.81	5.46	6.04	6.95	5.71	5.95	6.41	5.96
6.37	6.73	5.4	5.6	6.95	5.71	6.43	6.41	6.24
6.2	5.06	5.57	6.42	5.21	6.21	5.01	6.16	6.18
5.73	6.72	5.57	5.96	6.21	5.21	5.61	5.66	5.1
5.92	4.19	5.31	5.74	6.21	4.97	5	5.66	5.66
5.34	6.07	5.75	5.57	5.96	5.21	4.59	3.91	4.9
4.15	6.31	5.29	5.37	2.73	5.21	4.8	4.16	4.53
6.98	5.36	4.99	6.34	4.97	5.46	4.17	5.41	4.37
1.97	6.27	5.6	5.33	3.46	4.22	4.41	7.66	6.16
161.3	159.4	159.3	158.9	158.6	157.8	157.3	156.8	156.5

distances in km   Conversion factor   1.609344

Hour	Kouros (Mont)	Dowdle (Glos)	JGB (Laus)	JGB (Bkbn)	Pickard (Barn)	Kouros (N.Y.)	Barner (L.B)
2	15.192	12.585	11.813	12.440	13.164	14.790	11.459
3	14.790	12.810	12.038	12.183	13.132	13.985	10.927
4	14.388	12.730	12.344	12.489	12.666	13.599	10.895
5	13.985	12.521	12.102	11.845	13.245	11.990	11.072
6	13.599	12.440	11.990	11.764	12.714	13.181	11.523
7	13.197	12.376	11.233	11.957	12.730	12.794	10.992
8	12.794	12.167	11.636	11.941	12.424	11.990	11.442
9	12.392	11.587	11.700	11.442	11.732	10.799	11.555
10	11.990	10.799	11.716	11.056	12.086	10.783	11.507
11	11.587	10.992	11.732	10.718	11.217	10.799	10.895
12	11.990	10.815	11.732	10.976	11.072	11.185	11.265
13	11.990	10.944	11.845	11.153	11.137	10.380	10.364
14	11.587	10.944	11.941	10.445	10.203	10.799	10.718
15	11.587	10.879	12.054	10.380	10.815	10.783	11.619
16	11.185	11.217	11.539	11.169	10.332	10.396	11.974
17	11.185	11.282	11.442	11.185	8.208	8.787	11.072
18	10.799	11.314	10.477	11.410	9.366	7.194	10.718
19	10.799	11.780	10.606	10.863	7.242	3.589	10.895
20	10.799	9.833	9.914	11.008	8.787	7.194	10.992
21	10.396	9.334	10.010	10.284	10.058	11.587	10.589
22	10.396	10.525	9.833	10.026	10.171	9.994	9.350
23	10.396	10.783	10.268	8.674	8.835	10.783	8.739
24		10.895	10.445	6.003	9.205	10.364	9.608
Overall	283.566	274.393	272.623	264.093	263.450	262.645	261.197
Avg	12.137	11.372	11.322	10.931	10.893	10.771	10.877
Stdev	1.478	0.928	0.794	1.378	1.740	2.434	0.764
Min	10.396	9.334	9.833	6.003	7.242	3.589	8.739
Max	15.192	12.810	12.344	12.489	13.245	14.790	11.974
Avg2	11.815	11.433	11.359	11.004	10.977	10.944	10.883
1st half, hours 1-12	145.903	131.821	130.035	128.812	136.183	135.893	123.533
2n half, hours 13-24	121.119	129.729	130.373	122.600	114.360	111.849	126.639
ratio 2nd/1st	83%	98%	100%	95%	84%	82%	103%

JGB (Coet)	Bentley	Hayward	Boussiquet	Pickard	Newton	Bream	Newton	Macke	Heinrich
11.990	13.084	13.744	13.261	12.183	12.392	12.392	13.003	12.730	11.796
11.990	13.229	13.776	13.293	12.006	12.392	13.599	13.245	12.328	11.990
11.990	13.164	13.245	13.148	12.295	12.794	12.392	13.197	12.730	12.215
11.185	12.810	12.810	12.955	12.215	12.392	13.197	12.746	11.925	12.038
12.794	13.181	12.698	13.068	12.279	12.392	11.990	12.843	12.328	12.134
11.587	12.682	11.507	12.311	12.778	11.990	11.587	13.068	11.121	11.684
11.298	11.925	11.410	12.633	11.153	11.990	11.990	12.392	10.316	11.813
10.799	11.185	11.925	12.376	11.684	11.587	11.587	10.525	9.914	11.780
11.185	12.183	11.603	12.279	11.233	11.587	11.185	12.086	11.523	11.539
10.799	10.412	9.769	11.861	10.767	11.587	11.185	11.298	11.121	11.507
9.994	11.137	11.636	11.265	10.445	11.185	11.185	11.040	11.121	10.734
9.994	10.541	7.821	9.012	10.316	10.799	11.185	10.284	9.914	10.525
9.994	11.072	10.123	6.502	9.930	10.799	9.994	10.815	9.914	10.396
10.799	10.332	5.086	10.107	9.962	10.799	9.994	9.399	9.914	10.203
10.396	10.670	10.960	8.787	9.720	11.185	9.189	9.576	10.316	9.592
10.396	10.252	10.831	8.690	9.012	11.185	9.189	10.348	10.316	10.042
10.139	9.978	8.143	8.964	10.332	8.385	9.994	8.063	9.914	9.946
10.541	9.222	10.815	8.964	9.592	9.994	8.385	9.028	9.109	8.208
10.091	9.527	6.743	8.546	9.238	9.994	7.998	8.047	9.109	9.109
10.396	8.594	9.769	9.254	8.964	9.592	8.385	7.387	6.293	7.886
10.396	6.679	10.155	8.513	8.642	4.394	8.385	7.725	6.695	7.290
9.994	11.233	8.626	8.031	10.203	7.998	8.787	6.711	8.707	7.033
9.704	3.170	10.091	9.012	8.578	5.568	6.791	7.097	12.328	9.914
260.231	259.587	256.529	256.368	255.725	255.242	253.954	253.150	252.345	251.862
10.802	10.707	10.578	10.558	10.588	10.564	10.459	10.431	10.421	10.408
0.821	2.326	2.203	2.120	1.304	2.162	1.825	2.183	1.721	1.606
9.704	3.170	5.086	6.502	8.578	4.394	6.791	6.711	6.293	7.033
12.794	13.229	13.776	13.293	12.778	12.794	13.599	13.245	12.730	12.215
10.843	10.816	10.689	10.682	10.655	10.635	10.581	10.548	10.514	10.494
125.609	134.992	134.123	138.452	129.037	132.288	132.288	135.442	127.154	129.230
122.841	111.270	109.162	104.382	114.489	110.691	108.277	104.479	112.525	110.144
98%	82%	81%	75%	89%	84%	82%	77%	88%	85%

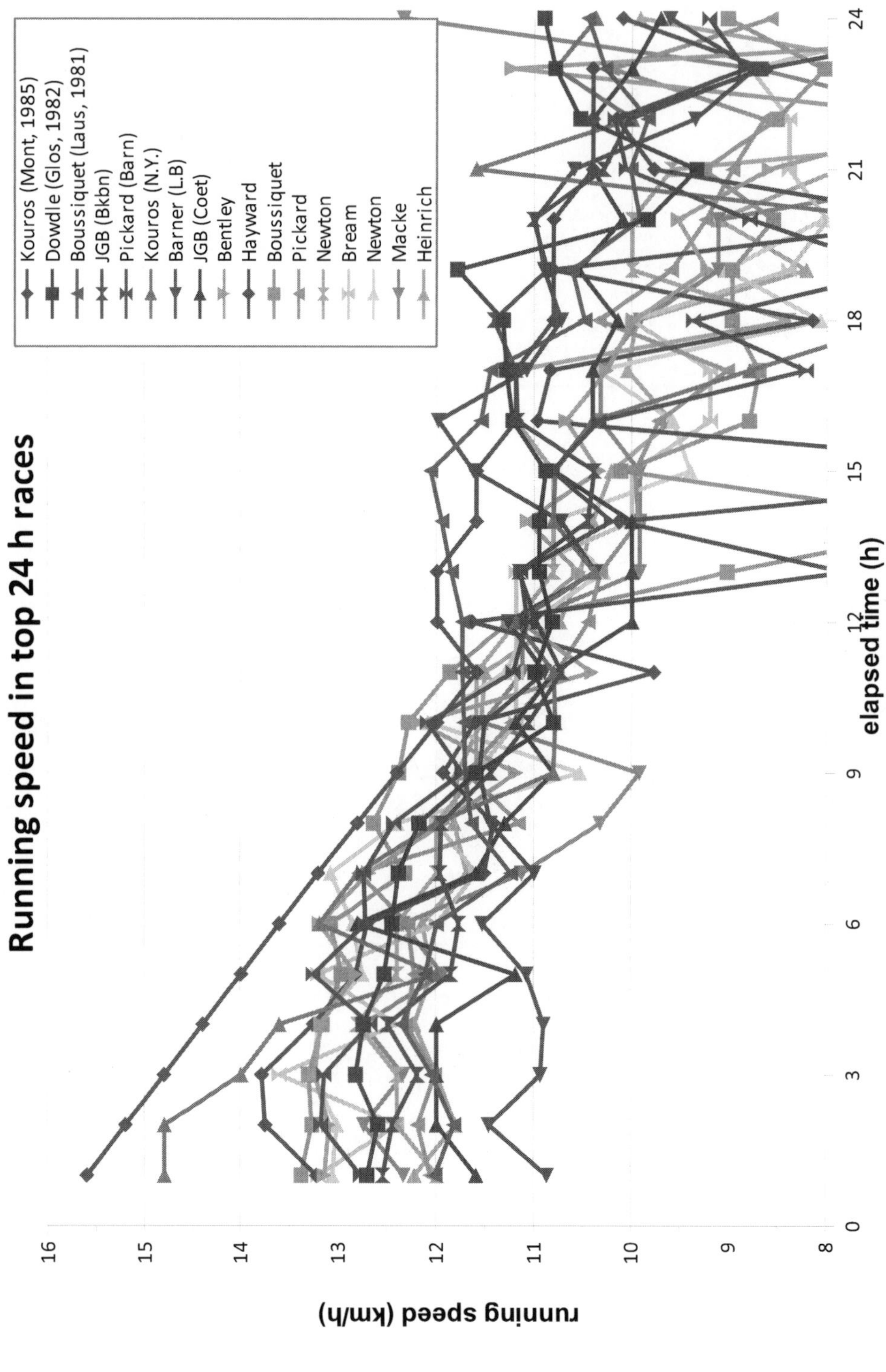
Running speed in top 24 h races
Kouros (Mont, 1985)
Dowdle (Glos, 1982)
Boussiquet (Laus, 1981)
JGB (Bkbn)
Pickard (Barn)
Kouros (N.Y.)
Barner (L.B)
JGB (Coet)
Bentley
Hayward
Boussiquet
Pickard
Newton
Bream
Newton
Macke
Heinrich
running speed (km/h)
16
15
14
13
12
11
10
9
8
elapsed time (h)
0
3
6
9
12
15
18
21
24

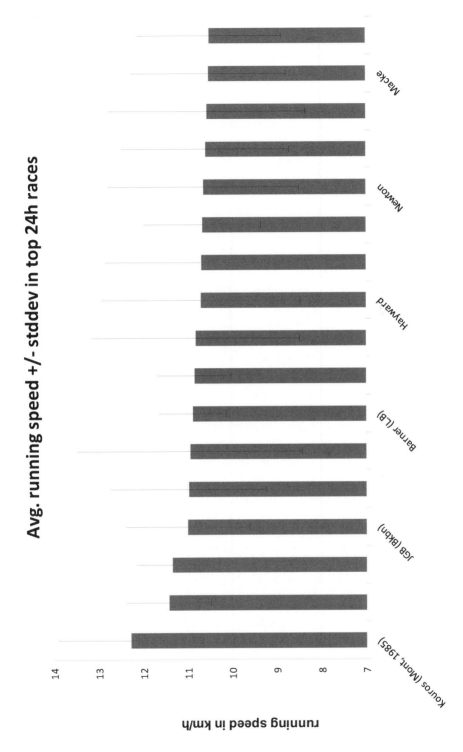

Avg. running speed +/- stddev in top 24h races

running speed in km/h

Kouros (Mont, 1985)

JGB (Bkbh)

Barner (LB)

Hayward

Newton

Macke

14 13 12 11 10 9 8 7

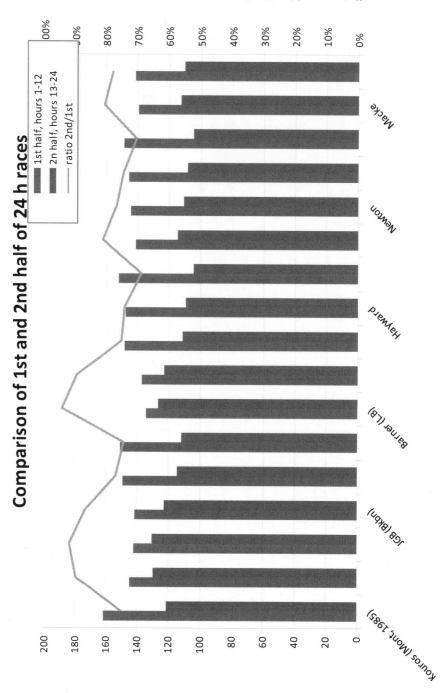

Comparison of 1st and 2nd half of 24 h races

distance of 2nd half compared to 1st half

km covered in 12 hours

Legend:
- 1st half, hours 1-12
- 2n half, hours 13-24
- ratio 2nd/1st